I0812847

IMAGES
of America

CARTHAGE
MISSOURI

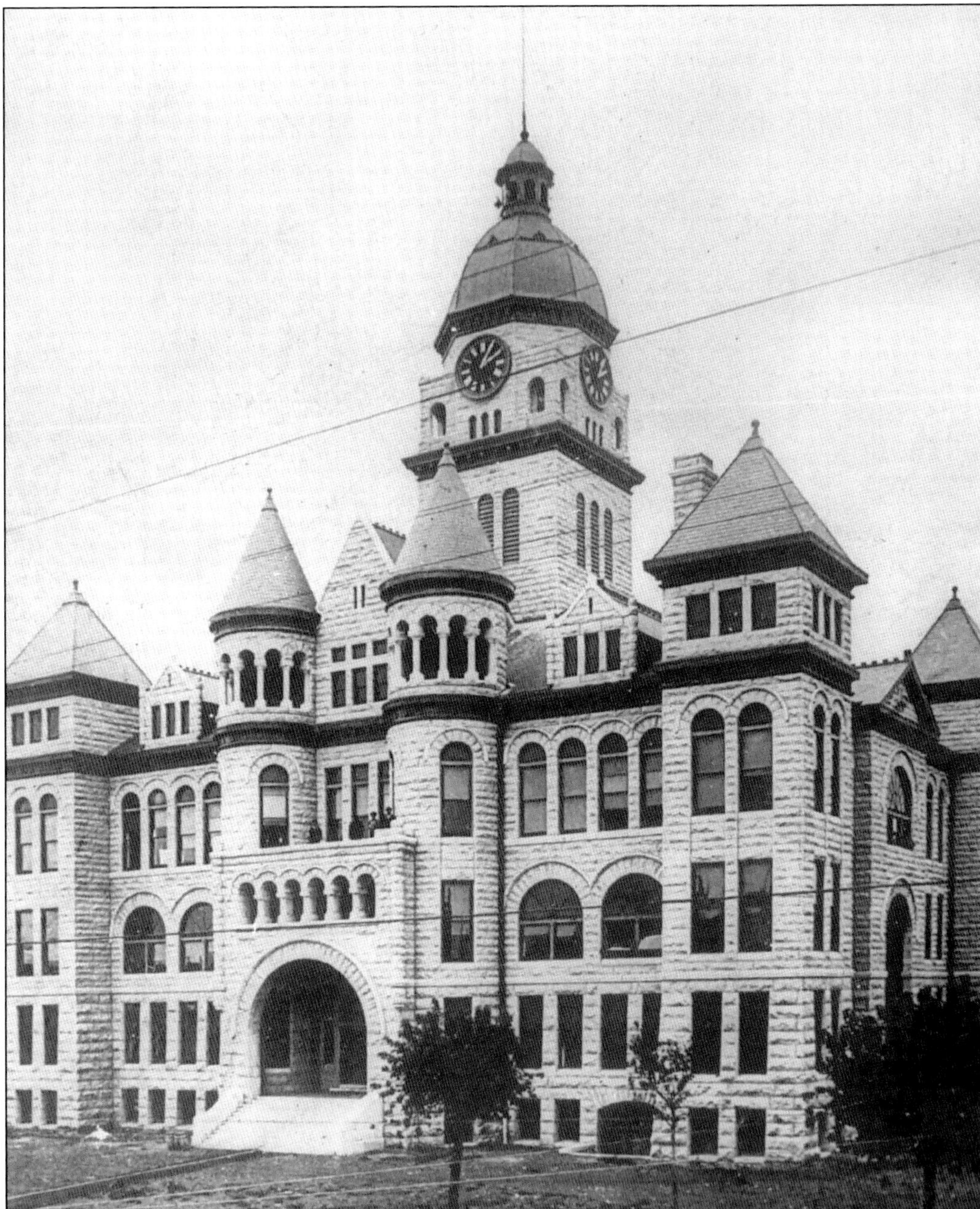

JASPER COUNTY COURTHOUSE, 1895. Since its establishment in 1842, the Carthage Public Square has been the town's focal point. With the completion of the massive limestone structure in 1895 (to replace the courthouse destroyed during the Civil War), the square has been anchored with a magnificent "Temple of Justice" and has served as the town's governmental, commercial, and social hub.

IMAGES
of America

CARTHAGE
MISSOURI

Michele Hansford

ARCADIA
PUBLISHING

ISBN 978-0-7385-0765-1

Published by Arcadia Publishing
Charleston, South Carolina

Printed in the United States of America

Library of Congress Catalog Card Number: 00105297

For all general information contact Arcadia Publishing at:
Telephone 843-853-2070
Fax 843-853-0044
E-mail sales@arcadiapublishing.com
For customer service and orders:
Toll-Free 1-888-313-2665

Visit us on the Internet at www.arcadiapublishing.com

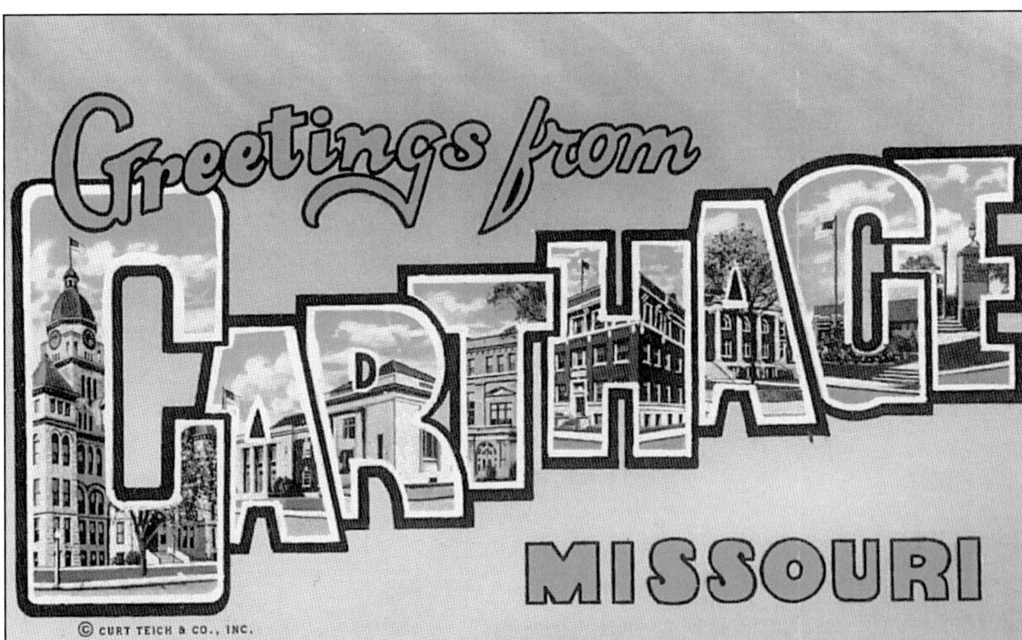

WELCOME TO CARTHAGE, C. 1940. The Jasper County Courthouse is the first of the buildings presented in this "big letter" postcard of Carthage (from left to right): Memorial Hall, Carthage Post Office, Carthage High School, YMCA, First Baptist Church, Bathhouse at Municipal Park Swimming Pool, and Municipal Park entrance. (Permission to publish this card courtesy of Lake County Museum (IL), Curt Teich Postcard Archives.)

Contents

ACKNOWLEDGMENTS

One purpose in undertaking a project like this was to provide wider access to some of the photographic and other pictorial holdings of the Powers Museum, so in selecting items to include in this book, a preference was given to images held by the Powers Museum. Since the museum has no permanent exhibits, it focuses on rotating artifacts, archival pieces, and information; once these pieces have been displayed, they are stored away for future research and use. This publication will make some of those images previously exhibited more accessible.

Of course the Powers Museum does not hold every image of Carthage ever produced, and a few photographs were borrowed to fill in certain time periods or subjects. The Powers Museum is grateful to the following for the loan of images for this book: Carthage Public Library, Carthage Red Cross, Darrel and Sheri Smith, and Mary Louesa Estes. Also acknowledged are Charlyn Hubbard, Donna Pfenniger Crocker, Patsy Pfenniger Hendrickson, and William Putnam Jr., whose courthouse images used in the 1994 Jasper County Courthouse Centennial Souvenir Program and companion 1995 Powers Museum exhibit, are reprinted here.

Selected images donated to the Powers Museum over the last ten years have been used as well, and include those given by Beverly Cody, Becky Thomas, Merle Little, Agnes Wilson, Eleanor Coffield, George Boyd, Virginia Shaver, Jane Jensen, Peggy Morrow, Helen Chickering, Sue Bailey, Mary Helen Eggenberger, the Elizabeth Wright Estate, the Ellen Davis Estate, Mercantile Bank, Nations Bank, Maryetta White, Harriet Kennedy, and the Carthage R-9 Schools. Since text space is limited by this book's format, I hope everyone will forgive me for not acknowledging ownership of specific photographs directly with the borrowed or donated image. The greater portion of the identification and caption information for this volume has come from resources at the Powers Museum, but I wish to thank the following for their assistance with some of the images: Mary Jane Conrades, John Cooper, the State Historical Society of Missouri, SLM & Associates, Sue Vandergriff, and Flanigan, Lasley, & Moore.

Finally, I would like to acknowledge Jeanie Hill of the Carthage Public Library for her help, along with the production assistance of the museum's staff including Elizabeth Sanderson, Wanda Youngblood, and Erica Boyd. Thanks also goes to the museum's best volunteer (even if not always by choice), my husband Gary, who gave his support during this project and in making those frantic last-minute deliveries of photographs and text.

Michele Newton Hansford
Director, Powers Museum
June 2000

INTRODUCTION

A century ago, it was said that "Carthage, with its broad streets, its fine residences, its beautiful parks, its magnificent courthouse, and its enchanting environments, may truthfully be said to be the most handsome city in the Southwest...." Those words, from the February 1900 *Southwest Developer Illustrated* magazine, are still true in 2000, evidenced by the remarks of today's tourists, who always comment on the castle-like courthouse, the beautiful Victorian homes, and the tree-lined streets. For many, visiting Carthage is like taking a glimpse into the past.

The Powers Museum is proud to present the following collection of historical images representing our printed glimpse into Carthage's past. Most of the selections span a period of 80 years from after the Civil War to the late 1930s. Other than the reconstruction years of the late 1860s through the 1870s, the time frame selected corresponds closely with the residency of the Curtis Wright family, who, like many others in the 1880s, moved west seeking new lives and fortunes attracted by this area's economic opportunities springing from the earth in the form of lead, zinc, and limestone. The places where these citizens worked, played, worshiped, and went to school upon arriving in Carthage is the subject of this volume.

While many of the images presented in this volume were collected by Wright family members and their descendants, these views represent only a small sampling of the natural and built environments that were so often praised in literature of the past. It was not the intent of the Powers Museum nor the publisher to present an exhaustive pictorial history of either the museum's archival holdings or other private collections, but merely to offer a brief visual reminiscence of the town known for many years as the "Queen City of the Southwest and the prettiest city in the entire state."

Also included here is a random sprinkling of Carthage ephemera such as trade cards and letterheads from the Powers Museum archival holdings. While the photographic and postcard images of popular attractions, major buildings, and special community events are numerous, material representing smaller industries, stores, and churches is often difficult to locate. By including some of these items, the museum hopes that readers will reconsider the significance of those pieces of ephemera (*i.e.* tickets, programs, brochures, receipts/invoices, broadsides, advertising handbills, etc.) when confronted with them.

Although each illustration presented is identified and is a historical document, in no way does this little volume aspire to be a comprehensive text outlining Carthage's history. For those wishing to read further on that subject, they should consult the following titles listed in order of publication.

History of Jasper County, Missouri by F.A. North. Des Moines, Iowa: Mills Publishing Company, 1883. (Reprints available from Jasper County Historical Society, call 417-358-2667 for details.)

Biographical Record of Jasper County, Missouri by Malcolm G. McGregor. Chicago: Lewis Publishing Company, 1901.

A History of Jasper County & Its People by Joel T. Livingston (two volumes). Chicago: Lewis Publishing Company, 1912.

Jasper County in the Civil War by Ward L. Schrantz. Carthage, Missouri: Kiwanis Club, 1988 reprint of 1923 original text. (Write P.O. Box 567, Carthage, MO 64836 for purchase information.)

Jasper County: The First Two Hundred Years by Marvin L. Vanglider. Carthage, Missouri: author and Jasper County Commissioners, 1995. (Call 417-358-0421 for purchase information.)

A few months after the courthouse was completed in 1895, it was remarked in the *Carthage Press* newspaper, "[t]hat the court house is to the people of Jasper [C]ounty like the story that never grows old. There is scarcely an hour of the day that visitors may not be found . . . viewing [it] with interest and curiosity . . ." To all the readers of this view book, it is hoped that these images never grow old and will spark renewed interest and curiosity in Carthage.

READERS NOTE: *The date used in bold captions for for an illustration denotes the year in which the building was constructed, or if a photograph of an event or people, the actual year when the image was taken. If c. (for circa) is used with a year, that designates the approximate year of the general view. Addresses in captions correspond to current numbering systems.*

One

Carthage Square

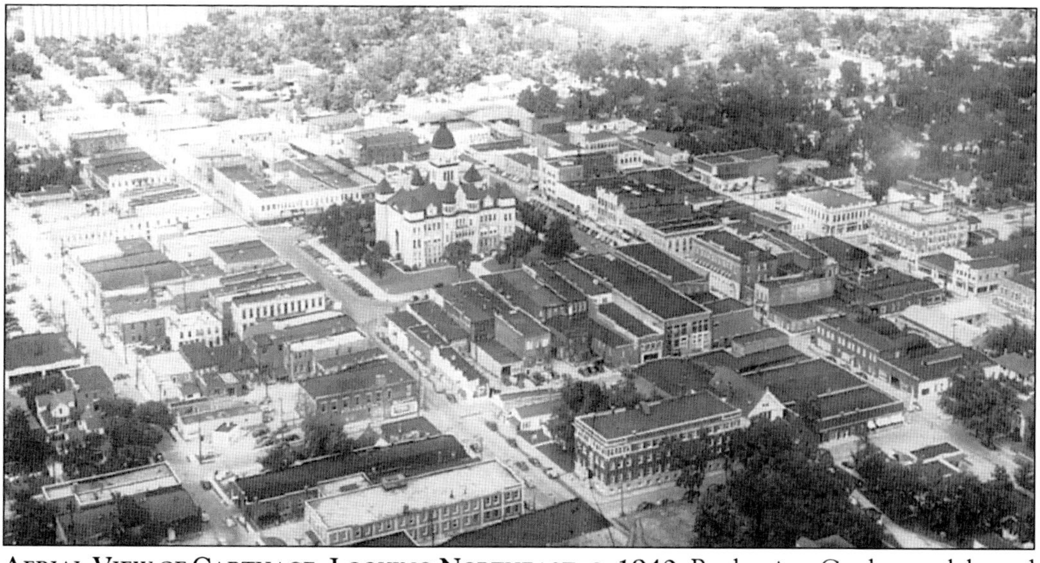

Aerial View of Carthage, Looking Northeast, c. 1940. By the time Carthage celebrated her centennial in 1942, she had grown to a city of approximately 12,000 people. At the city's center was the Jasper County Courthouse, looming over a business district that stretched for blocks in all directions from the square.

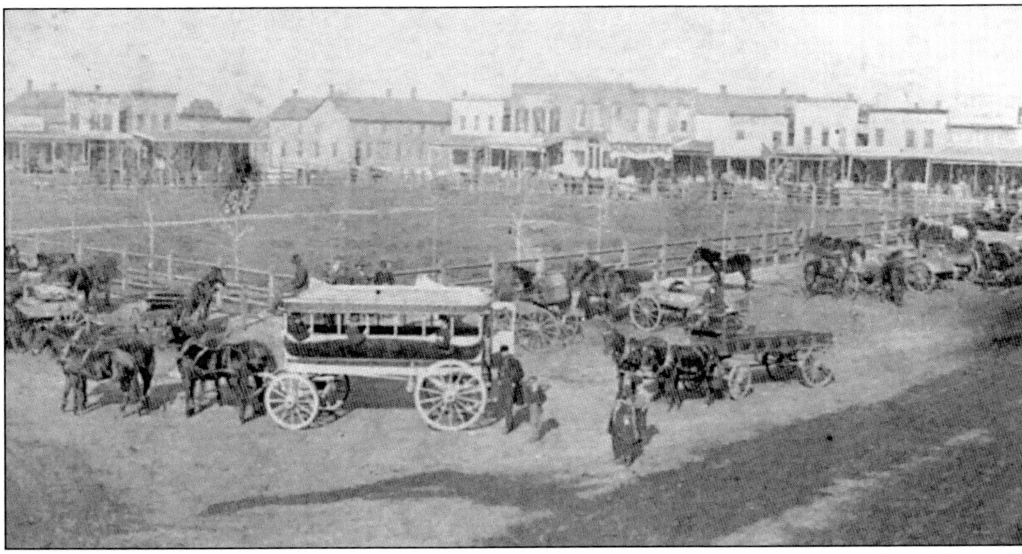

Partial Views of North and East Sides of Square, c. 1872. The growth of the town in the few years following its destruction during the Civil War is illustrated. Even though the former brick courthouse is gone, leaving the square empty, new and returning merchants built simple frame and brick structures on all the original town lots, including the Aetna House hotel at the northeast corner (straight up from the horse-drawn bus).

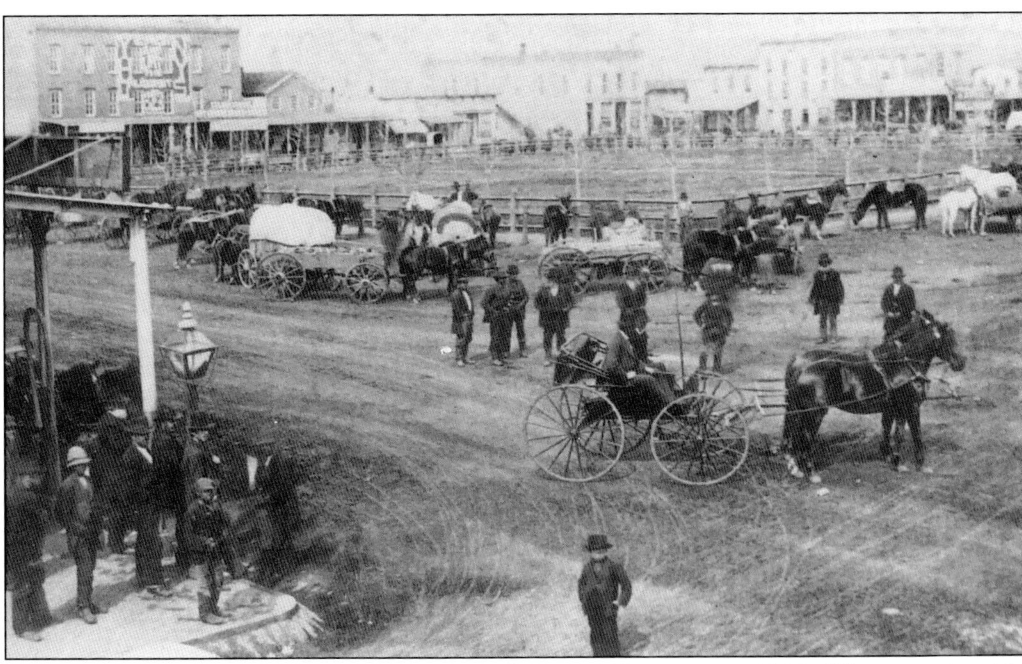

Partial Views of the West and North Sides of Square, c. 1879. The opposite sides of the square are seen here as well as the carriages and wagons hitched to the fence, where the former courthouse stood. The area inside the fence had been a public common used for parking, but this prevented grass from growing and made for a very dusty town. After the area was fenced in, trees were planted around the perimeter.

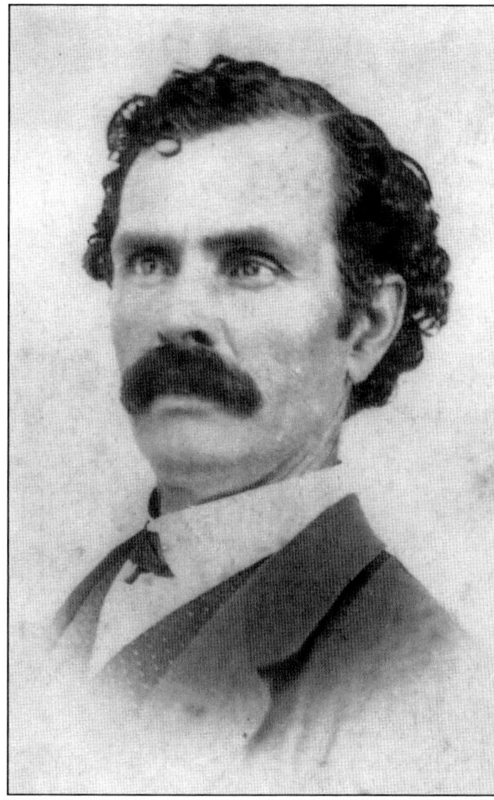

George Rader, c. 1870. When residents returned to Carthage after the Civil War, they found a destroyed courthouse and a town that was described by future judge Malcolm McGregor as a "haunt for wolves and owls." George Rader, undaunted by the surroundings, was the first merchant to return and set up his grocery and dry goods establishment near 6th and Grant Streets. He also was postmaster from 1866 to 1879 and mayor of Carthage in 1879.

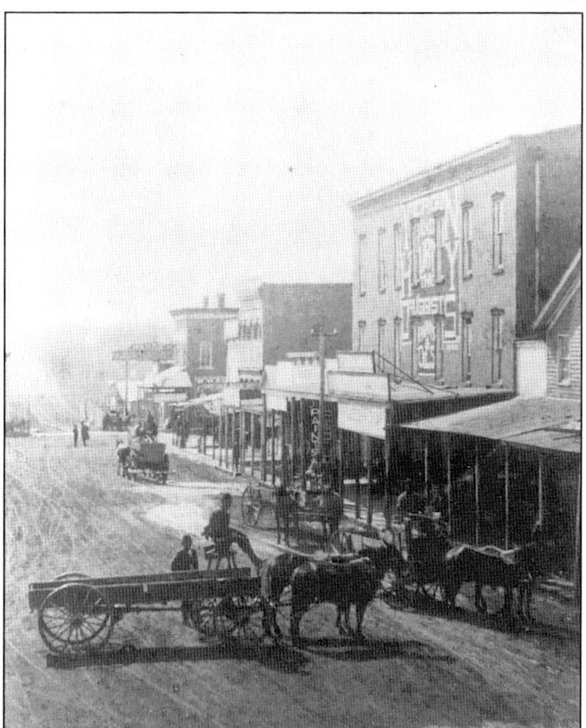

Partial View of West Side of Square, c. 1875–79. Timothy Regan's three-story brick building dominated the block once it was built in 1868. On the facade was the painted sign of Yergin and Hurty Druggists, one of three merchants on the first floor. The second floor housed professional offices, and the third floor served as a public hall for lodges and fledgling churches. The other two-story brick buildings in this view are the Farmers & Dovers Bank (341 S. Main) and the Roessler Building (401 S. Main).

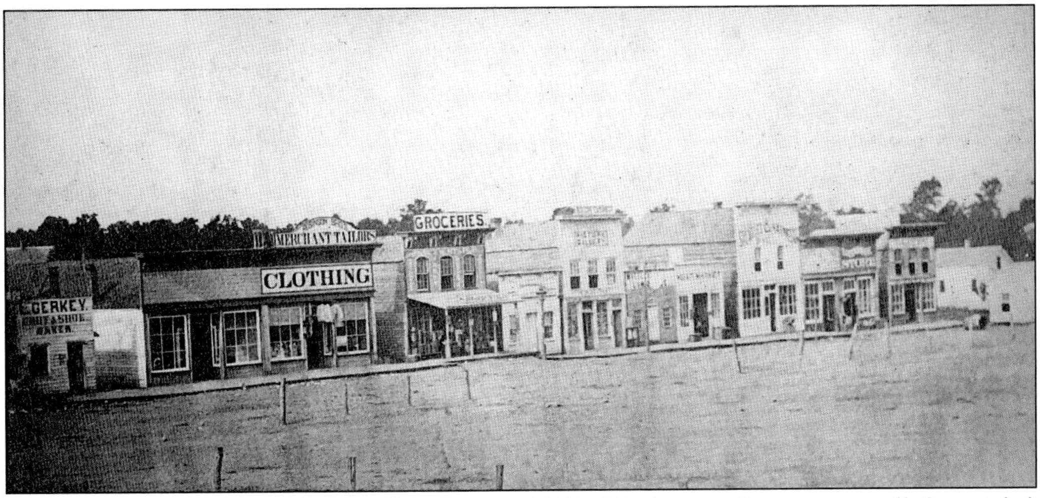

PARTIAL VIEW OF SOUTH SIDE OF SQUARE, C. 1870–72. Among the stores are (left to right) Louis Gerkey's shoe shop, ? store, Robinson Bros. Merchant Tailors, S.B. Griswold's grocery, ? store, W.S. Judd's Southwest Jewelry Emporium with Bulgin and Cashner Photography Studio above, two unknown stores, Peter Hill's harness and saddle shop, a music and book store, a queensware store, and Jerry Casey's bakery (at Main Street).

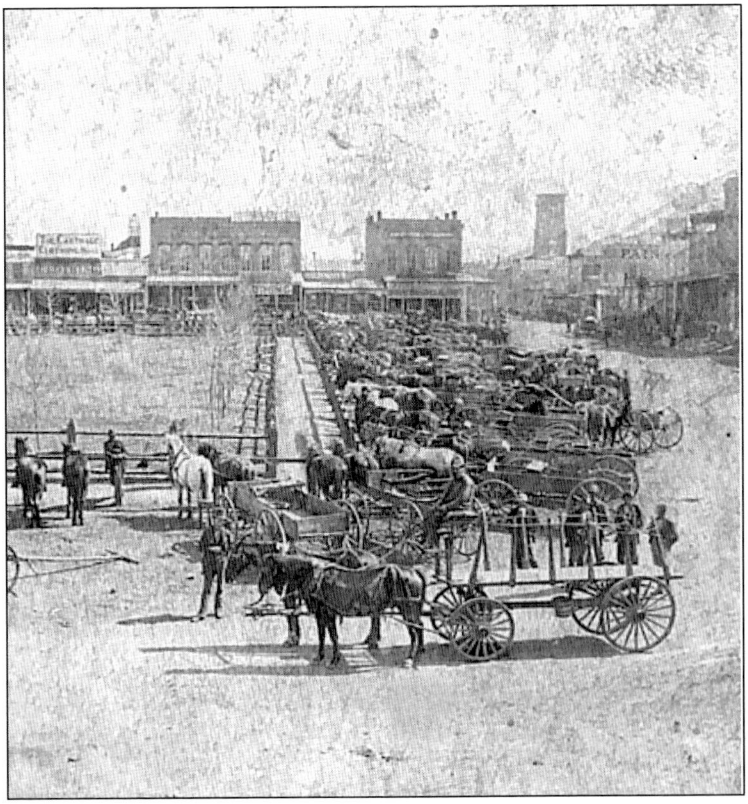

PARTIAL VIEW OF EAST SIDE OF SQUARE, C. 1878–82. Behind all the wagons are the stores of the southern half of the east side of the square—including the Farmers Exchange, J.E. Mobley's grocery, and probably J.J. Wells' grocery and Ruffin and McDaniel's dry goods store in the two-story building at Grant and 4th Streets. The tower of the 1870 Methodist Church can be seen in the distance (4th and Howard Streets).

BURLINGAME AND CHAFFEE OPERA HOUSE, 136 EAST 4TH STREET, 1877-78. By the late 1870s and early 1880s, many of the post-war frame structures were being replaced by more substantial brick buildings. Such was the case when Carthage's first opera house was built. In addition to the second floor being a 640-seat theater, the first floor housed the stores of R.H. Rose (left) and Maas and Cahn (right).

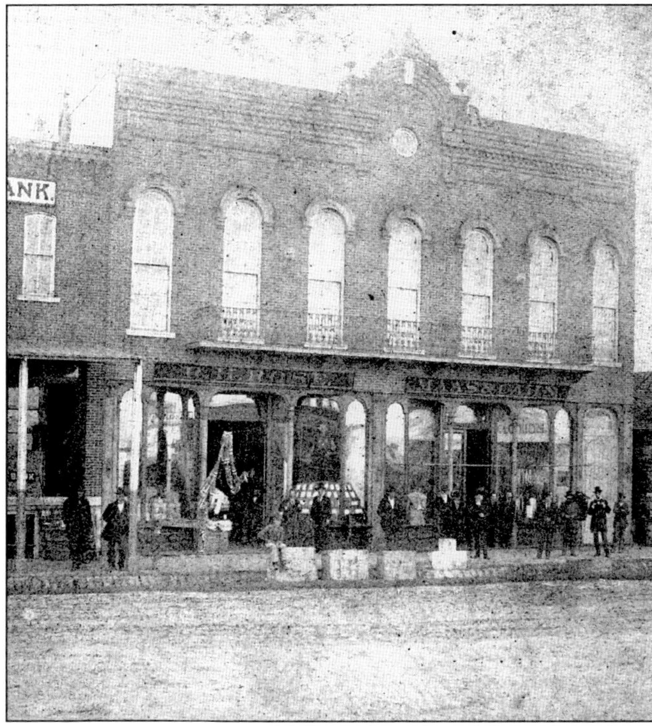

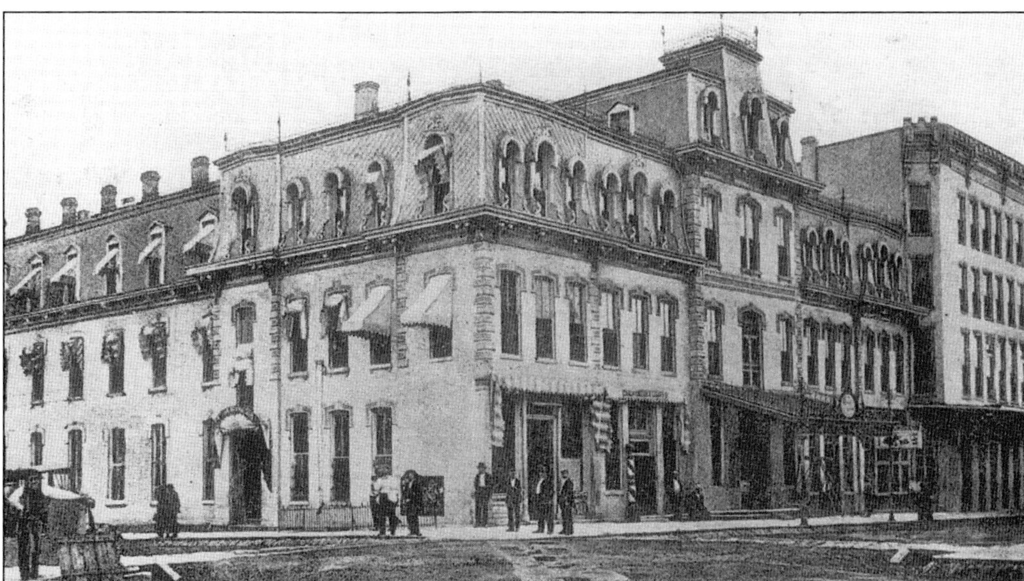

HARRINGTON HOTEL, 3RD AND GRANT STREETS, 1881–82. In the vicinity of East 3rd and Grant Streets, Charles Harrington built several new brick buildings after a disastrous fire in 1880 on the north side of the square. Included among his holdings was the Second Empire-style hotel that anchored the northeast corner of the square. Acquired by the Crane family in the 1920s, the structure was demolished in 1939 when the present building (originally Kroger Grocery) was constructed.

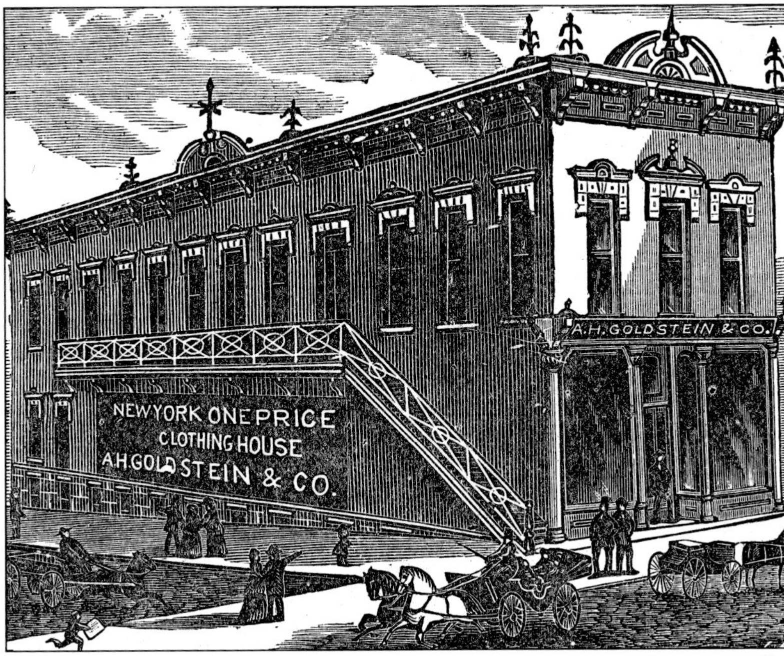

A.H. GOLDSTEIN STORE, 347 SOUTH MAIN STREET, 1879-80. The McCrillis and Allen Building was occupied by the firm of A.H. Goldstein, who specialized in men's clothing on a wholesale and retail basis. The McCrillis brothers went on to build a larger store at 146 East 4th Street in which they operated a hardware business.

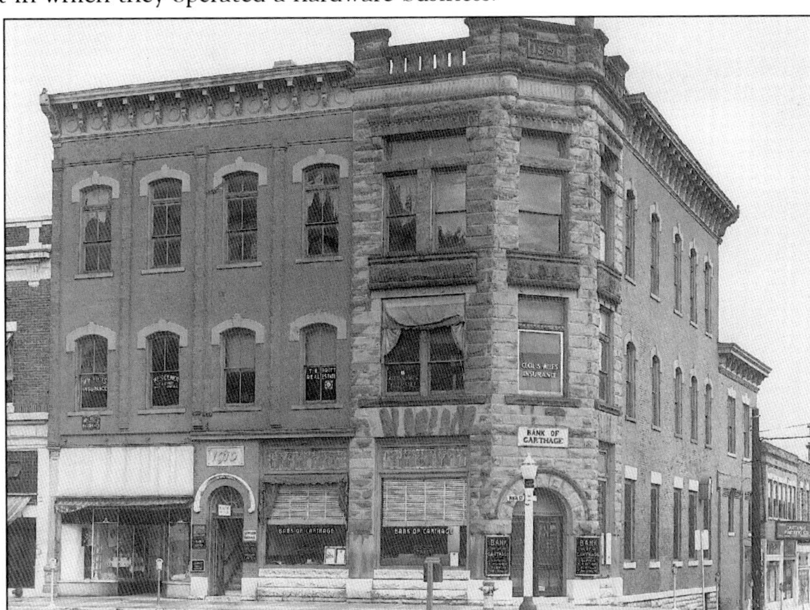

BANK OF CARTHAGE BUILDING, 300 SOUTH MAIN STREET, 1890. Built on the site of the first bank constructed after the Civil War, this brick and sandstone structure offered its second floor for professional offices, while the third floor served as the I.O.O.F lodge hall—other groups such as the Knights of Pythias and the Grand Army of the Republic used the area, too. Today the building (seen here in a 1940s photograph) survives without its third floor.

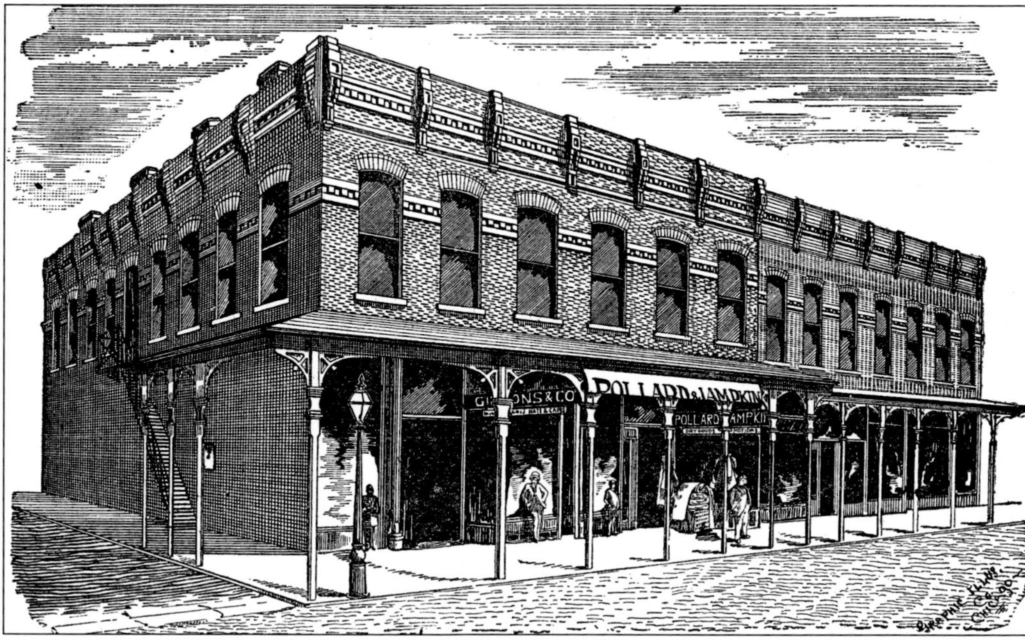

POLLARD BUILDING #1, 131–141 SOUTH MAIN STREET, C. 1880. Substantial buildings such as the Pollard, a series of four storefronts with offices and apartments above, were also built on the blocks approaching the courthouse square. Pollard and Lampkin Dry Goods and Gibbons & Company were early tenants.

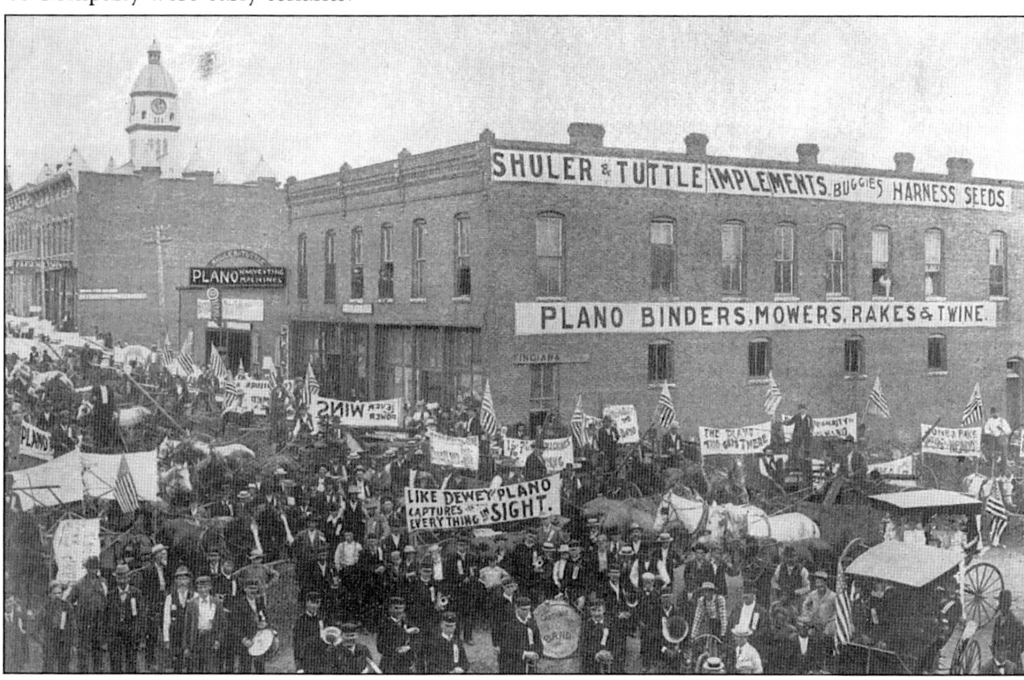

101-103 SOUTH GRANT STREET, C. 1893. Prior to housing the Shuler and Tuttle Implement store, the Modern Steam Laundry occupied this store building. The scene presented documents the largest delivery in 1899 of Plano harvesting machinery, which the company distributed to Kansas, Arkansas, and Indian Territory.

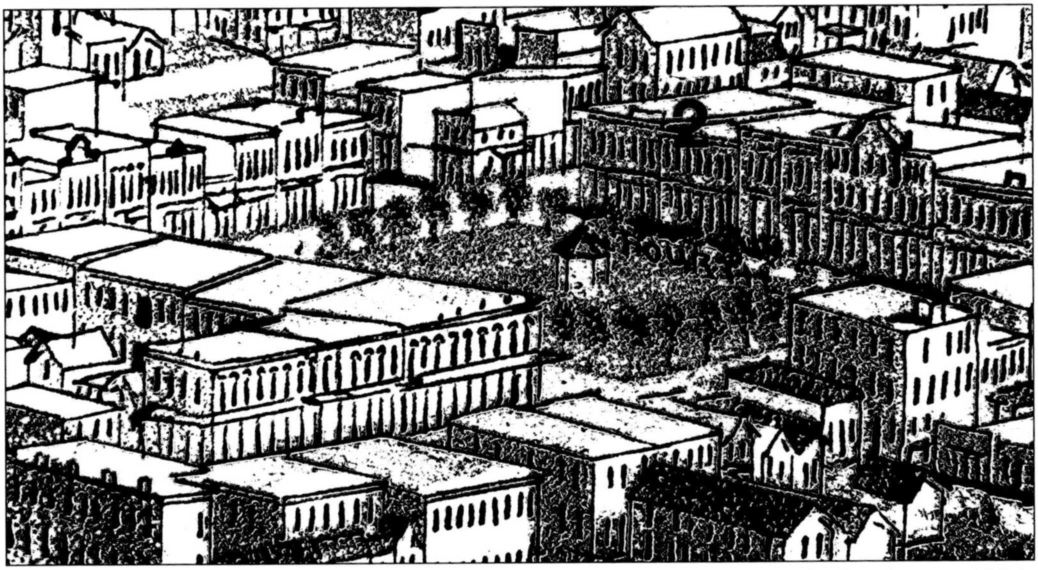

COURTHOUSE SQUARE DETAIL FROM THE ***Bird's-eye View of Carthage 1891.*** As construction of a permanent courthouse was debated and voted on four times in two decades, county offices hopscotched around the square. Among the several temporary office sites used were the Harrington and Sanderson Building (now 217 Grant Street) and the Burlingame and Chaffee Opera House (#2) on the square's south side.

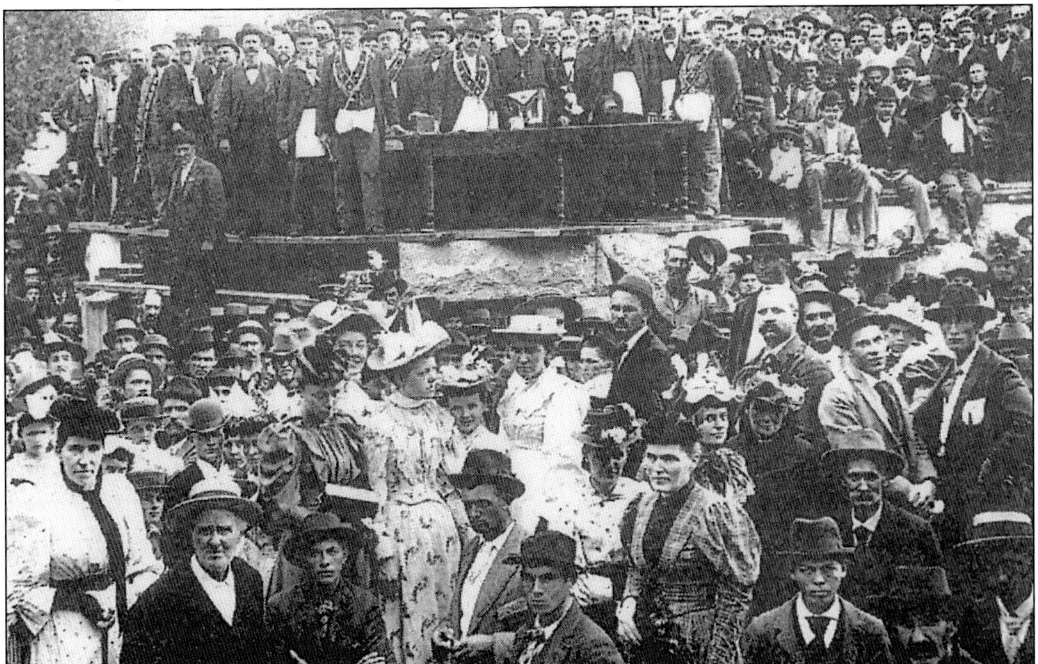

COURTHOUSE CORNERSTONE CEREMONY, AUGUST 21, 1894. After almost 30 years without a permanent county government building, construction of the Jasper County Courthouse began in the spring of 1894. By August 21, stone work was progressing far enough to allow a cornerstone ceremony to be held. Missouri Grand Master John Vincil and other Masonic officials presided over ceremonies, while Carthage's William H. Phelps was the featured orator.

FIRST NATIONAL BANK, 300 SOUTH GRANT STREET, 1891. The First National Bank, designed by C.W. Terry, was one of the first large-scale buildings constructed completely with local limestone. Prior to this, Carthage stone had been used primarily for foundations, sills, steps, and other building details. With the construction of this building and the courthouse, use of the local stone escalated. Architect Terry designed many structures in Carthage including the Westminister Presbyterian Church, E.O. O'Keefe's Cassil Place home, Dr. D.F. Flower's home at 901 Grant, and all-stone Myers-Garland Blocks on the square's east side.

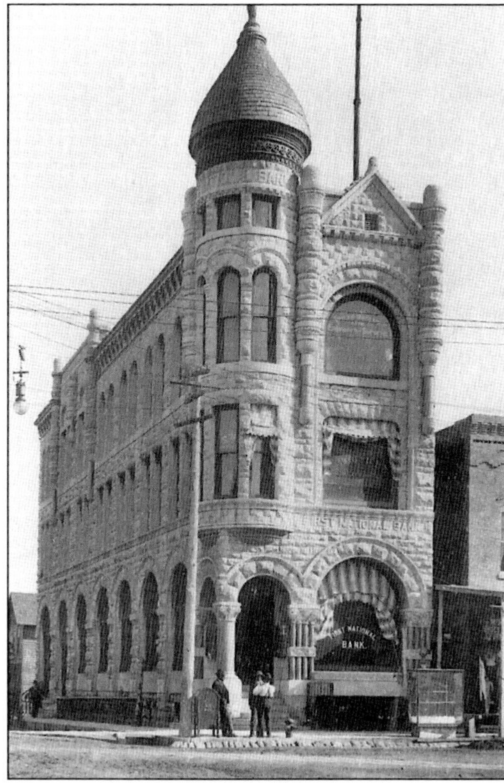

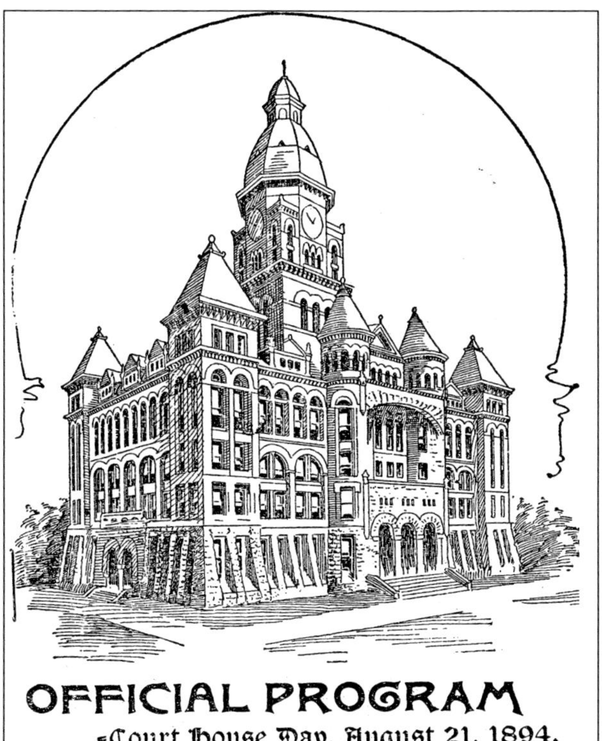

COVER OF CORNERSTONE CEREMONY PROGRAM. Text in the program lauded the "wonderland of agricultural and mineral resources, schools, churches, and happy homes" in Jasper County, a place of "60,000 people, with more lines of railroad, a larger school fund, and a greater exporter than any other county in the state." At the start of the 1890s, Jasper County was Missouri's third leading county in population and wealth.

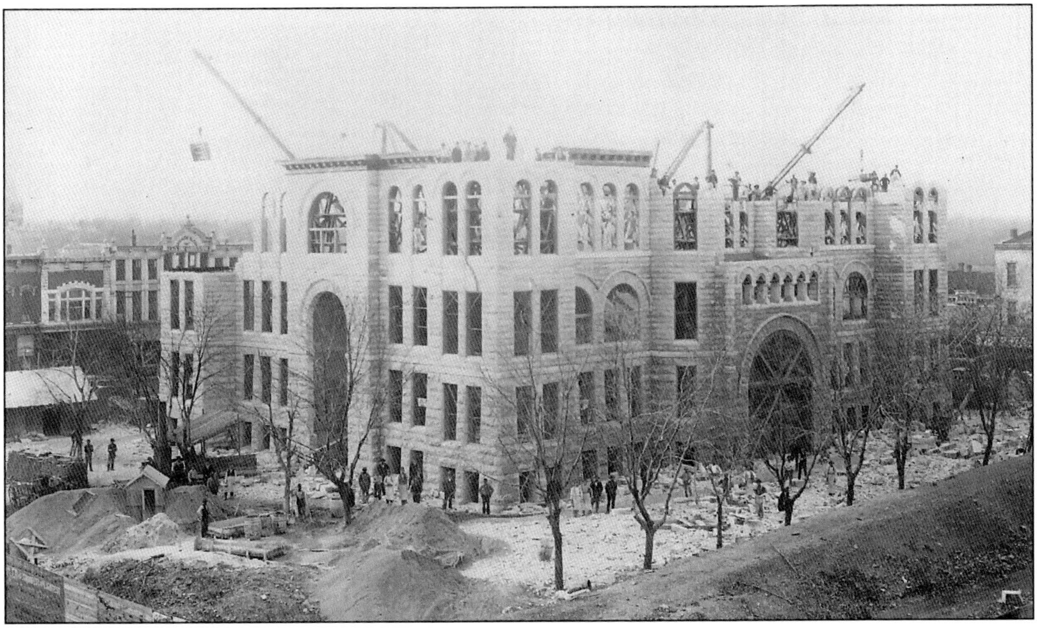

Jasper County Courthouse Under Construction, Date Unknown. Although E.C. Thym of Kansas City supervised the stonework, many local stone masons were employed on this project, including Rudolph Pfenniger who is in this view but not identified. Stone was provided by Carthage Stone Company, which had to operate six days a week, 24 hours a day from March 1894 to October 1895 to keep up with demand for this project and orders elsewhere.

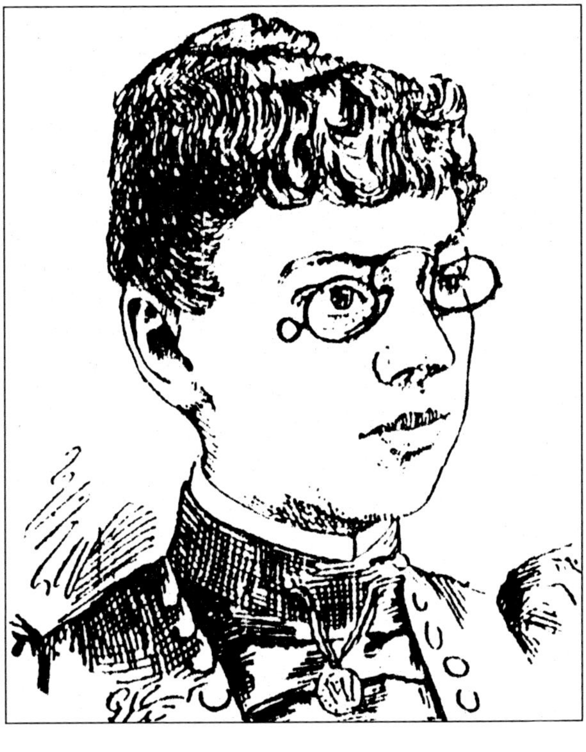

Annie Baxter (1864–1944). Believed to be the first female county clerk in the United States and first elected female official in Missouri, Mrs. Baxter served from 1891–1894 when courthouse construction began. Her name, like her fellow county officers, is found on the building's cornerstone as well as on a commemorative marker on the courthouse lawn.

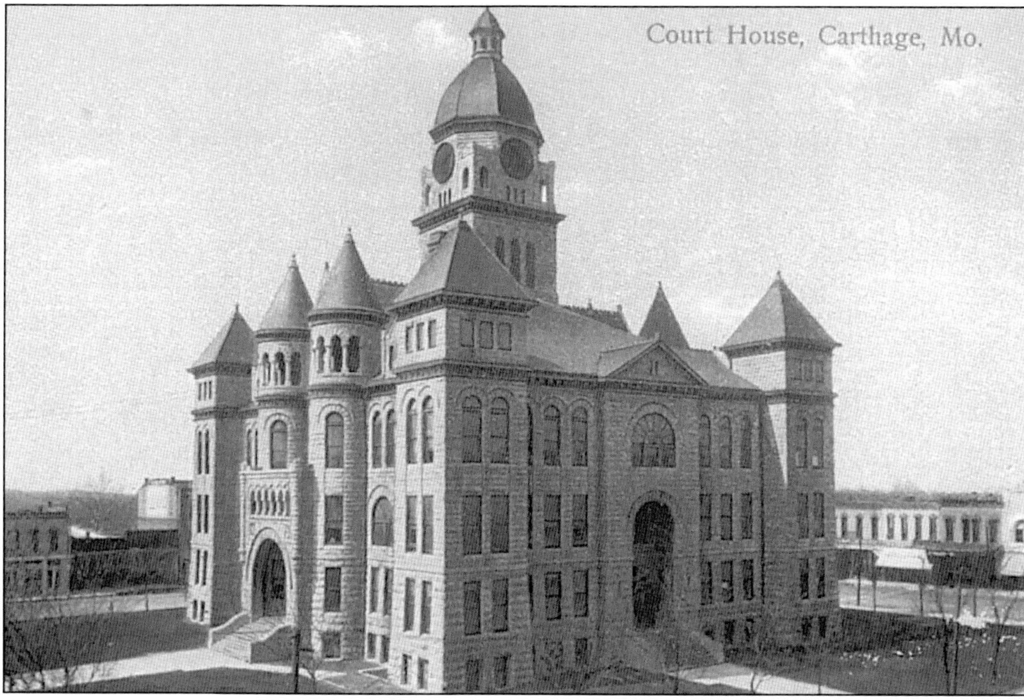

JASPER COUNTY COURTHOUSE, C. 1905. The courthouse was designed in the Romanesque Revival style by architect M.A. Orlopp Jr. of Little Rock, Arkansas, and New Orleans, Louisiana. He later worked in Dallas and designed the Dallas County Courthouse in a similar design. The builder was L.W. Divelbiss of Olathe, Kansas, who also constructed the Kansas courthouses of Franklin County in Ottawa and Miami County in Paola.

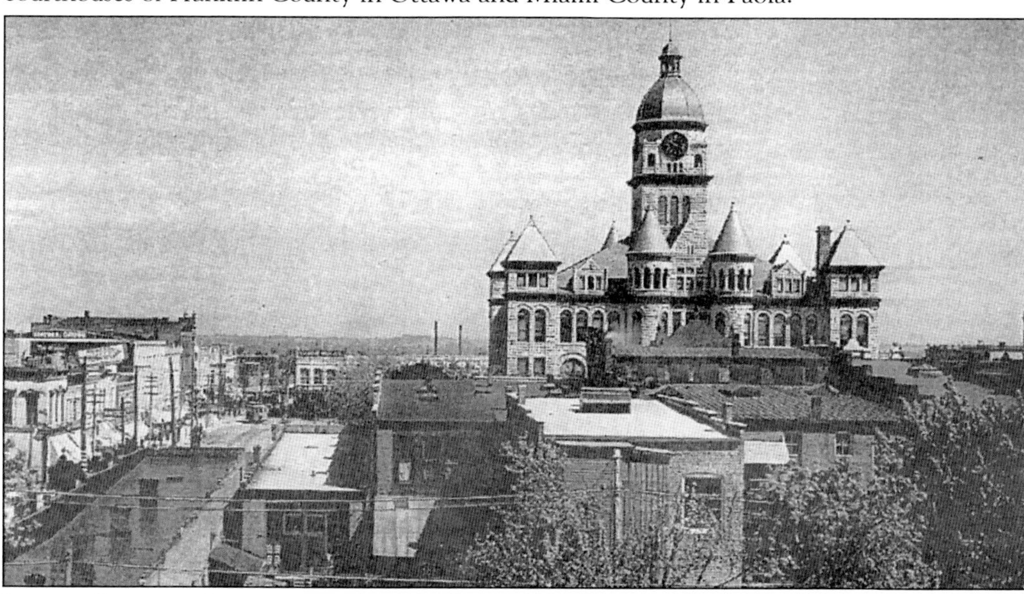

JASPER COUNTY COURTHOUSE ABOVE BUSINESS DISTRICT, C. 1910. Once completed, the courthouse became the dominating structure of town. In the foreground of this view are the roofs and backs of stores on East 4th Street, while Main Street is to the left. The courthouse cost $100,000 to build and still serves as home to Jasper County government.

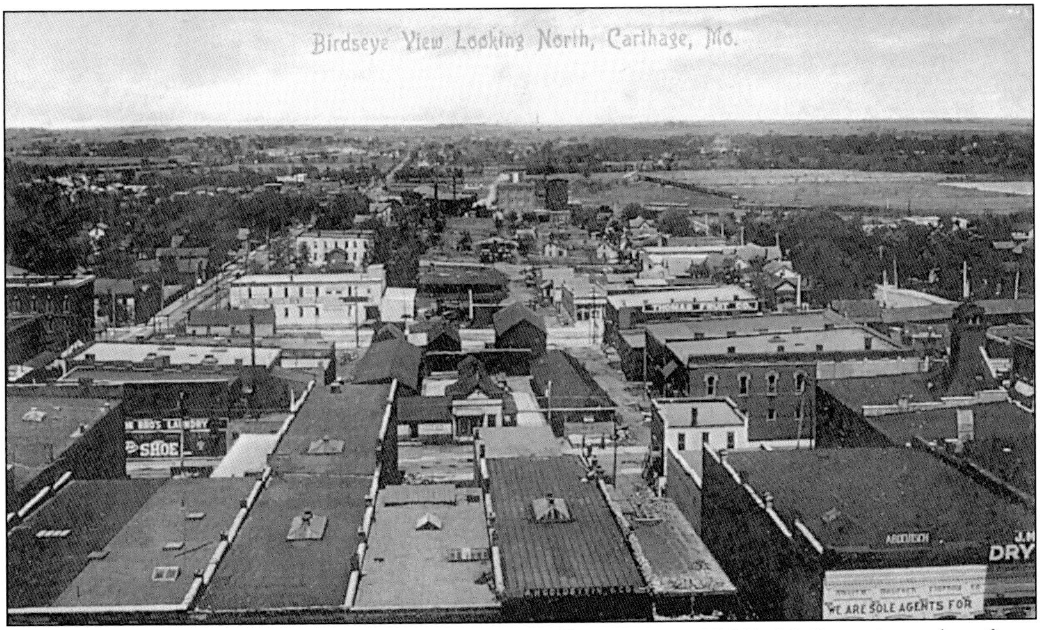

NORTH SIDE OF SQUARE AND BUSINESS DISTRICT BEYOND, C. 1905–10. In a view taken from the courthouse, Carthage's main industrial area is in the distance beyond the storefronts of the north side. In the center of this view on 2nd Street between Main Street (left) and Grant Street (right) is the lumberyard of Calhoon-Putnam Company.

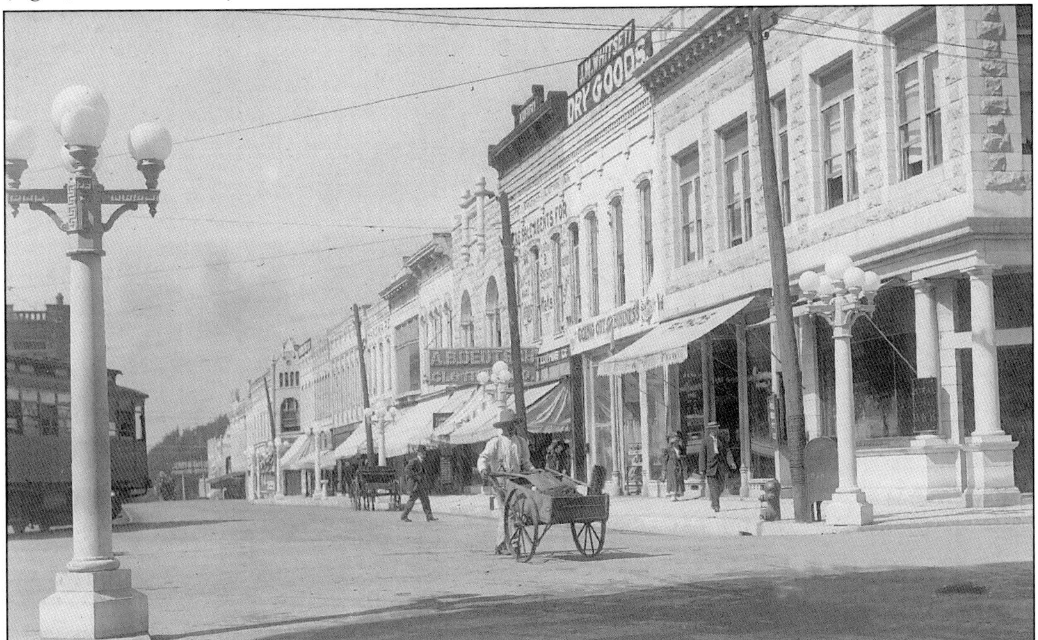

NORTH SIDE OF SQUARE LOOKING WEST FROM GRANT STREET, C. 1910. A.B. Deutsch Clothing Company and J.M. Whitsett dry goods store are beyond Charles Dumar's Music Store and F.G. Bishop's Photograph Studio. Dumar's is the left storefront next to the Central National Bank at the corner, which refaced its older building with Carthage stone in 1910. A street worker cleans up after horses while the trolley goes by behind him.

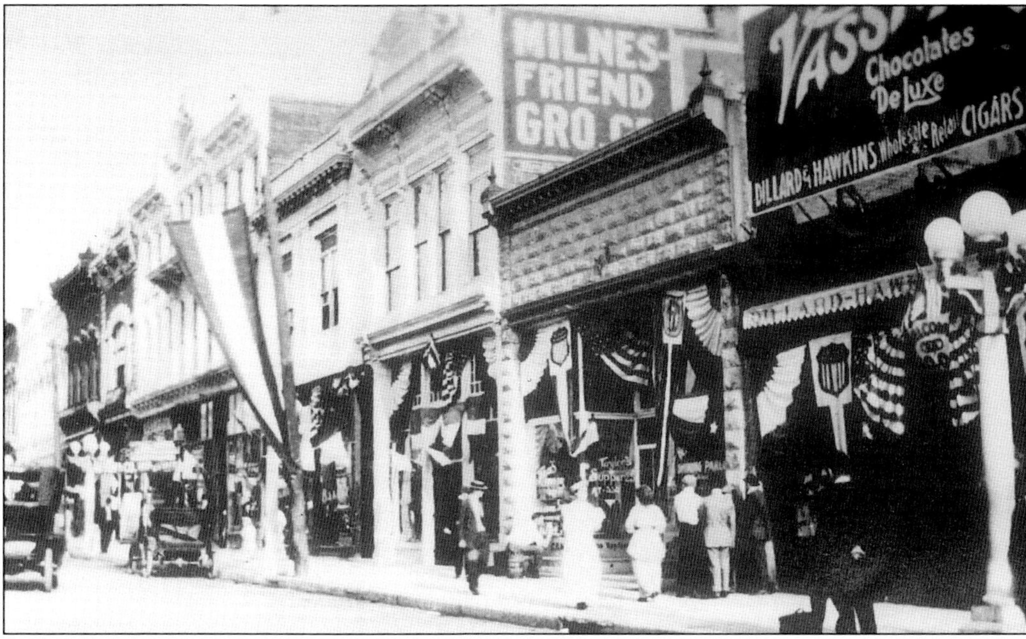

South Side of Square Looking East From Main Street, c. 1914. Decorated for a patriotic holiday, these stores are decked out with flags, shields, and bunting. Pictured here from right to left is the Dillard and Hawkins Tobacco Shop and Confectionary, Carthage Shining Parlor, John Taylor's Confectionary, and Milnes-Friend Grocery in the center. Midway down the block in the three-story Cassaday Building was the Delphus Movie Theatre.

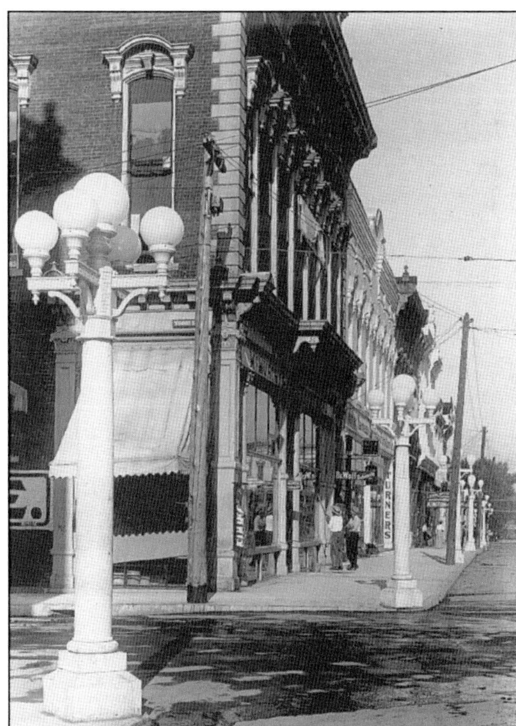

South Side of Square Looking West From Grant Street, c. 1910. The town's "White Way" of Carthage stone light posts and sidewalks is touted on this real photo postcard. McMurtry's Department store is visible in the 1885 McCrillis Building at the corner, while Turner's Harness, Carriage, and Furniture Company is just beyond in the former Burlingame & Chaffee Opera House building.

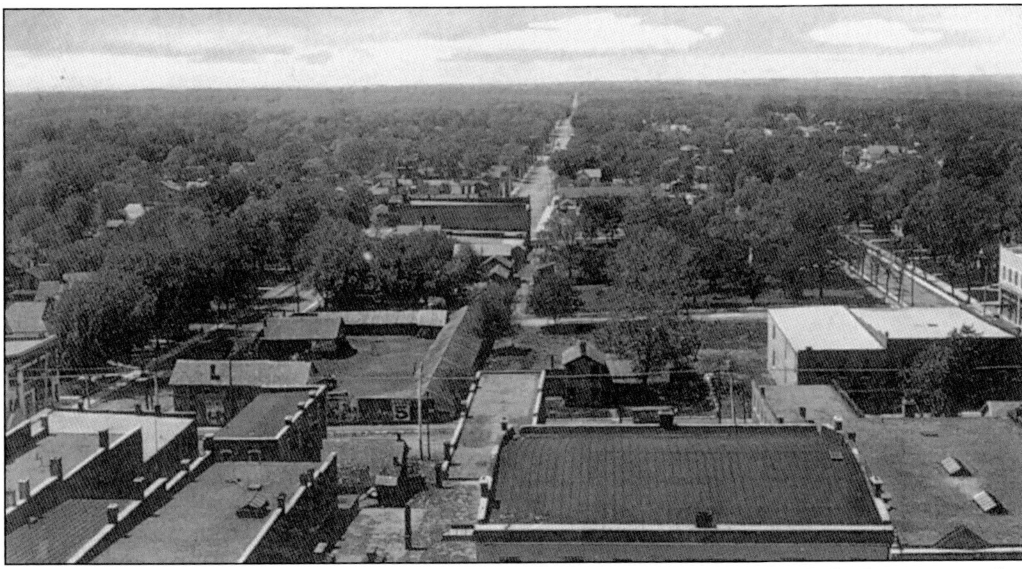

WEST BUSINESS DISTRICT AND RESIDENTIAL AREA, C. 1906–08. Oak Street stretches westward in the center of this postcard, while on Lyon Street (behind the storefronts of the square), the Southwest Feed, Sale, and Wagon Yard still stands at 4th Street—even though the former 3rd Street Livery, Board, and Sale Stables has been cleared for future.

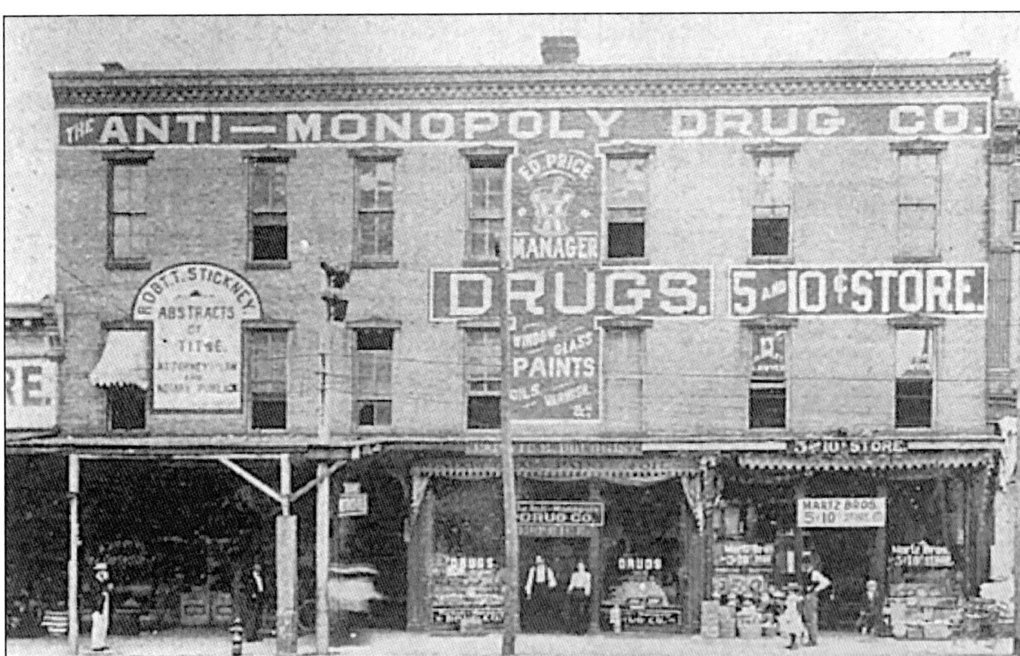

REGAN BUILDING, 317–325 SOUTH MAIN STREET, C. 1900. At the new century, the Regan now housed Ed Price's Anti-Monopoly Drug Company and the Martz Brothers Five and Dime store, while upstairs Robert Stickney had his office along with other professional tenants. Remodeled and renamed Center Building in the 1920s, this structure has lost its third floor like the Bank of Carthage building.

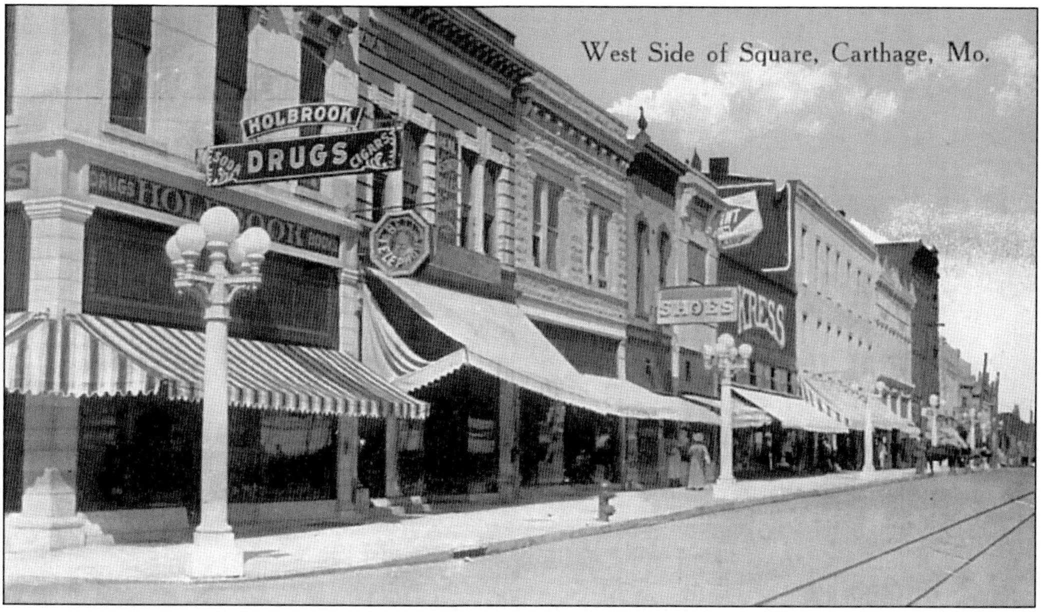

West Side of Square, c. 1910. Located in the middle of this block was the 1907 Kress store, which replaced the frame structure of the former post office and its companion, P.O. Bookstore. Carthage's store marked the first Kress 5–10 and 25¢ Store in Missouri. At 4th Street was Holbrook Drugs, the successor to the P.O. Bookstore, run by James R. Holbrook and son Newell. Other merchants in the first-floor storefronts about this time (left to right) were: Blankenship & Owens Men's Clothing, H.P. Hall Jewelry & Music, McCutcheon & Hughes Shoes, unknown merchant, Kress, Electric (?) Theatre, Gunther Drugs, Ramsay Brothers' Dry Goods, C.T. Hall's Shoes, Morris Goldstein Jewelry, and the Bank of Carthage.

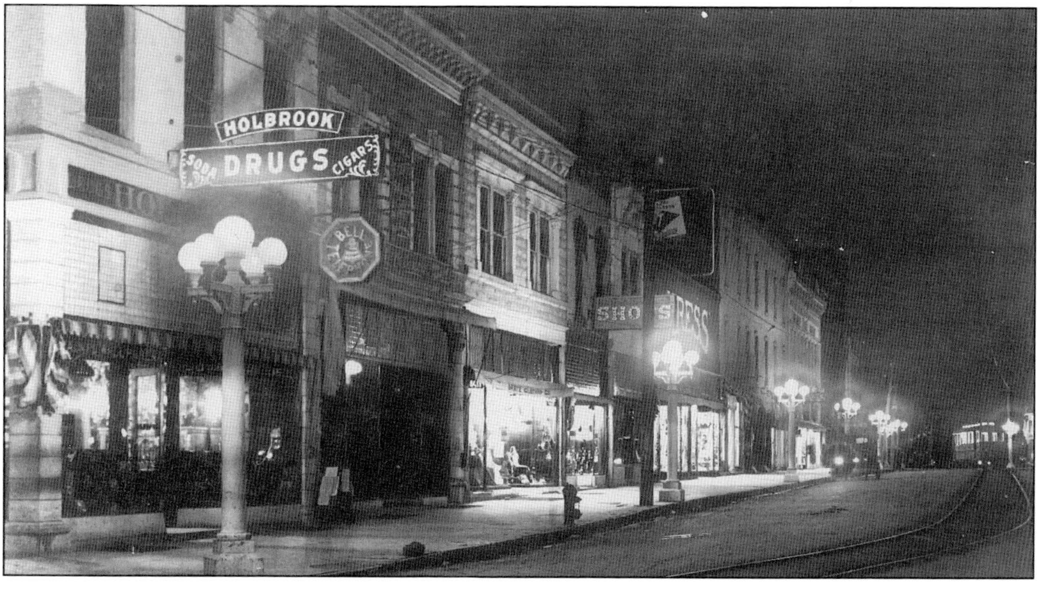

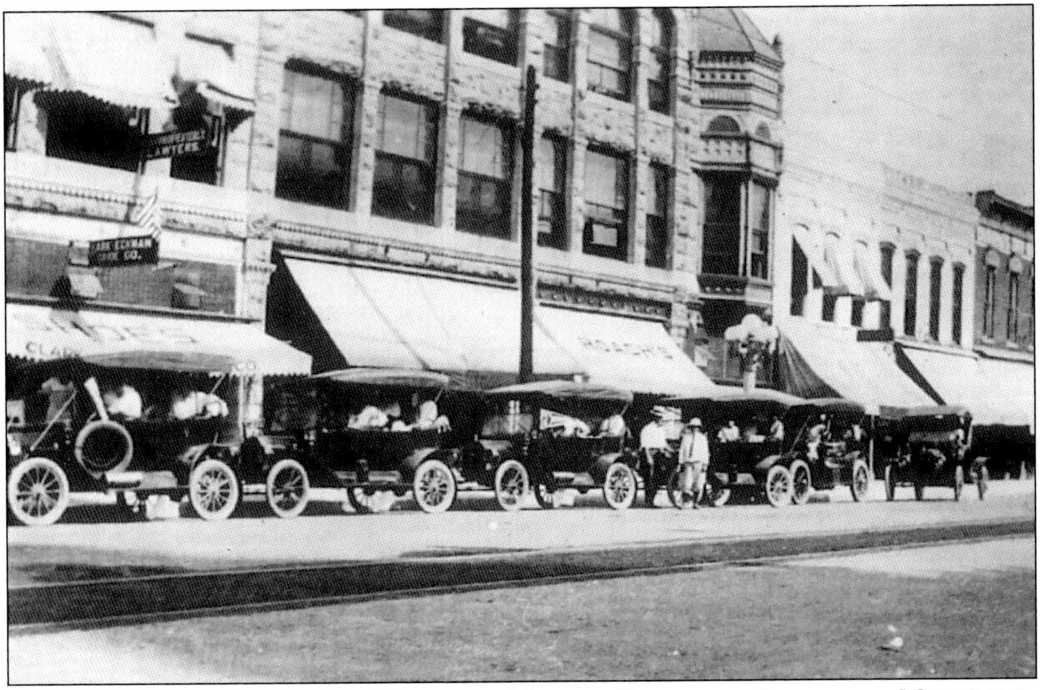

EAST SIDE OF SQUARE WITH NEWTONIA-NEOSHO-CARTHAGE EXCURSION MOTORISTS, C. 1914–15. Scenic excursion trips were favorite pastimes of early automobile owners, including this group parked on the east side of the square. Store awnings behind the travelers announce the Clark-Eckman Shoe Company (left) and W.T. Roach's Jewelry and Queensware store (middle).

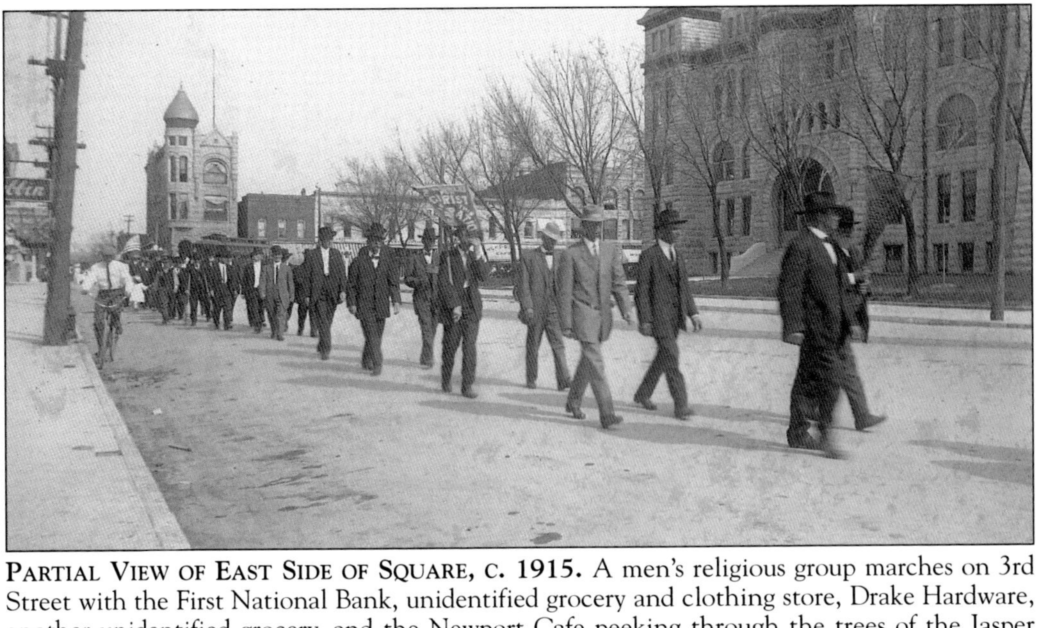

PARTIAL VIEW OF EAST SIDE OF SQUARE, C. 1915. A men's religious group marches on 3rd Street with the First National Bank, unidentified grocery and clothing store, Drake Hardware, another unidentified grocery, and the Newport Cafe peeking through the trees of the Jasper County Courthouse to the right.

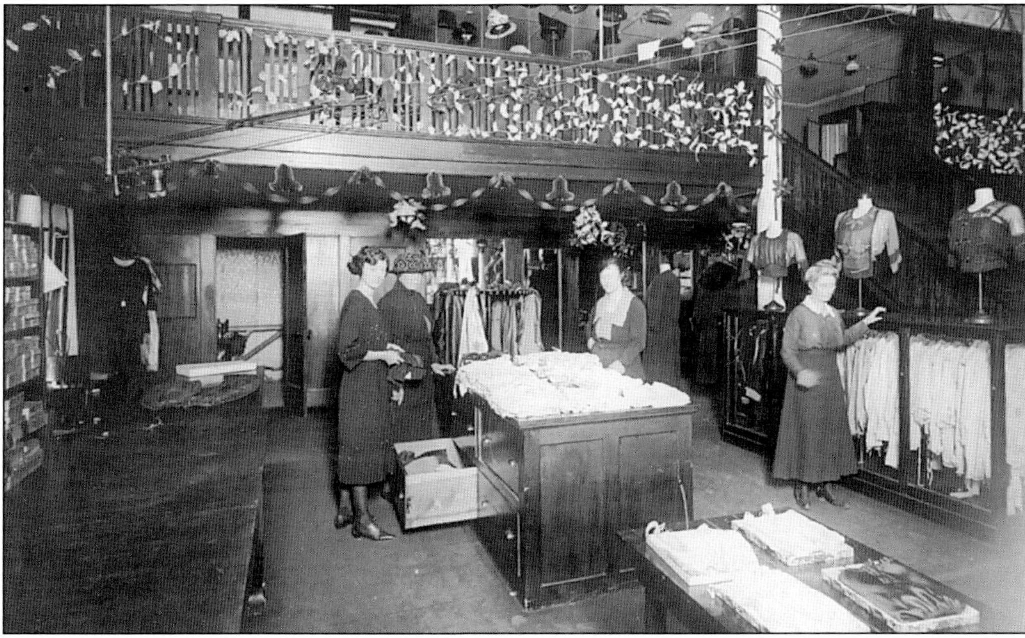

INTERIOR OF BURKETT-ANDREW'S DEPARTMENT STORE, 146 EAST 4TH STREET, 1921. Decorated for the Christmas season, these ladies are inspecting women's shirtwaists. The millinery department is located on the upper mezzanine, whose balustrade is decorated with holly garland, while chenille roping, crepe paper, and honeycomb tissue paper bells decorate other areas of the store. Among the women are Jewell Chumbley and Mrs. Ward.

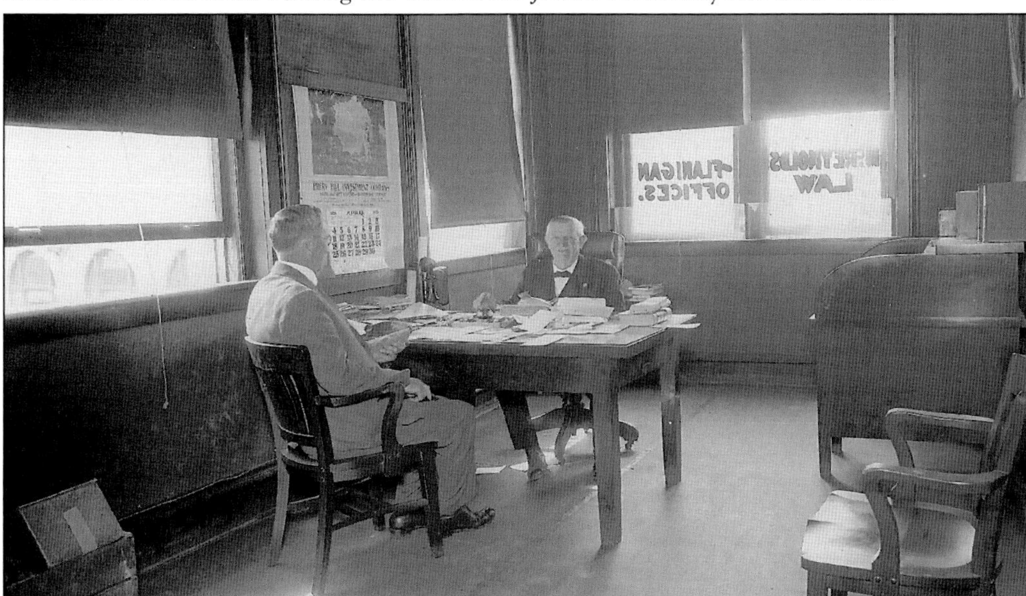

INTERIOR OF MCREYNOLDS AND FLANIGAN LAW OFFICE, SECOND FLOOR, 149 EAST 3RD STREET, 1920. Professionals such as doctors, dentists, lawyers, insurance, and real estate agents inhabited many of the rooms above the storefronts surrounding the square. Attorney Sam McReynolds sits facing the photographer. At his death in 1931, he was chairman of the Central National Bank above which this office was located. The other gentleman is unidentified.

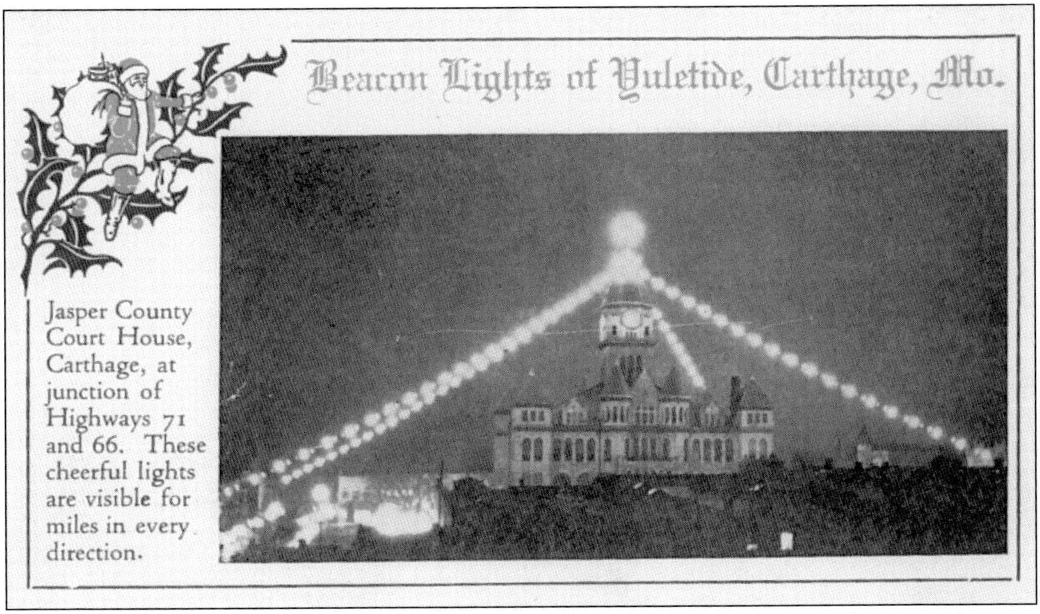

CHRISTMAS GREETING CARD, C. 1925. Christmastime lighting of the courthouse and square has been a tradition since the first municipal tree on the courthouse lawn in 1916. This greeting card entitled "Beacon Lights of Yuletide," shows the string of lights that continue to form a canopy over the square at the holidays.

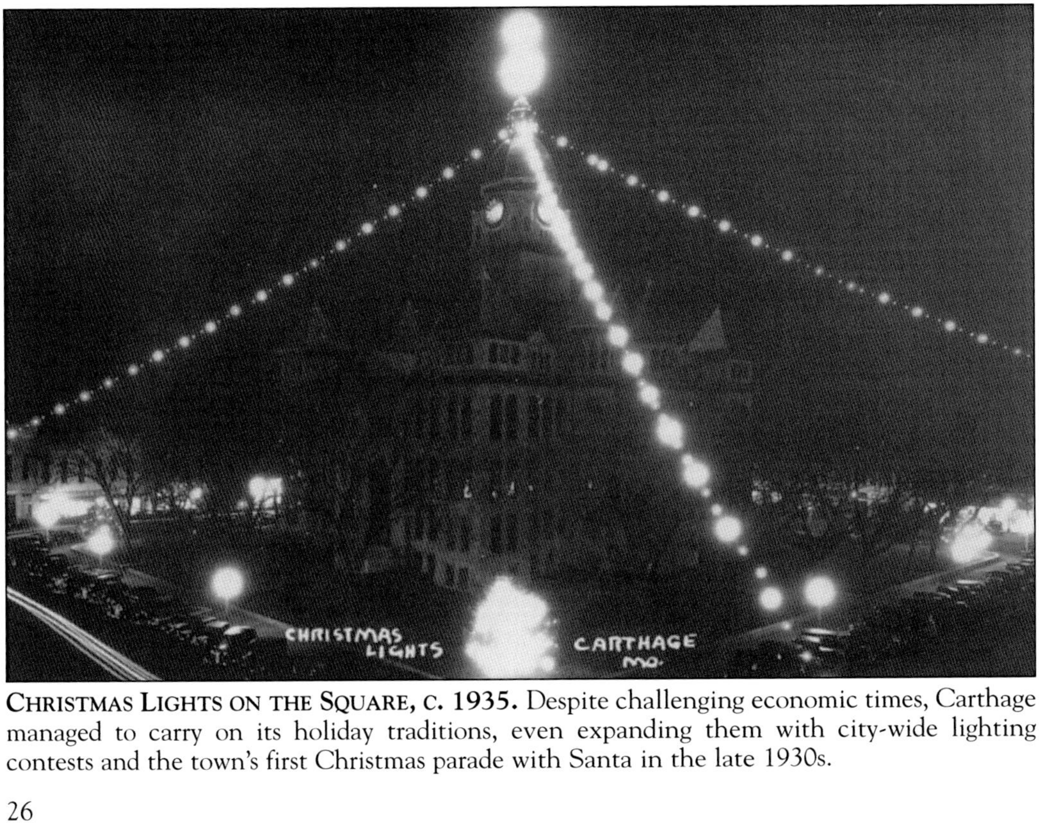

CHRISTMAS LIGHTS ON THE SQUARE, C. 1935. Despite challenging economic times, Carthage managed to carry on its holiday traditions, even expanding them with city-wide lighting contests and the town's first Christmas parade with Santa in the late 1930s.

Two

EDUCATION

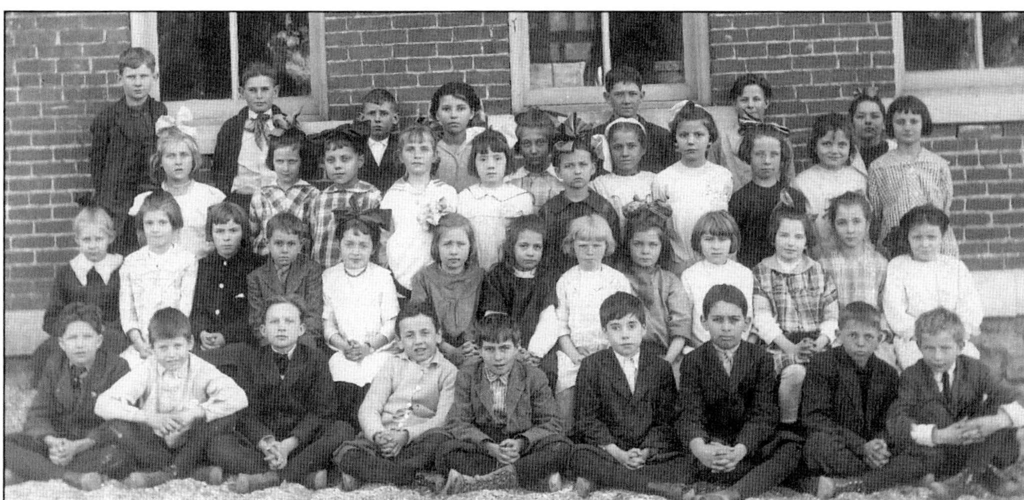

MISS HOLIDAY'S 4TH GRADE, FRANKLIN SCHOOL, 1914–15. Pictured from left to right are (starting on front row): Raymond deFries, Leland Stebbins, Eugene Gunther, Milo Johnson, Marcus Dolph, Carter Bishop, Paul Wisegarver, Clyde ?, T.J. Gilbert; (second row) Elizabeth Caulkins, Esther Baker, unidentified, Robert Strohm, Virginia Murphy, Della ?, Harriet Webster, Ruby Erickson, Eugenia McBean, Pearl Ellis, Marian Powers, Mildred Jenkins, unidentified; (third row) Dorothy ?, Lois Wood, unidentified, Martha Sharon, Susan Wallace, Martha Seaver, Charlotte Ralston, Beulah ?, Alberta Webster, unidentified, Helen Van Hoose; (back row) Alan ?, Sam McReynolds, Allen ?, unidentified, Todd ?, Curtis Wright, and Juanita Wheeler.

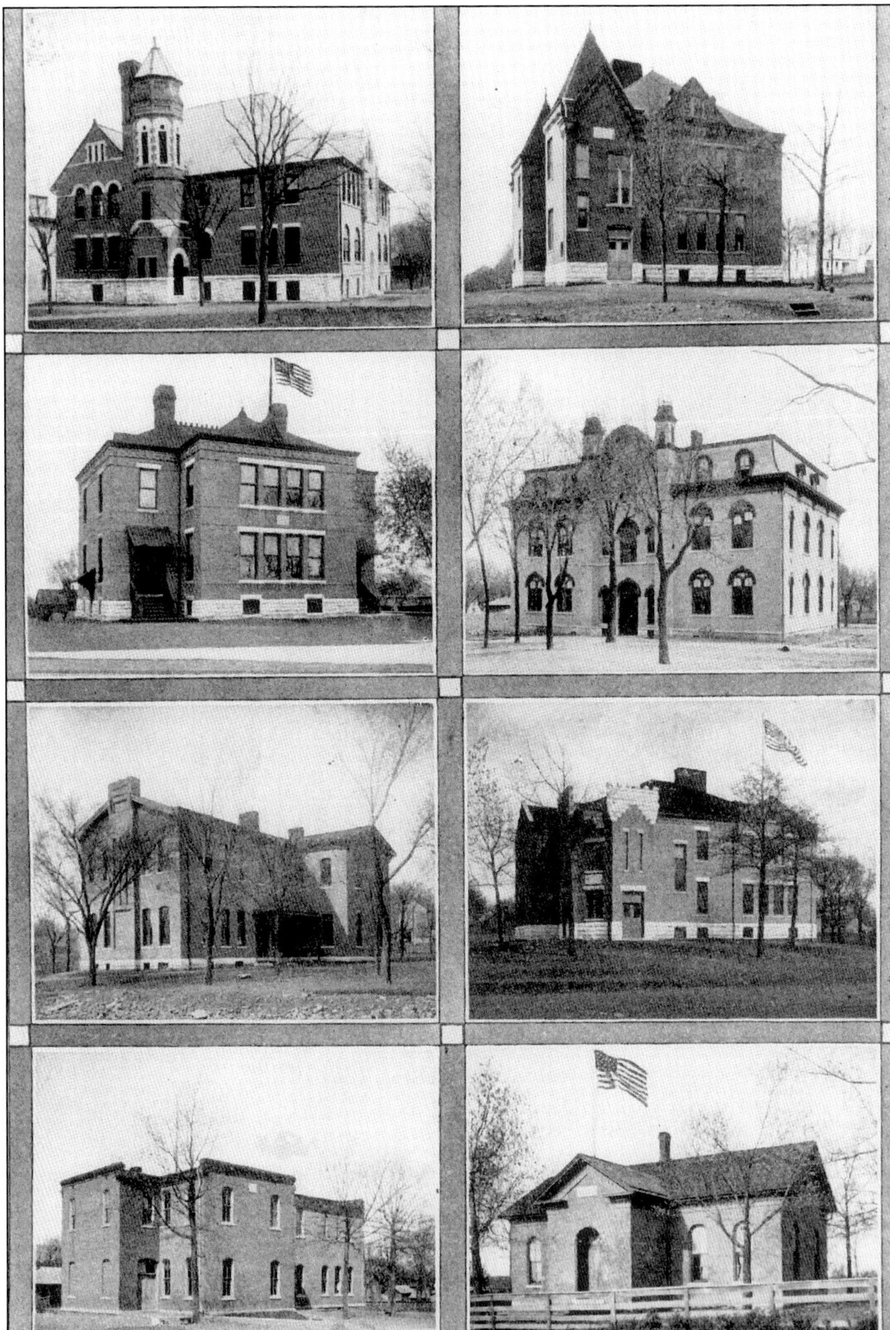

Carthage Schools, c. 1904. Pictured from the top, left to right, are: Carthage High School at Main and Chestnut Streets, Columbian on West Chestnut Street, Irving at 3rd and Orchard Streets, Central at 700 South Main Street, Washington at 823 Fulton Street, Benton at McGregor and Mound Streets, Franklin at Miller and Maple Streets, and Lincoln at High and Garrison Streets. Except for Central, all these schools were built in the 1880s–90s amid the town's population explosion.

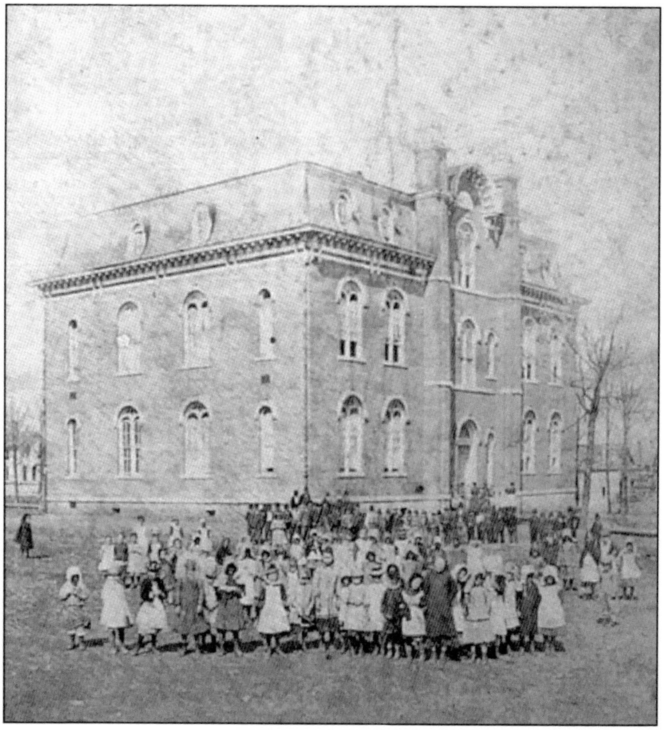

CARTHAGE GRAMMAR AND HIGH SCHOOL, (LATER CENTRAL SCHOOL), 700 BLOCK SOUTH MAIN STREET, 1870. Photographed by W.S. Johnson of Springfield, this stereopticon view finds all the students out on the lawn of the brick school, which was built on the site of the former Carthage Academy that had been destroyed during the Civil War. Myrabelle Shirley—later known as Belle Starr—was the earlier school's most famous student.

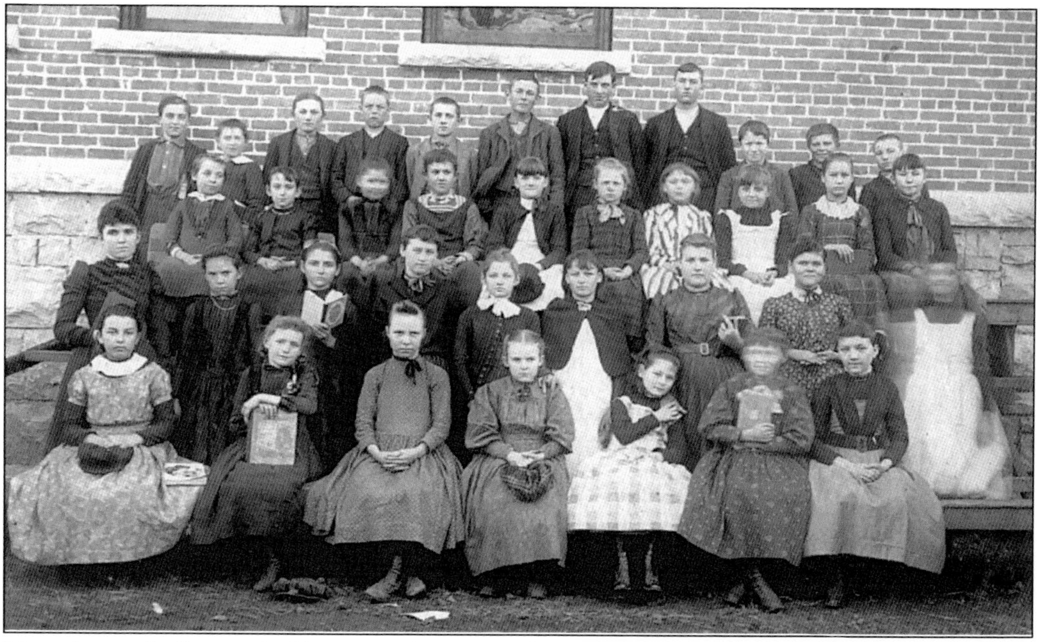

MISS LOWEN'S ROOM 6, CENTRAL SCHOOL, 1890. Among the students in this unidentified photograph is Marian "Mamie" Wright, seen in the plaid jumper in the first row, third from the right. At the close of the school year, Marian sang at the high school and at Central, probably marking the first public appearance for this future professional coloratura soprano.

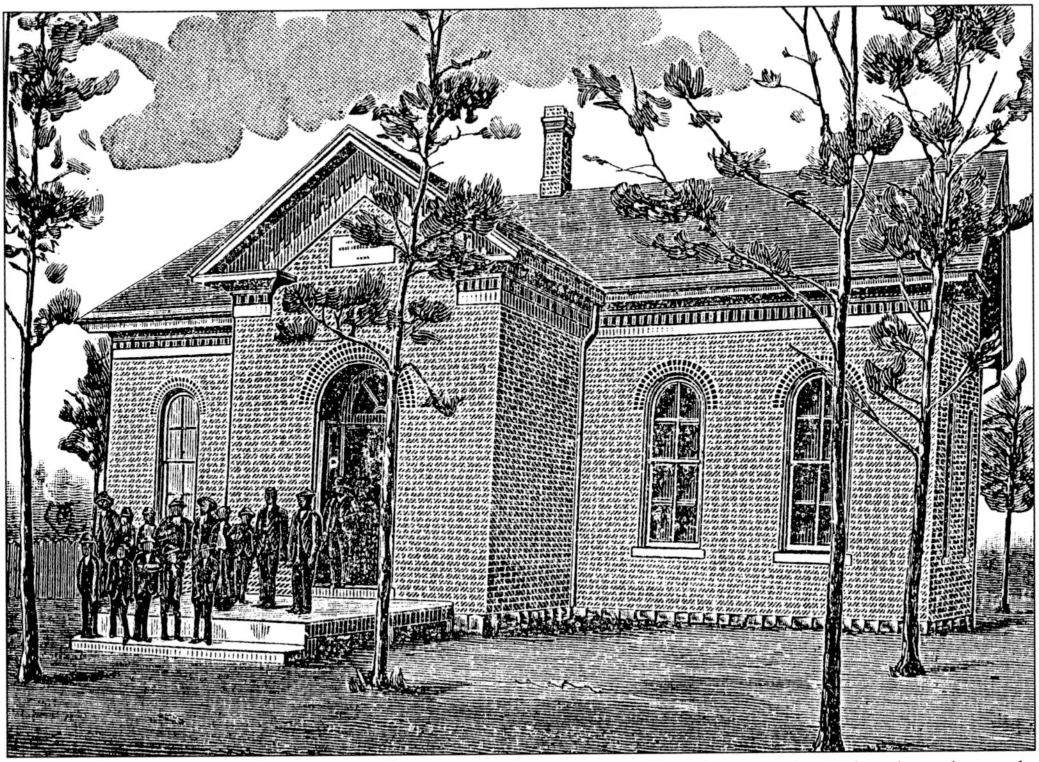

LINCOLN SCHOOL, 525 NORTH GARRISON STREET, C. 1880. Lincoln School is the only pre-1900 school still in existence, although it has been remodeled with stucco covering the original brick facade. In an 1876 "Report of the Board of Education of the City of Carthage," Lincoln was noted as having 53 African-American students under R. Dobyns then DeMott Woodmansee, who had taken over for Alonzo Hubbard, the school's early teacher.

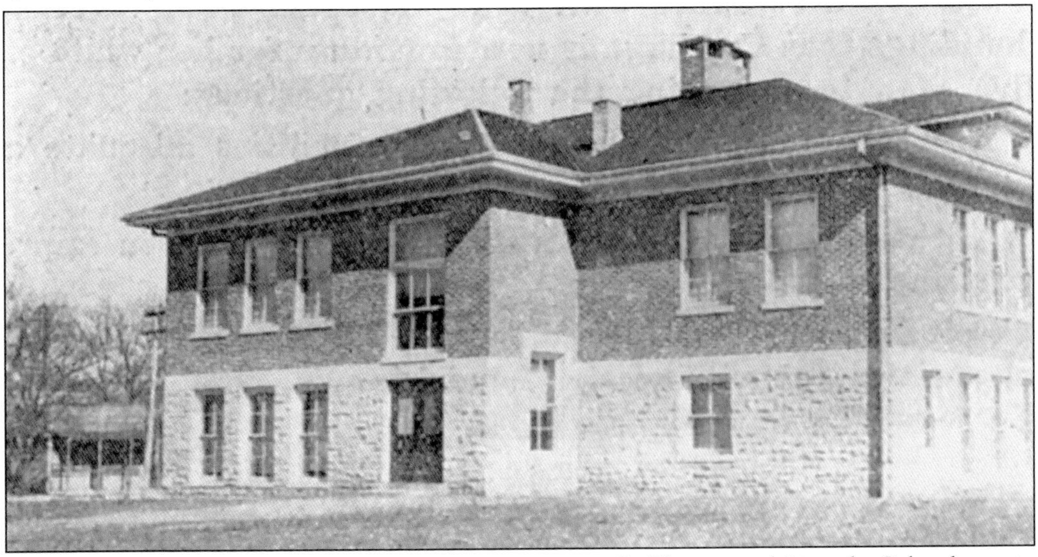

LINCOLN SCHOOL, 6TH AND RIVER STREETS, 1914–15. The second Lincoln School was in use for less than two years when the structure burned. It was replaced and served until 1955 when schools were desegregated.

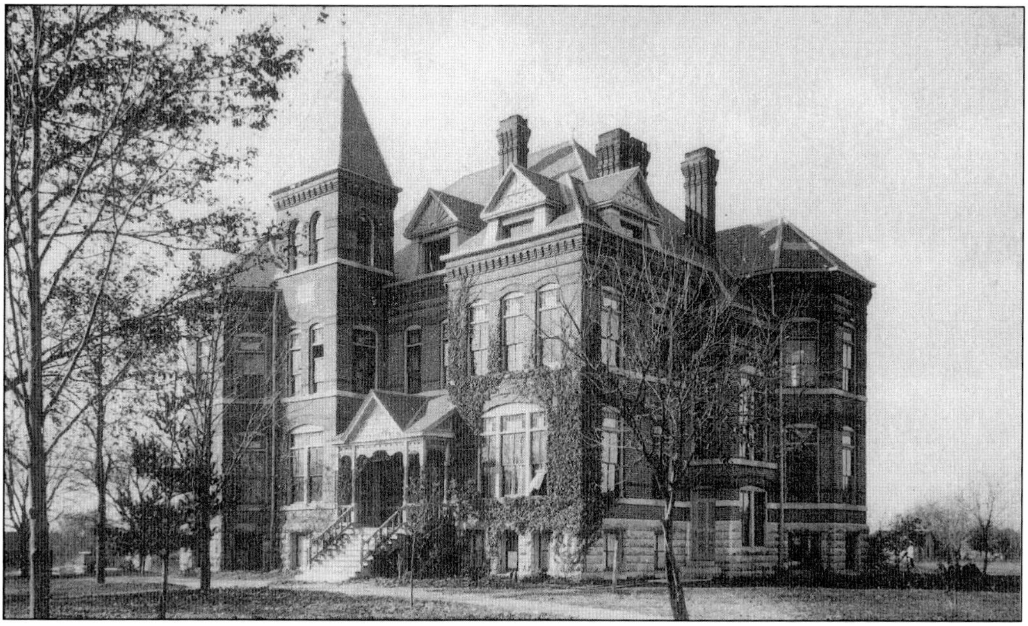

CARTHAGE COLLEGIATE INSTITUTE, WIGGINS AND MAIN STREETS, 1887–88. Designed by St. Louis architect J.B. Legg, this massive brick and stone building housed Carthage's first college, which was established in 1884. Affiliated with the Presbyterian Church, business, "normal" (teacher training), and academic courses were offered, with tuition ranging from $10-18 per term. The college closed in 1908.

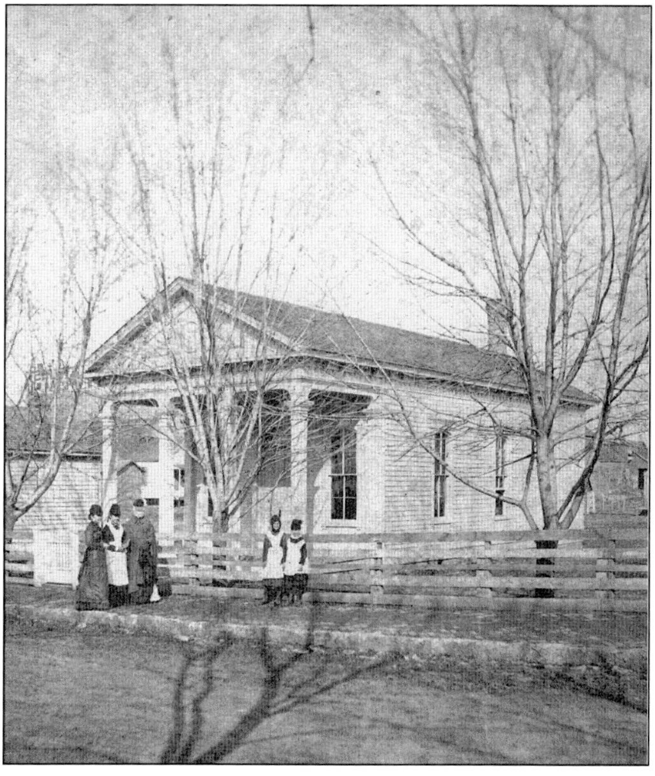

CARTHAGE LIBRARY, 506 SOUTH MAIN STREET, 1870. The ladies of Carthage organized the Carthage Library Association around 1870, and by the early 1880s they had over one thousand books that members could borrow for 10¢ a week per title. Amazingly, the pediment of this library building is still visible, although the remainder of the structure has been altered greatly. The library was only at this address one year before moving to various locations around the square.

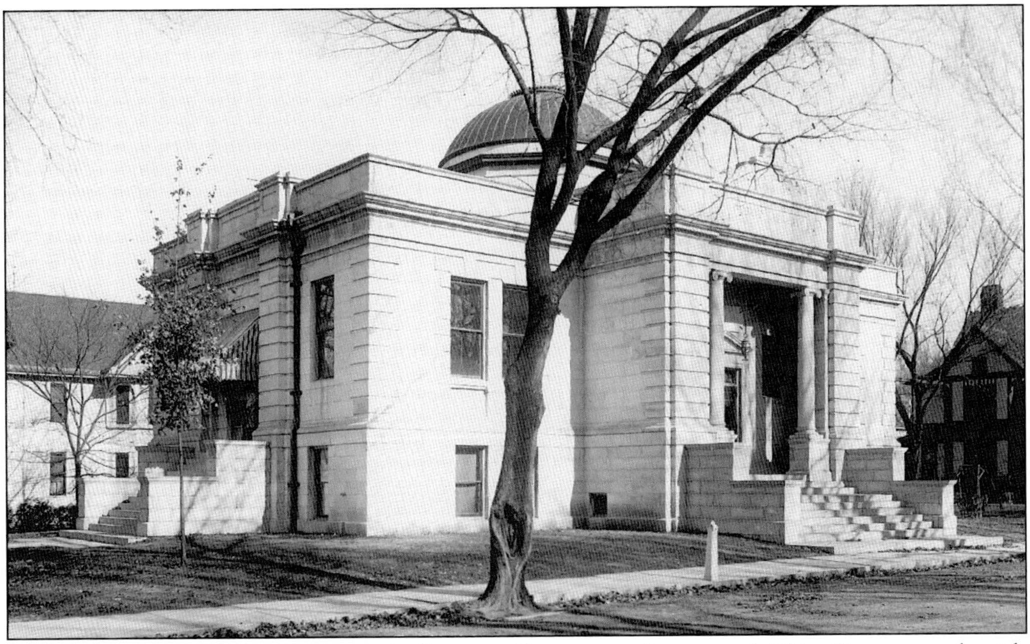

CARTHAGE PUBLIC LIBRARY, 612 SOUTH GARRISON STREET, 1904. Constructed with $25,000 from Andrew Carnegie, this Neo-Classical, Carthage stone building was designed by F.C. Gunn of Kansas City. Final costs exceeded the donated amount, but Carnegie declined to give more, stating through his representative that the original amount was sufficient for a library in a town the size of Carthage. The library opened in February 1905.

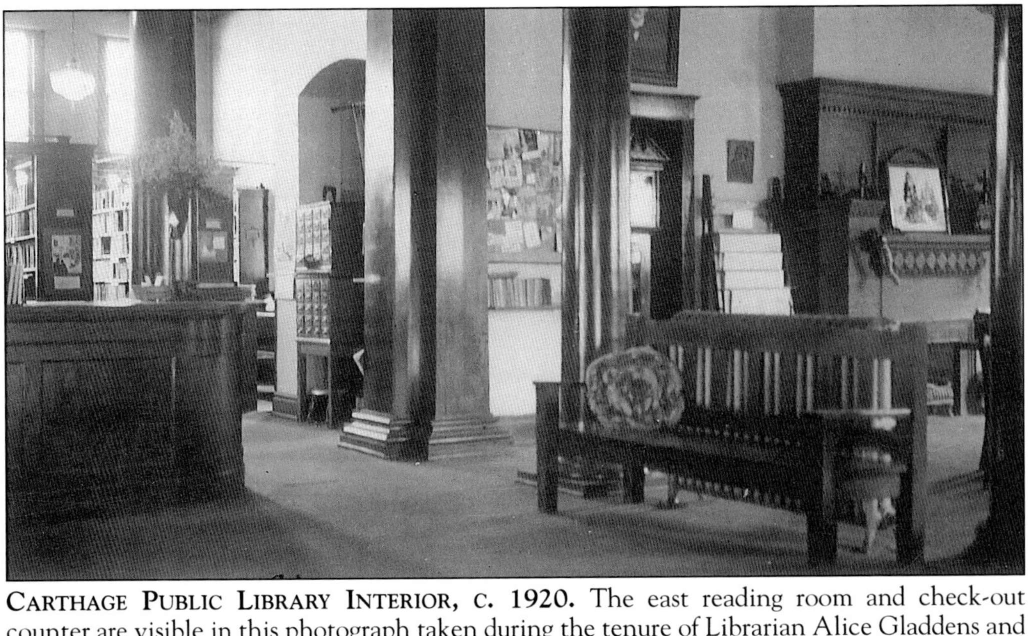

CARTHAGE PUBLIC LIBRARY INTERIOR, C. 1920. The east reading room and check-out counter are visible in this photograph taken during the tenure of Librarian Alice Gladdens and Assistant Librarian Laura May Wood. The interior appears today much as it did in this view.

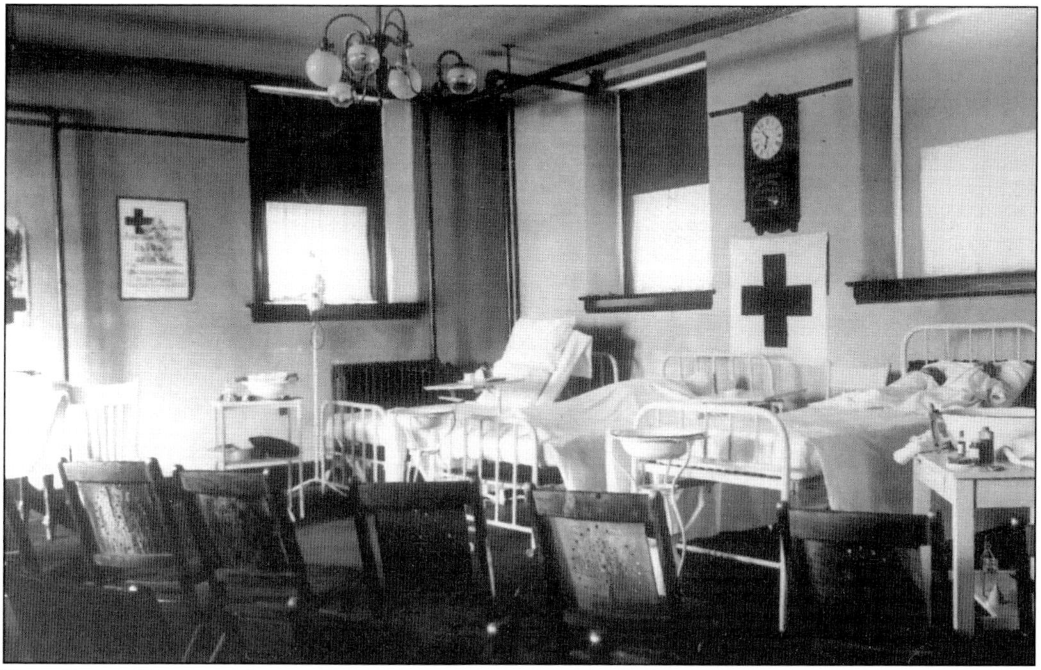

RED CROSS ROOMS, CARTHAGE LIBRARY, 1917. When the library was first built, provisions were made to provide a lecture hall and club rooms on the lower level for civic use, but no one could have foreseen these spaces being turned into the Red Cross production and classrooms during World War I. While most of these Red Cross volunteers learning first aid are unidentified, Marian Wright Powers is believed to be sitting at the far right administering a wrist bandage.

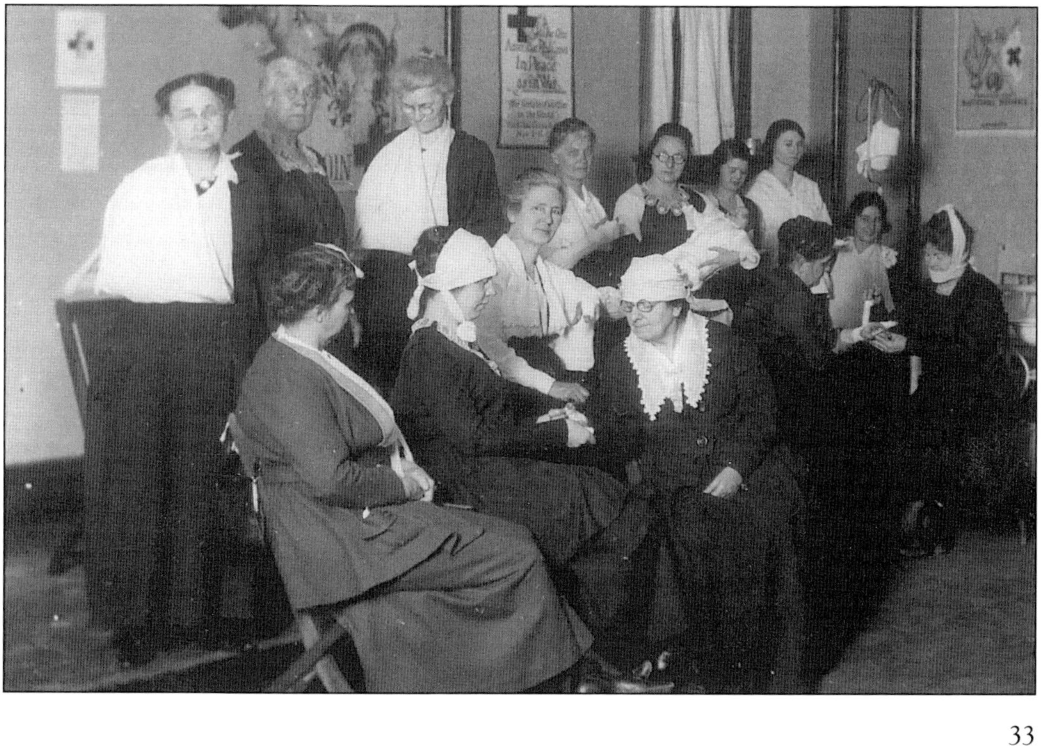

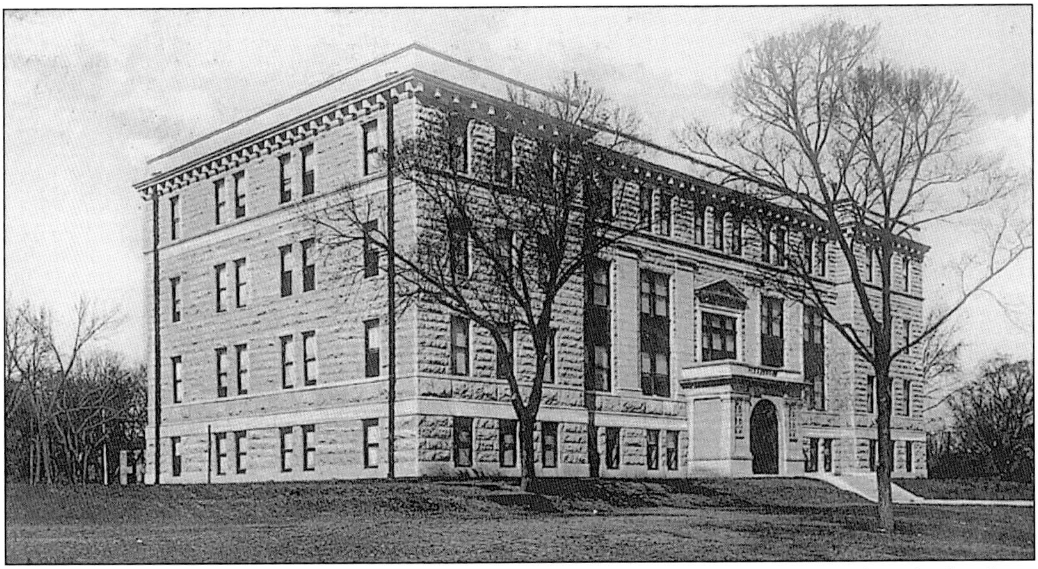

CARTHAGE HIGH SCHOOL, 714 SOUTH MAIN STREET, 1904–5. Overcrowding had a long history in the Carthage school system as the city grew. By the turn of the century, high school classes were being held in the attic of the old high school as well as in Central. With the decision to construct another school, bonds were arranged, and the cornerstone was placed November 29, 1904. Originally, stonework was to be smooth-faced but orders were changed, and Ellis Jackson superintended the laying of rock-faced, local stone.

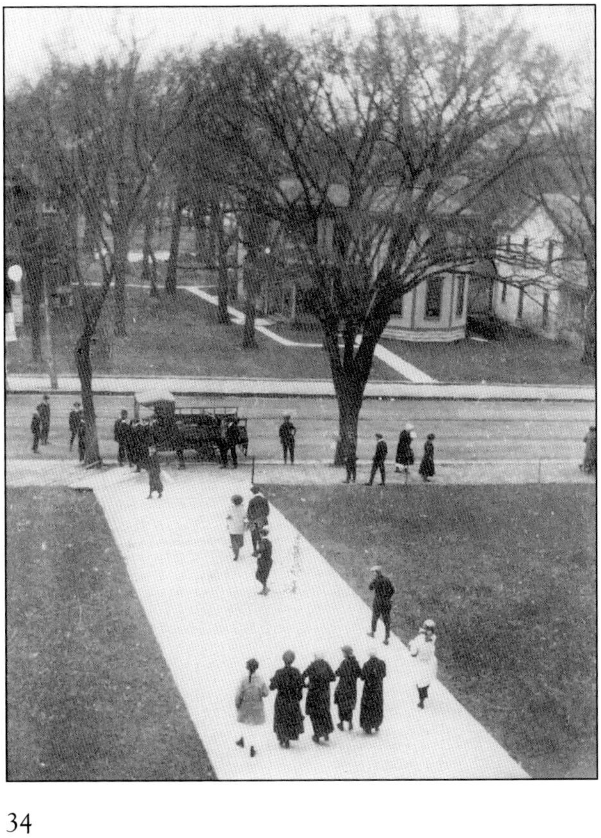

VIEW FROM MISS PRATT'S ROOM, CARTHAGE HIGH SCHOOL, C. 1914. Esther Pratt taught at CHS for 37 years and organized the English department, expanding it to include classes in grammar, rhetoric, composition, and literature, which she felt was the most important subject of all. An accomplished poetess, she wrote "Fair Carthage," the school's song. Homes at 701 and 703 South Main are visible in the background.

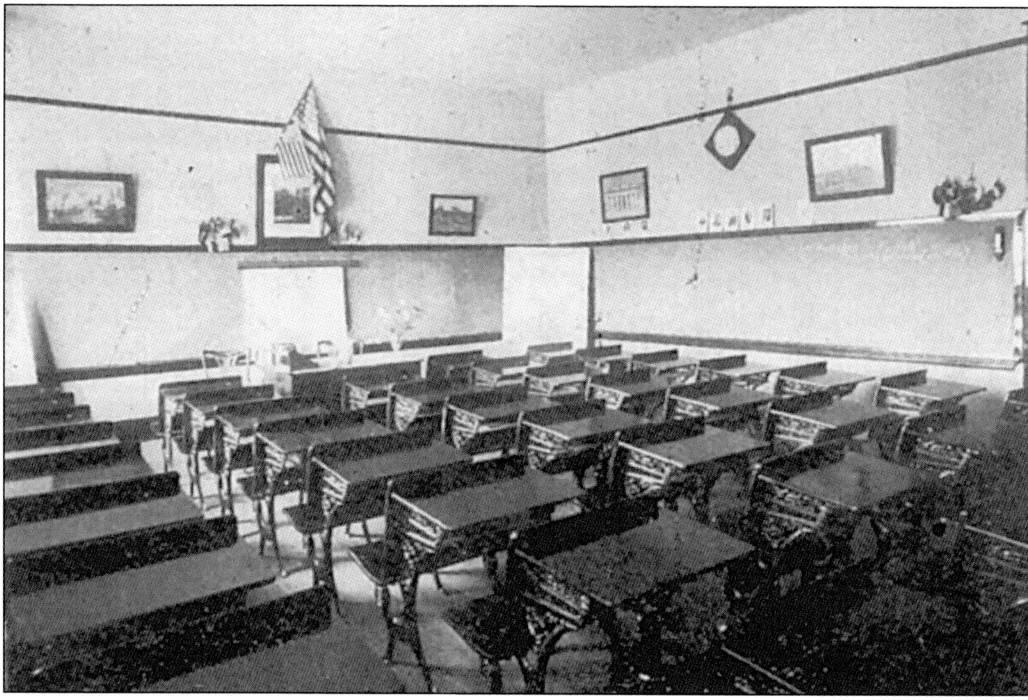

CARTHAGE HIGH SCHOOL, HISTORY (ABOVE) AND ENGLISH (LOWER) ROOMS, 1906. With other change orders, it soon became evident there would not be enough money to adequately furnish and equip the interior of the school, and another special election was held to add $30,000 to the original construction bonds. The first classes were held February 26, 1906, and the former high school, which was built in 1890, eventually became the Manual Arts building.

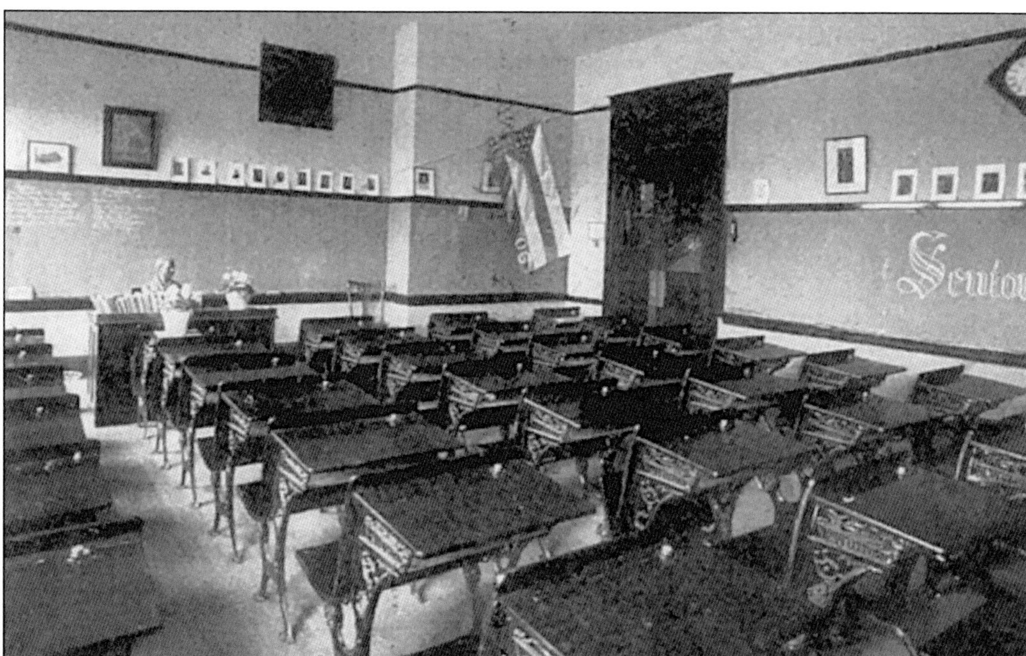

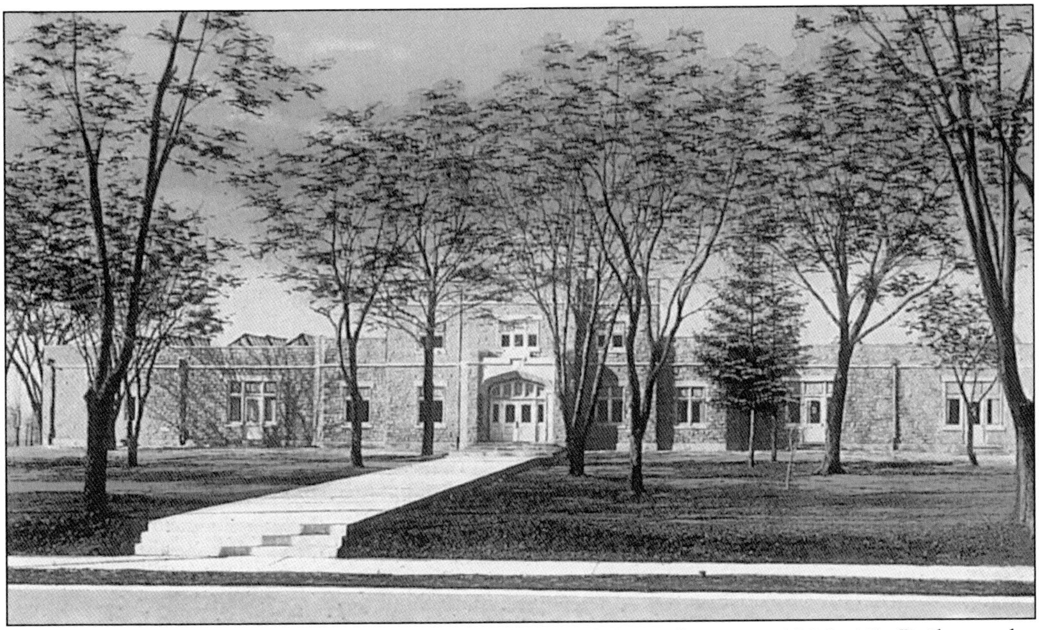

Mark Twain Elementary School, 1435 South Main Street, 1916–17. Built on the site of the Carthage Collegiate Institute, this school replaced the ward schools of College and Franklin. Miss Daisy Rankin was the principal when the first classes were welcomed to the stone structure designed by Percy Simpson, in conjunction with J.H. Felt and Company.

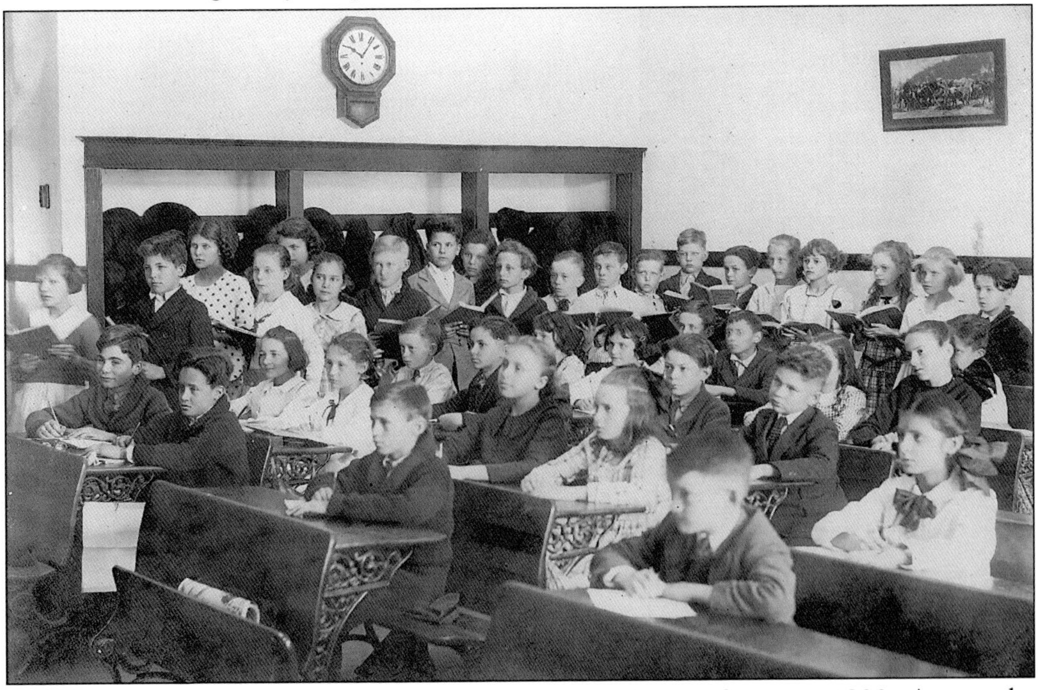

Unidentified Students of the 5th Grade, Mark Twain School, 1922. Among the students in this group is Elizabeth Wright, believed to be sitting at the right edge of the picture with a bow in her collar. As an adult, Miss Wright returned to the Carthage school system and served as a longtime teacher and music supervisor.

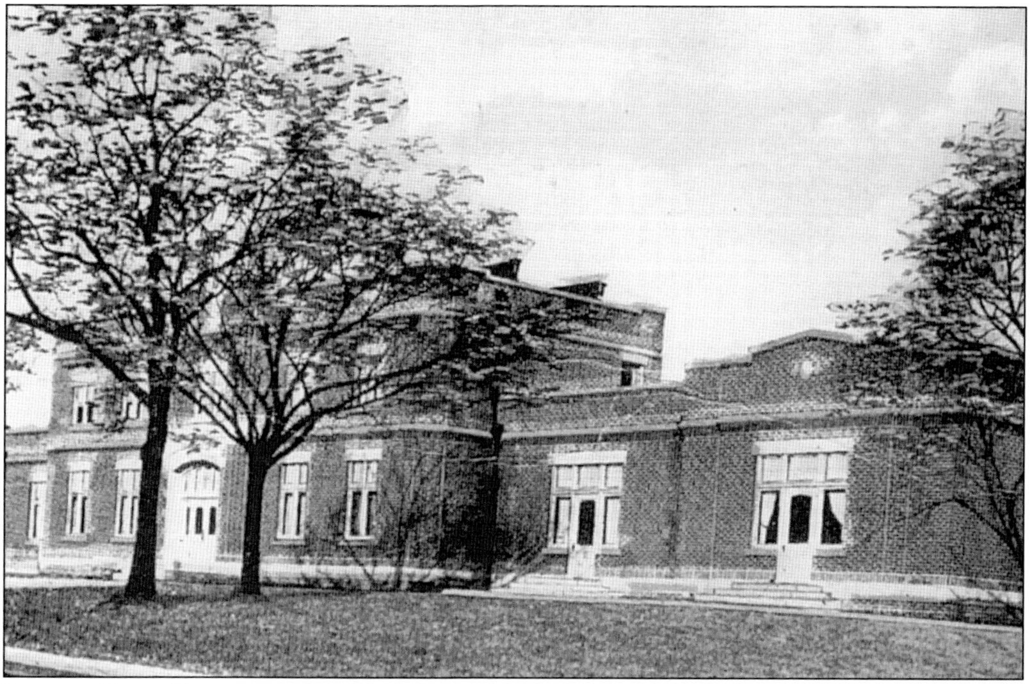

EUGENE FIELD ELEMENTARY SCHOOL, 1916–17. This structure was built to replace the older ward schools of Washington and Irving on the east side of town. Lula Stanley was the first principal. When originally proposed, both Mark Twain and Eugene Field were said to have an existence of 50 years. Mark Twain is still in use, and Eugene Field closed after 80 years in 1997.

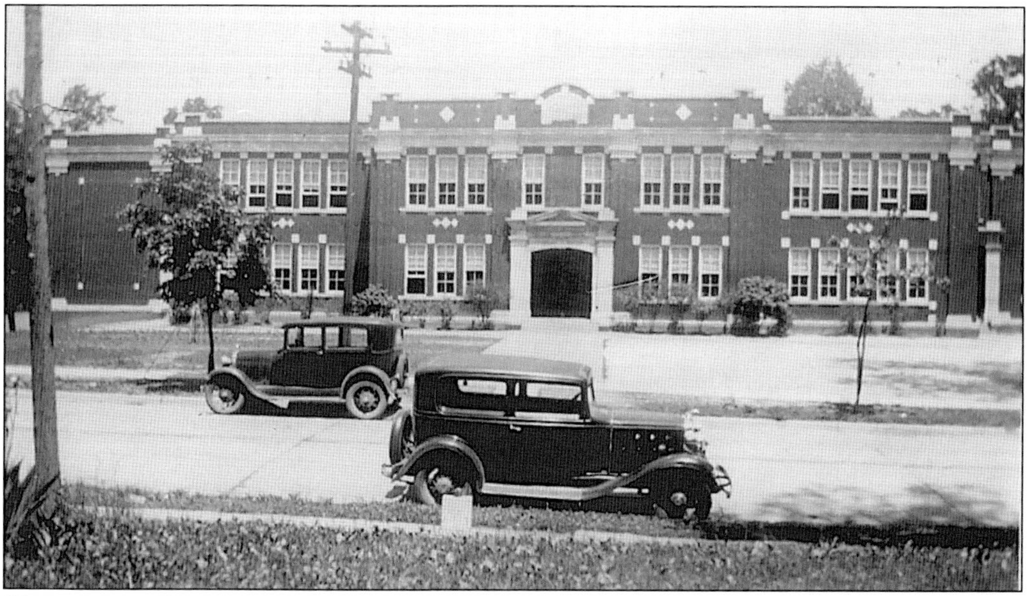

HAWTHORNE ELEMENTARY SCHOOL, 1921–22. Hawthorne was intended to replace Benton School, but it took several New Deal construction programs to complete the facility designed by Percy Simpson. Benton continued to serve as a school until it became the Federal Emergency Relief Administration office in 1935 and was not torn down until 1949–50. Hawthorne served until 1997 and was destroyed in 1999.

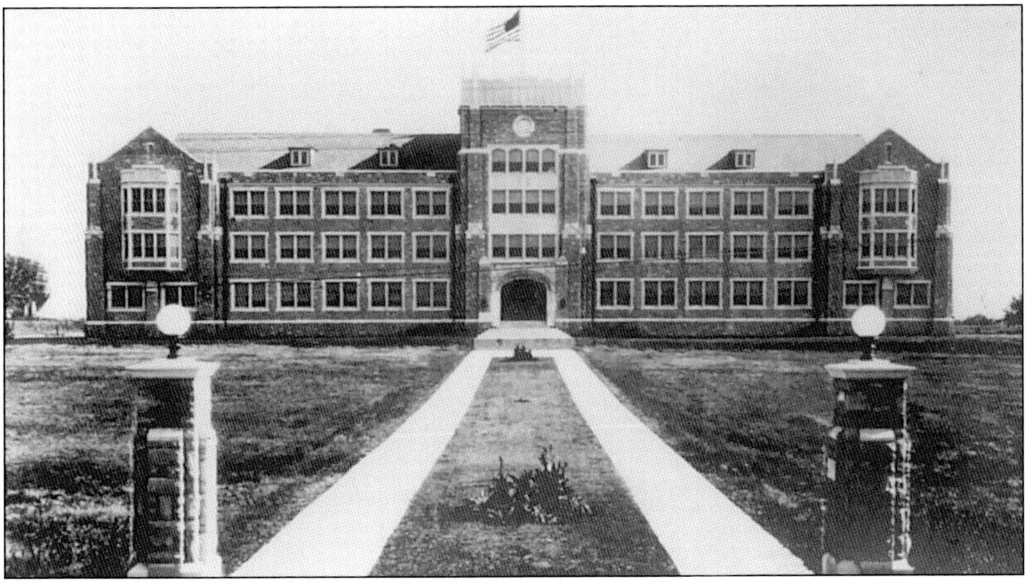

OZARK WESLEYAN COLLEGE, 1900 GRAND AVENUE, 1925–26. In 1924, 30 acres on Grand Avenue between Highland and Fairview Streets, were selected for OWC, and within a year, this imposing structure was begun. After serving as The College of Our Lady of the Ozarks (1944–1971), the Vietnamese-American Congregation of the Mother Co-Redemptrix settled in the former OWC building. Their annual religious festival, called Marian Days, brings over 50,000 people to a town with a normal population of 11,000.

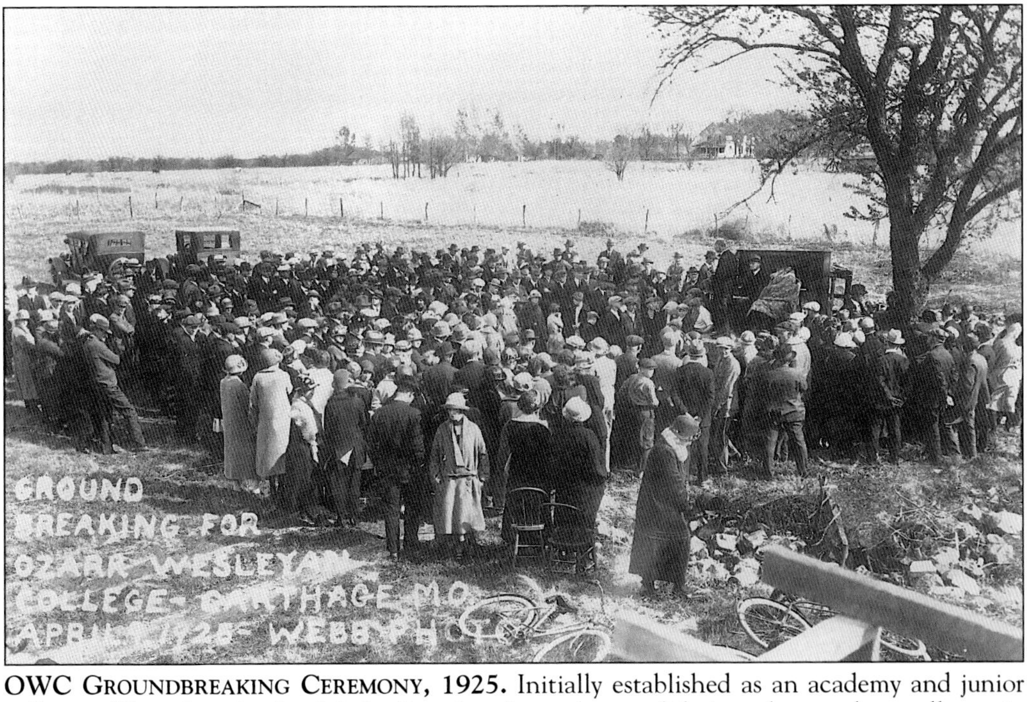

OWC GROUNDBREAKING CEREMONY, 1925. Initially established as an academy and junior college affiliated with the Methodist church, and consolidating three other colleges in Marionville and Farmington, Missouri, as well as Siloam Springs, Arkansas, ground was broken on April 9 for the permanent college structure, pictured above.

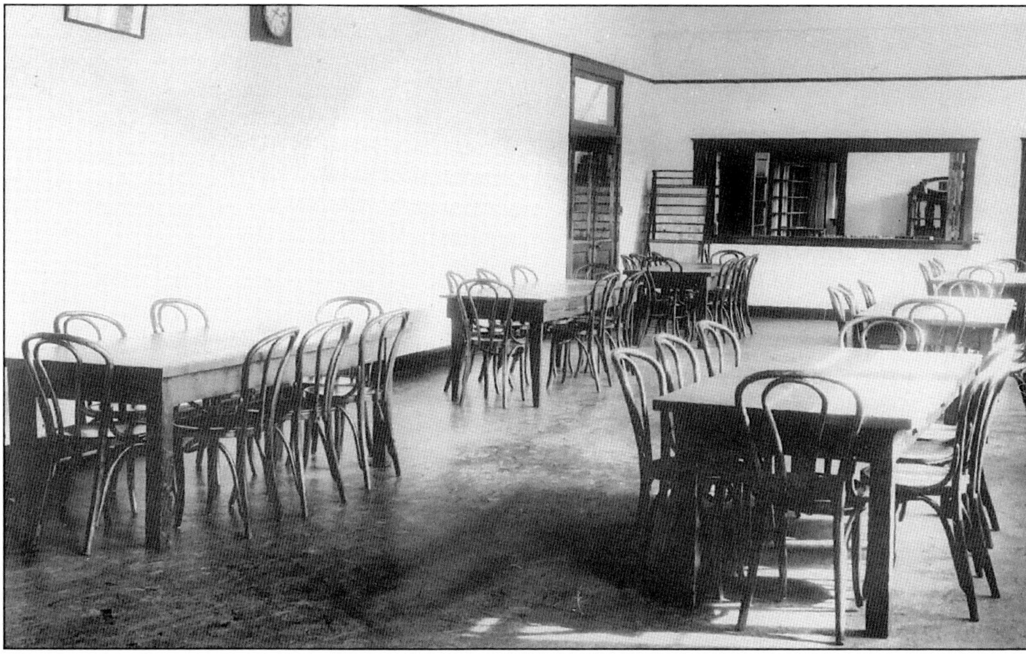

OZARK WESLEYAN COLLEGE READING ROOM, 1926. With the completion of this building that housed classrooms, a gymnasium, laboratories, and a library, OWC became a four-year institution. Always confronted with financial difficulties, it became Ozark Junior College until 1934–35, then the National Youth Administration used the structure as a girl's dormitory in 1936–37. An attempt to acquire the property for a local high school in 1938 failed.

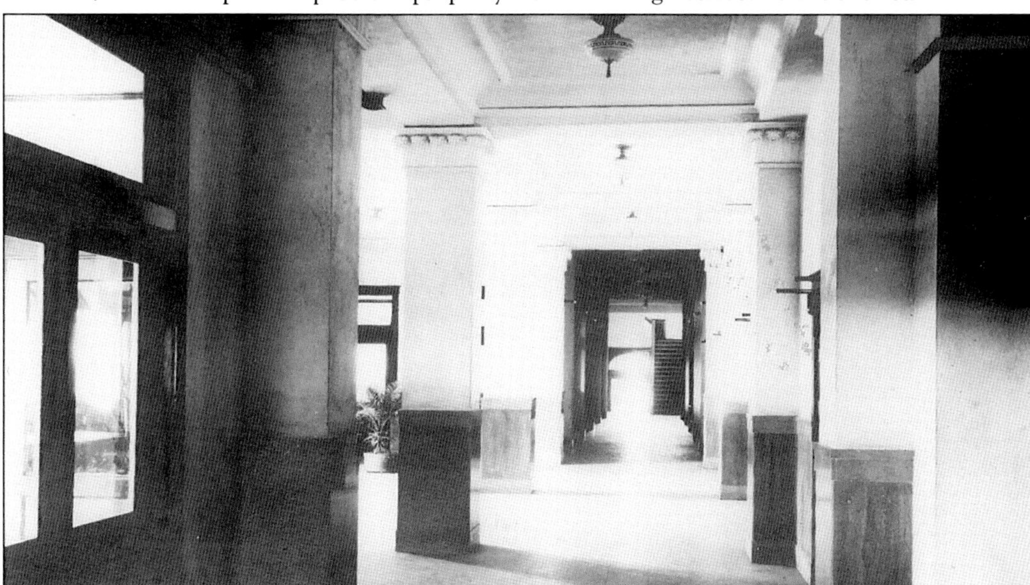

OZARK WESLEYAN COLLEGE, ADMINISTRATION BUILDING INTERIOR, 1926. Built of ashlar-cut stone provided cooperatively by the local quarries and processed by Spring River Stone Company, this structure was designed by Percy Simpson in conjunction with Bonsack and Pearce of St. Louis. Among OWC presidents were William Wirt King and Grant Robbins; R. B. Hohn represented Ozark Junior College.

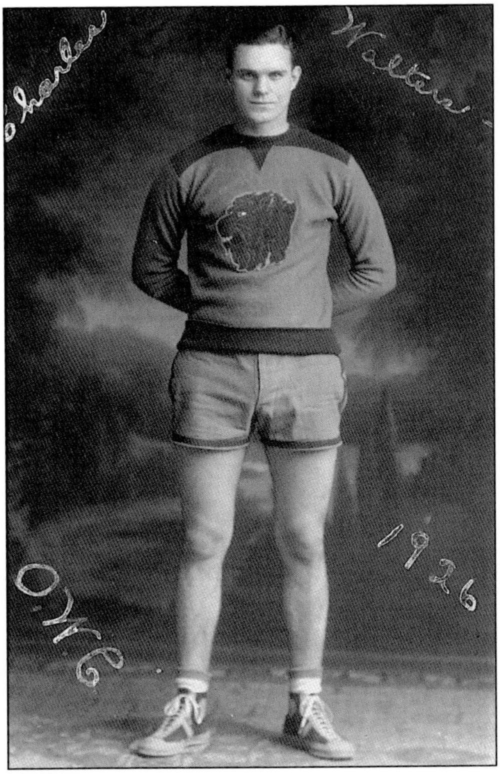

OWC BASKETBALL CENTER, CHARLES WALTERS, 1926. Other known members of the OWC basketball team in 1925–26 were Bennie Martin, Leroy Sours, Seth Gibbons, Otis McGaughey, Edward Knight, Ancell Lewis, and Garrett and Charles Cummings. Dr. Frank B. Moon was coach and OWC athletic director. Among the OWC Lions' opponents were Drury College in Springfield, Missouri, Southwest Baptist College and Fort Scott Junior College in Fort Scott, Kansas.

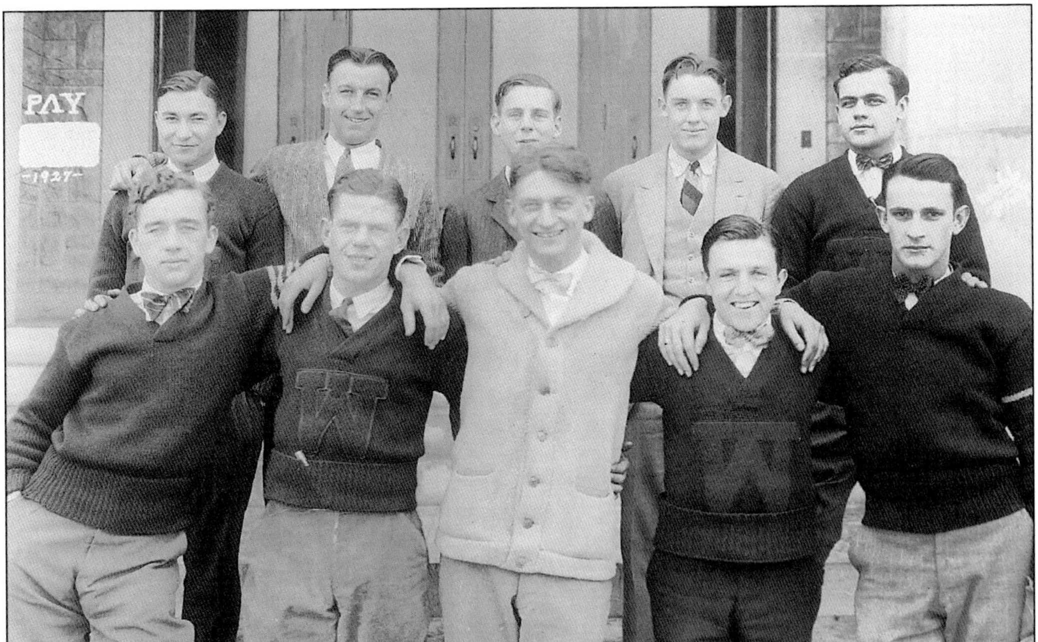

OWC MEN'S ORGANIZATION, 1927. Pictured here, from left to right, are: (back row) Charles Cummings, Cecil Murrel, Jim Logan, Paul Baker, Otis McGaughey; (front row) Basil Kirby, Garrett Cummings, W.L. "Bill" Winchester, Seth Gibbons, and Tom Harbour.

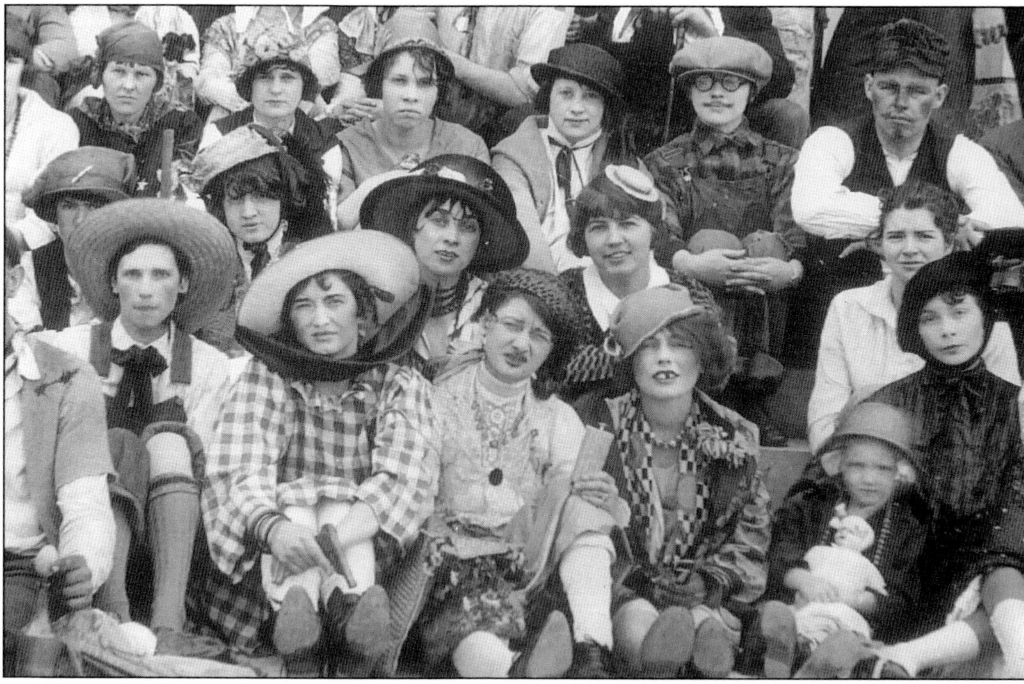

OWC Hobo Day, 1927. One of OWC's annual recreational events for students and friends was Hobo Day. After attending chapel, the student body was unleashed on Carthage to beg for food, the excess of which was consumed in a secret assembly later in the evening. In this detail from a larger photo, Marian Louisa Powers is in the checkered dress and all others are unidentified.

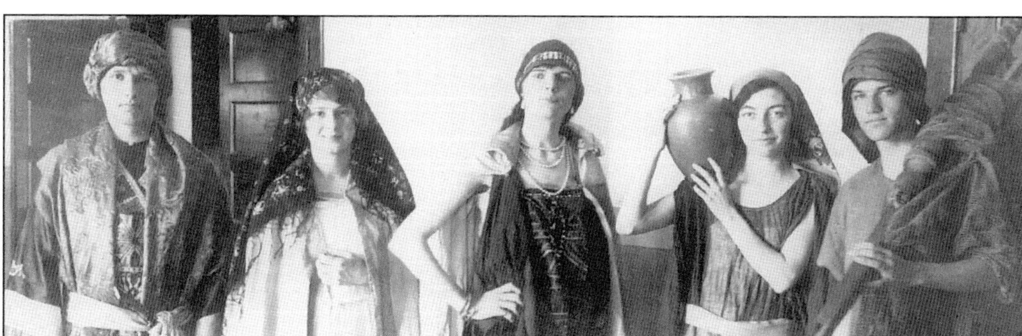

OWC Wesleyan Players, 1926. Among the cultural offerings of the college were theatrical performances and musical concerts involving the glee clubs, the orchestra, and Jefferies Concert Band. A music conservatory was held in a property across from the college (1819 Grand Avenue), and touring musical artists of the day, such as opera singer Ernestine Schumann-Heink, gave concerts in the school's auditorium and Carthage's Memorial Hall.

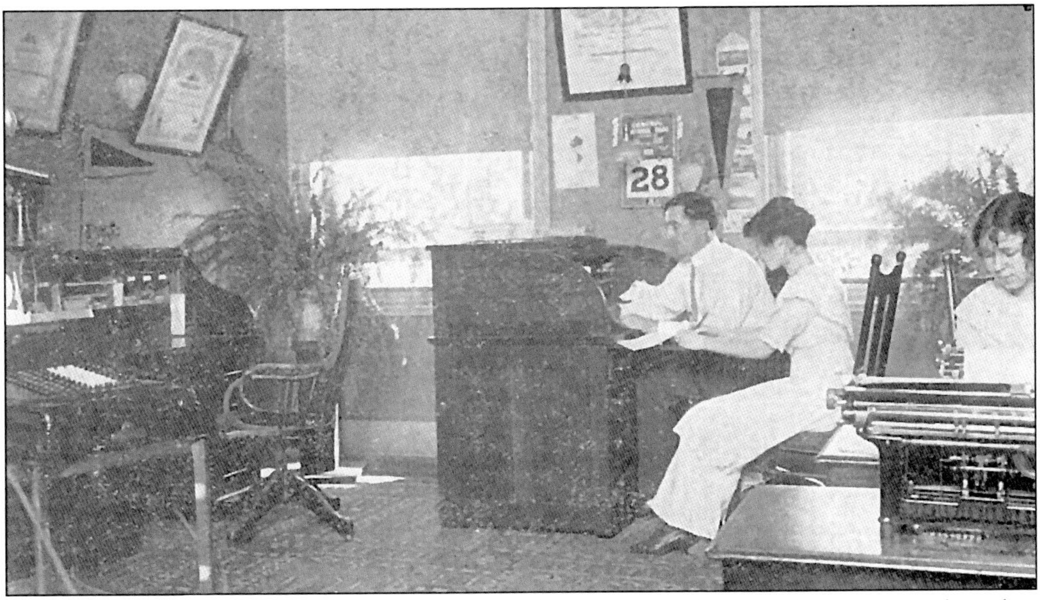

RUDE'S BUSINESS COLLEGE, 609 SOUTH MAIN STREET, . 1914. Over the years, Carthage has contained many specialty schools including a telegraph school, Carthage Commercial College on the south side of the square, Miss Hankin's Business College in the Taylor Building at the southwest corner of 4th and Lyon Streets, and Sarah Frank's Business School at 5th and Main Streets.

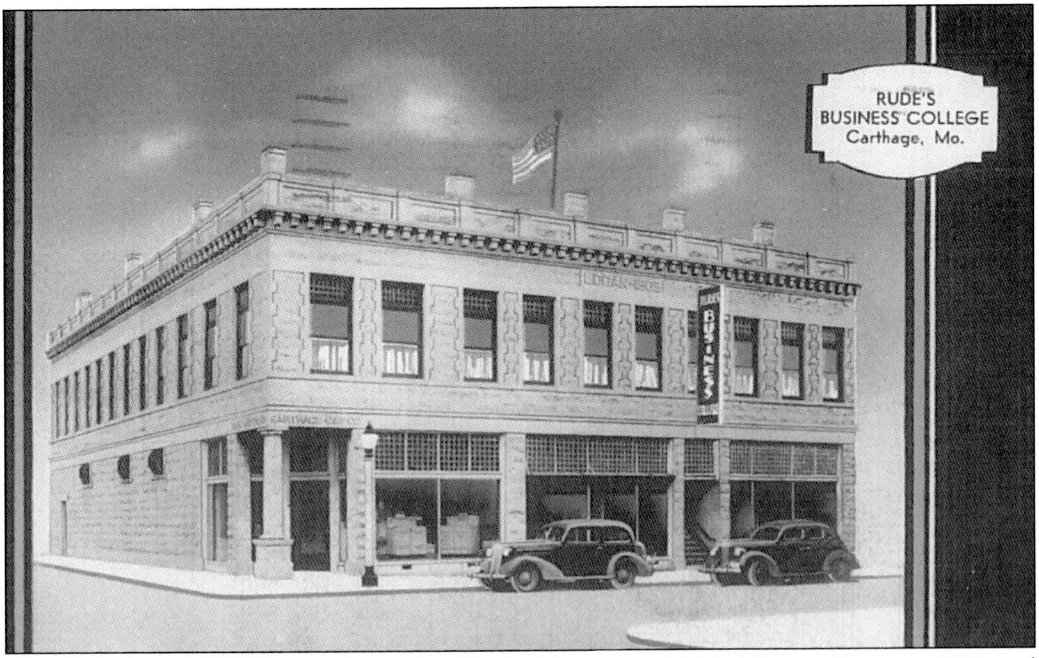

RUDE'S BUSINESS COLLEGE, 4TH AND HOWARD STREETS, 1941. Moving between 1937 and 1941, Rude's advertised on this postcard for its new location: "A good school in a good town, training good students for good positions at good salaries." Housed on the second floor of the Logan Building (built 1909), the Carthage Gas Company had its office on the first floor. (Permission to publish this card courtesy of the Lake County (IL) Museum, Curt Teich Postcard Archives.)

Three

WORSHIP

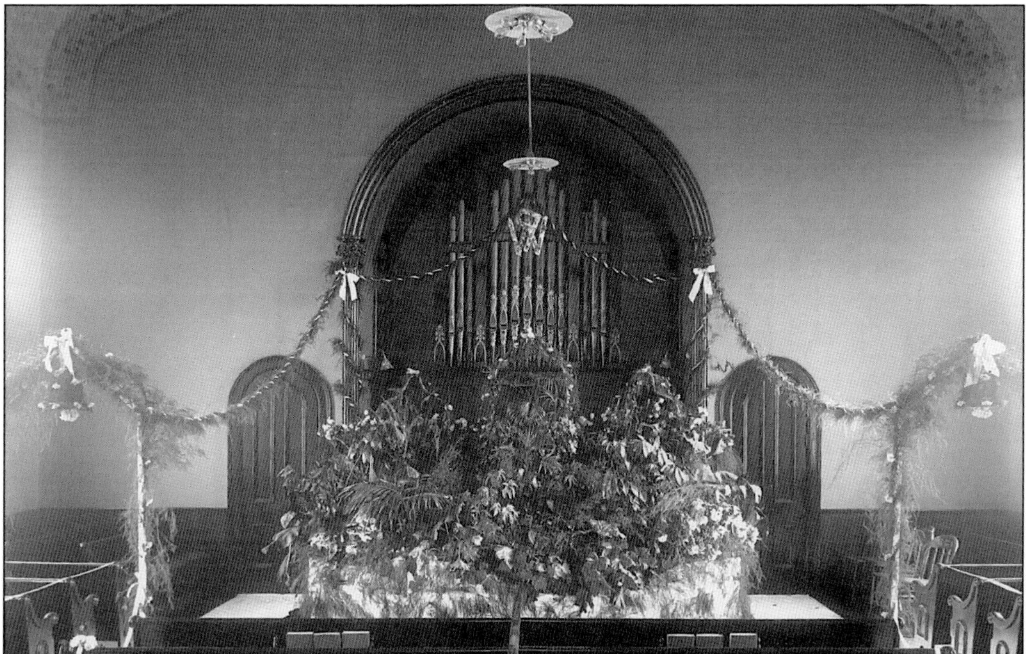

1ST PRESBYTERIAN CHURCH INTERIOR, 1903. The altar is decorated with foliage for the October 29 wedding of Marian Lucy Wright and Dr. Everett Powers. As the new Mrs. Powers wrote to her family immediately after the service, "[t]he church was prettier than I ever saw it, and I was mighty proud to come marching through it."

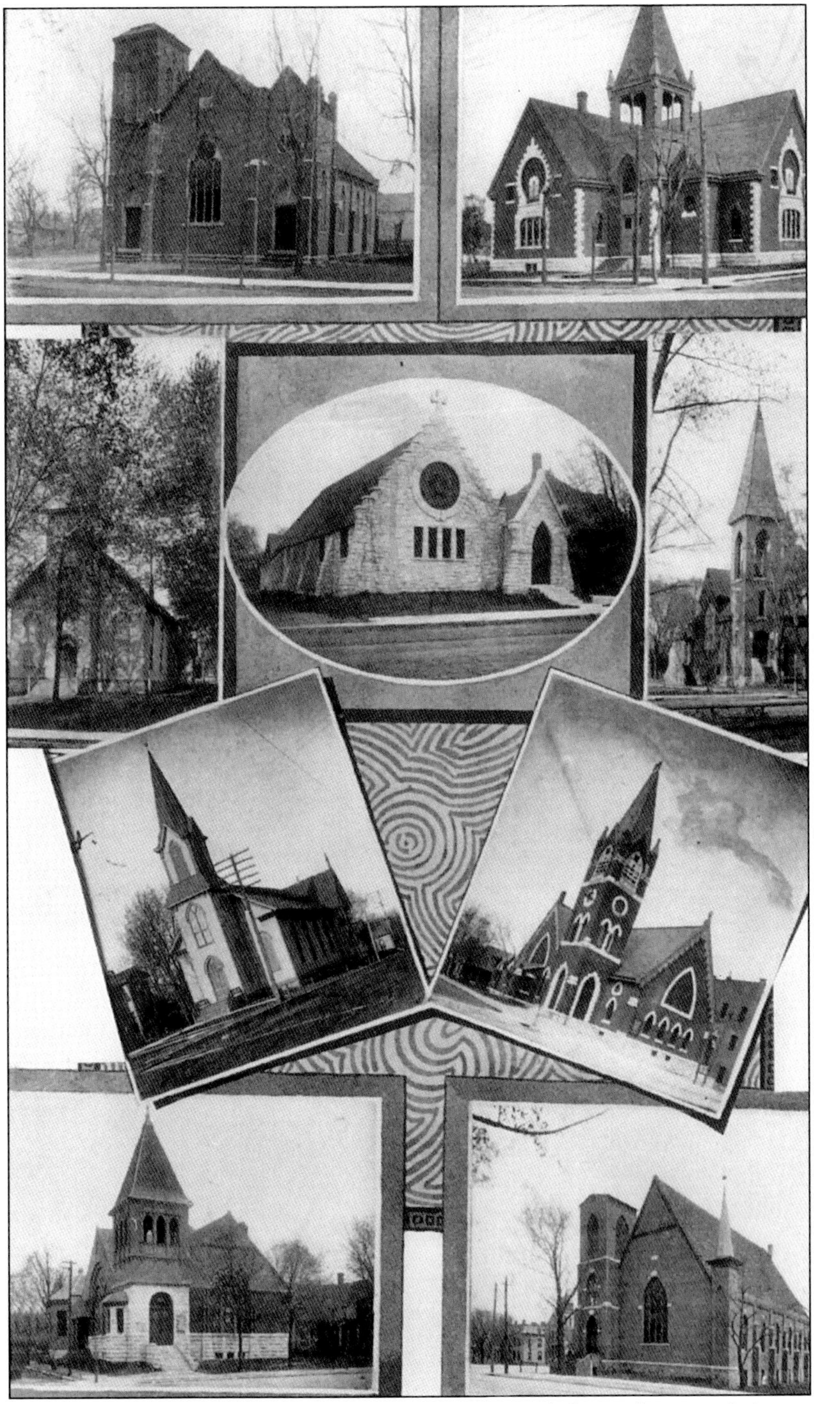

SELECTION OF CARTHAGE CHURCHES, C. 1904. Pictured from the top, left to right, are: Methodist Episcopal Church, South at Howard and Chestnut Streets, Cumberland Presbyterian at Main and 11th Streets, First Presbyterian, Grace Episcopal, Congregational, First Baptist at Central and Maple Streets, First Methodist Episcopal, Westminster or Second Presbyterian at Grant and Chestnut Streets, and Christian at Main and Chestnut Streets.

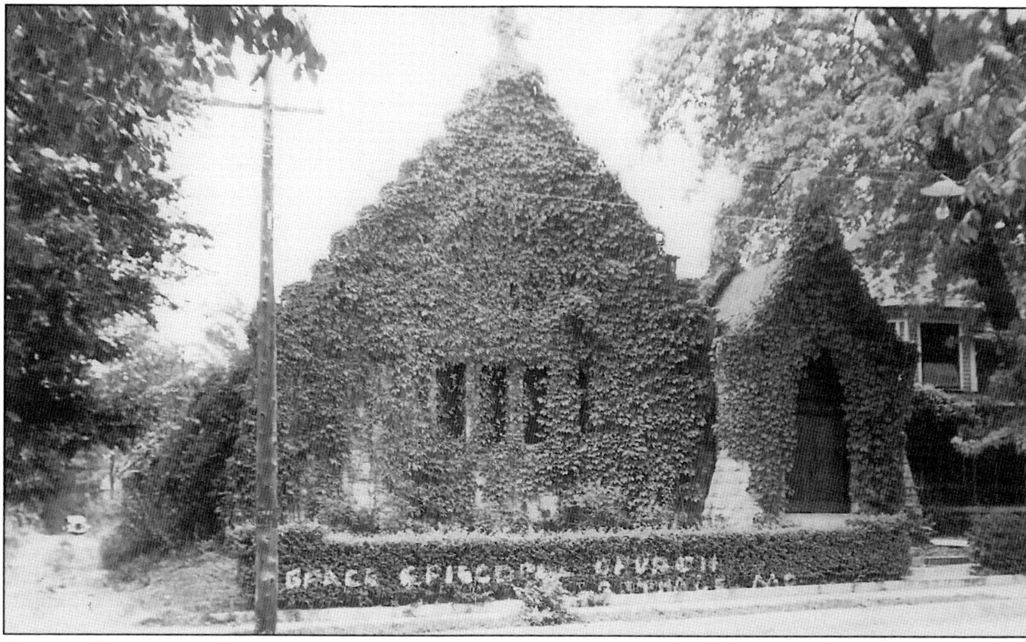

GRACE EPISCOPAL CHURCH, 820 HOWARD STREET, 1889. One of Carthage's oldest religious structures still in use as a church, it is almost hidden by vines in this 1920s view. Built of native stone in what WPA Historical Records Survey sheets of 1938 called the "small English parish church style," this building's first service was held December 22, 1889.

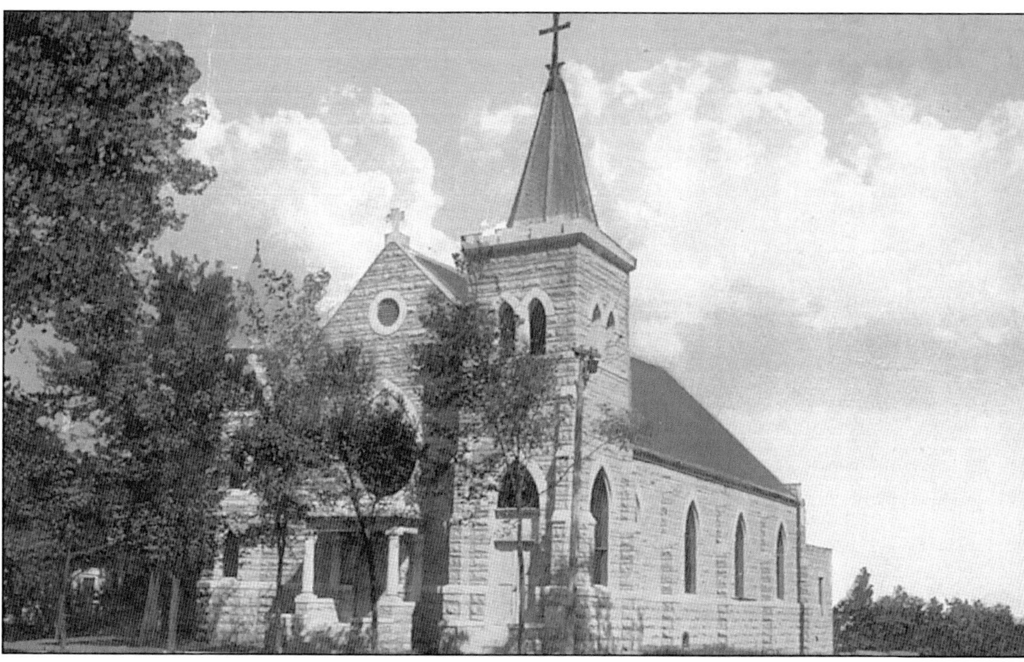

ST. ANN'S CATHOLIC CHURCH, 908 CLINTON STREET, 1910. When this church was completed, it was entirely debt-free, and half of the money used to build the church had come from non-Catholics in the community. Designed by Carthage architect George Raynor in the Gothic style, the building was made with stone from the F.W. Steadley and Company quarry.

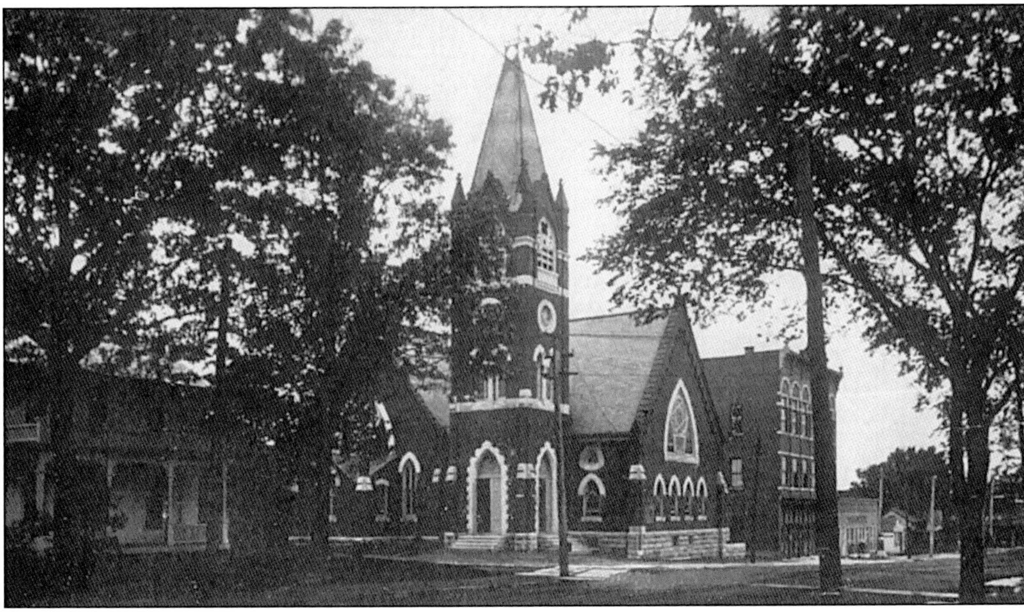

West side of 700–600 Blocks of South Main Street, c. 1910. Visible in this streetscape is a residence, First Methodist Episcopal Church, and Wells-Woodward Wholesale Grocery. The church was built in 1888–89 of brick and stone and stood until fire destroyed it in 1972. Prior to this in 1941, the congregation of the Howard Street Methodist Church (former M.E. Church, South) had united with this congregation.

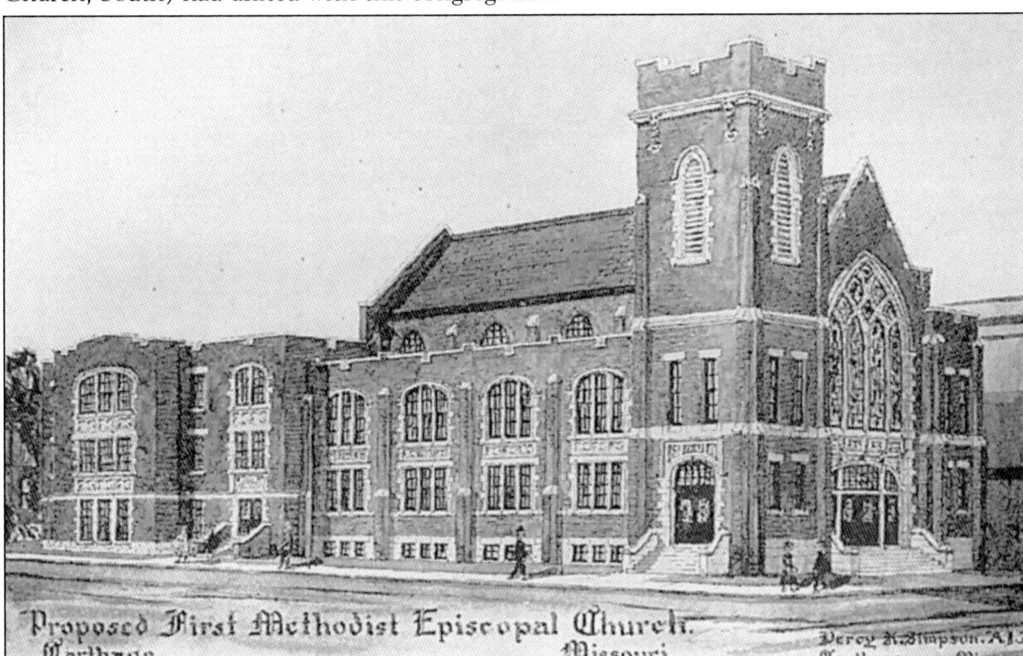

Proposed Remodeling of First Methodist Church, 617 South Main. Only part of this project, the Sunday School addition was built (completed in 1925). The cost was $65,000 and the addition was designed, like many of Carthage's schools and churches, by local architect Percy Simpson. The addition survived the fire and is still in use today.

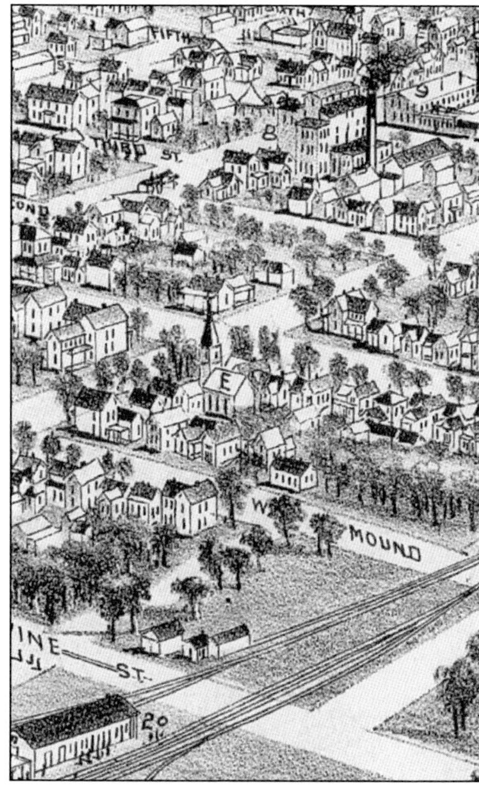

EVANGELICAL LUTHERAN CHURCH, 115 MCGREGOR STREET, C. 1891. Known as "Old Swede Church," this frame structure (#E) was built in 1877 under Pastor Charles Roos. Its members were Swedish Lutherans who held services in Swedish for many years. Once these families moved from town, the church disbanded, and the building was used by other denominations. It would be 1910 before another Lutheran church (Faith) would be established in Carthage. Also visible in this view are the Missouri Pacific Railroad (#20), Globe Flour Mill (#8) and the Carthage Foundry (#9), the latter two located at Oak Street and Garrison Avenue.

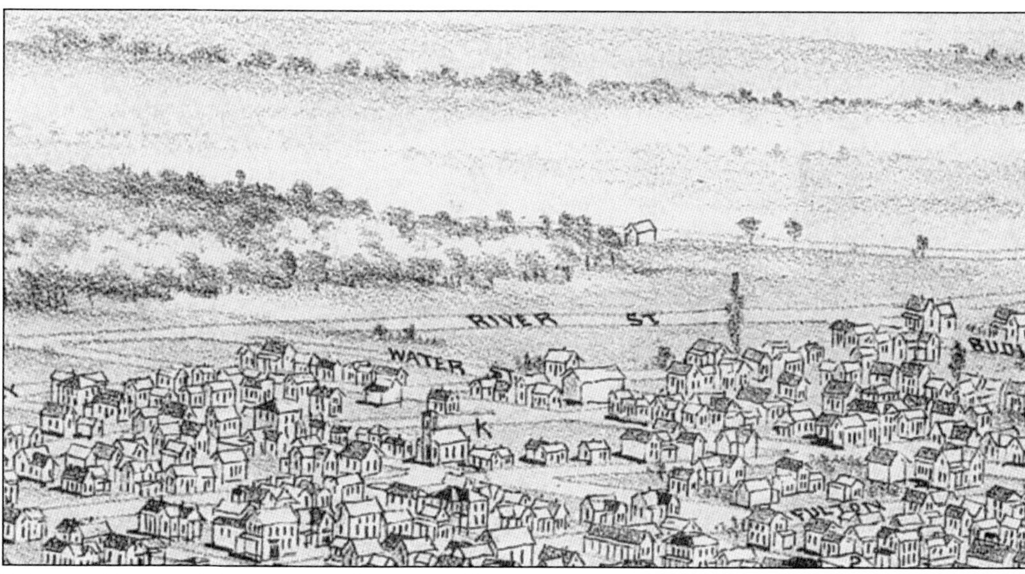

WESLEY CHAPEL METHODIST CHURCH (#K), 708 EAST 6TH STREET, C. 1891. Carthage's African-American Methodists built this church c. 1879 under Rev. A. Coleman. It served until a fire in 1899 left members to meet in the tack room of the livery building at the northeast corner of 4th and Garrison Streets. A new structure was finished in 1904 but was damaged by lightning after a few years. Another brick structure was built in 1923, which served the Methodists until the 1950s.

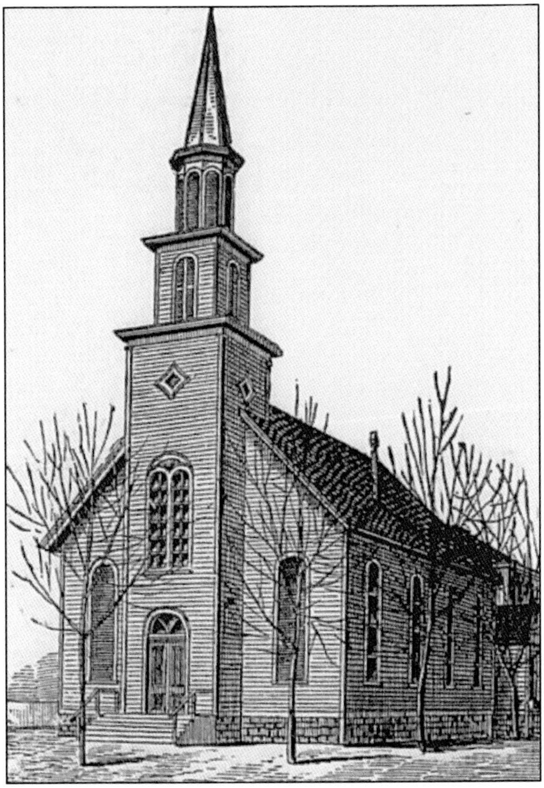

FIRST PRESBYTERIAN CHURCH, 616 SOUTH GRANT STREET, 1870. The Presbyterians had established a congregation in 1867 pastored by Rev. Pinkerton. This simple frame structure was built a few years later for the sum of $6,500. It was one of the pastors of this church, Rev. W.S. Knight, who was instrumental in founding the Carthage Collegiate Institute and until the college building on South Main Street was built classes were conducted here.

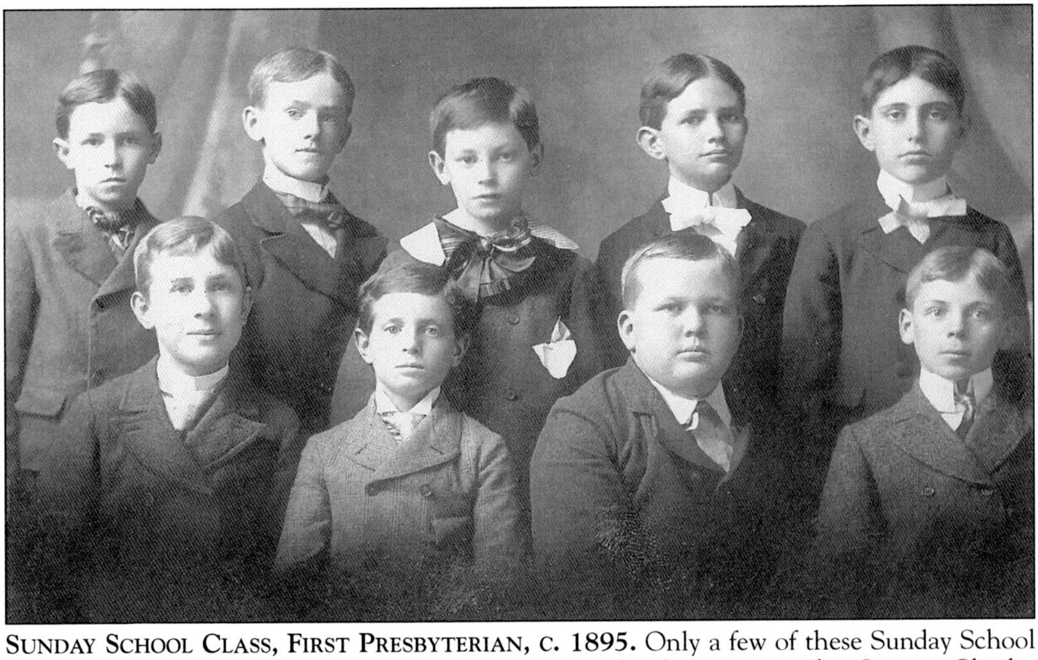

SUNDAY SCHOOL CLASS, FIRST PRESBYTERIAN, C. 1895. Only a few of these Sunday School boys are identified—Clayton Hough on the right in the front row, and ? Groves, Charles Bartlett, Bob Wright, unidentified, and Frank Kilgore from left to right in the back row (left to right).

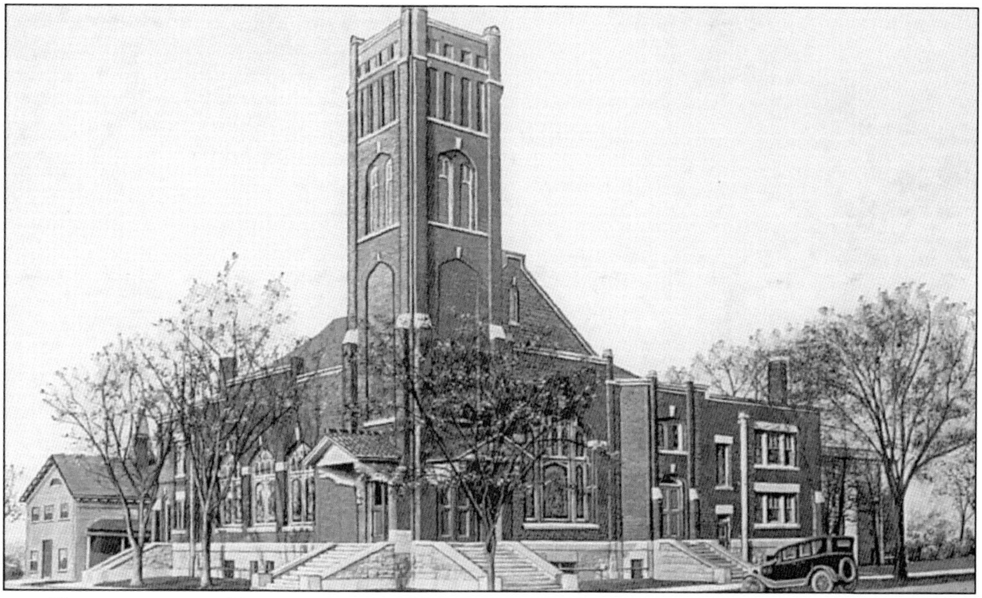

First Presbyterian Church, 115 West Chestnut Street, 1916–17. Built at a cost of $36,000 under the direction of Rev. J.D. McCaughtry, the First Presbyterian congregation and that of the Westminster Church had reunited in 1903 and occupied Westminster until constructing this brick edifice. The stone trim was provided by Spring River Stone Company.

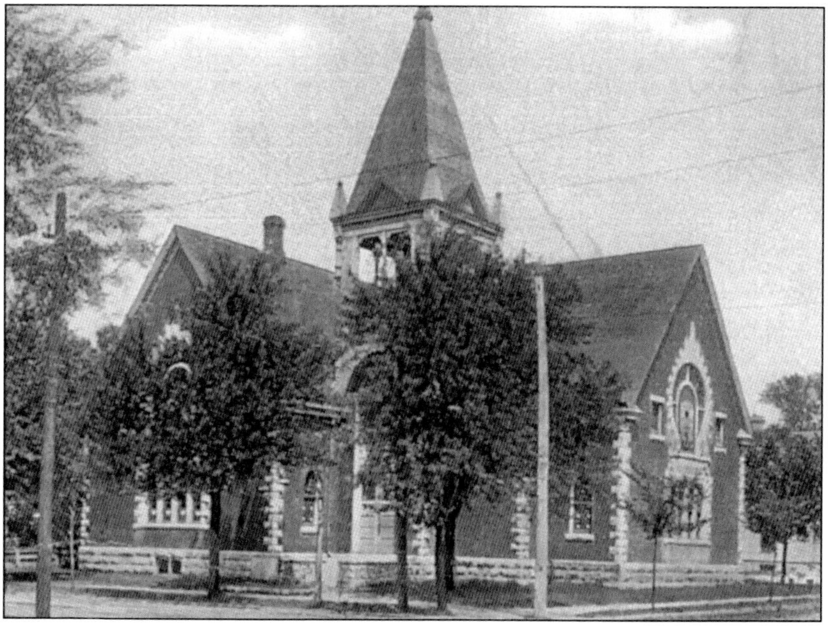

Main Street Presbyterian Church, 1014 South Main Street, c. 1922. Renaming the old 1892 Cumberland Church as the Main Street congregation, other denominations acquired the other former Presbyterian churches. In 1922, Nazarenes established a congregation in the 1892 Westminster Church, while the Church of God purchased the original frame Presbyterian Church and moved it to Budlong and Orchard Streets (along with another old church) and used the salvaged lumber to construct a new building.

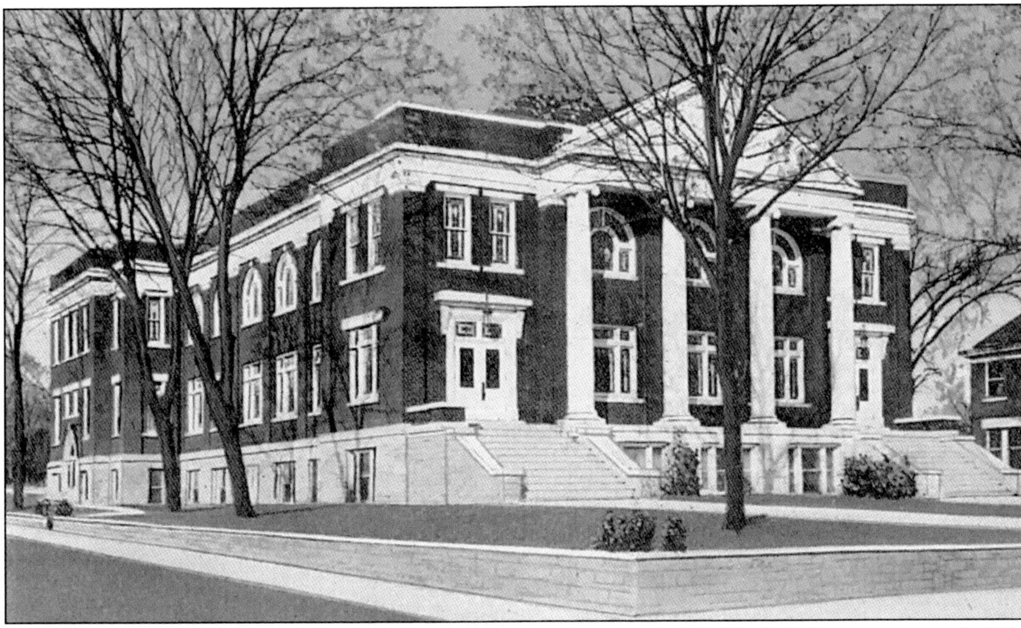

FIRST BAPTIST CHURCH, 631 SOUTH GARRISON, 1924–25. J.L. Berkebile superintended the construction of this brick and stone church that replaced the congregation's historic structure at Central and Maple Streets, built in 1872. The cost of the new structure was $76,000, and it was designed by Alabama architect James E. Greene.

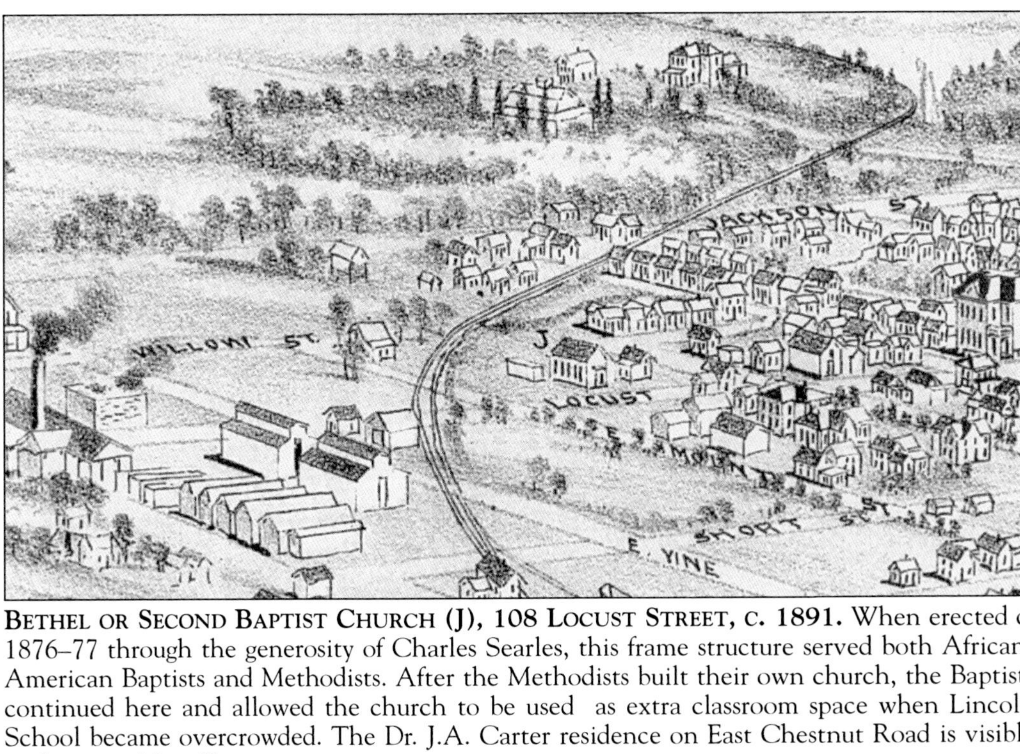

BETHEL OR SECOND BAPTIST CHURCH (J), 108 LOCUST STREET, C. 1891. When erected c. 1876–77 through the generosity of Charles Searles, this frame structure served both African-American Baptists and Methodists. After the Methodists built their own church, the Baptists continued here and allowed the church to be used as extra classroom space when Lincoln School became overcrowded. The Dr. J.A. Carter residence on East Chestnut Road is visible at the top of this illustration.

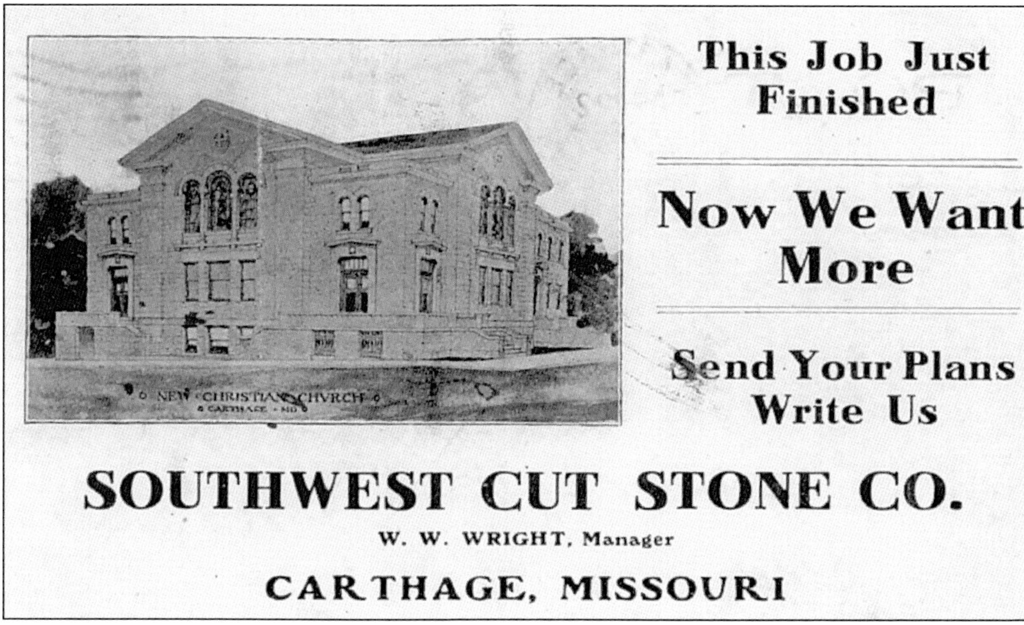

ADVERTISEMENT FOR SOUTHWEST CUT STONE COMPANY, 1910. William W. Wright, son of Carthage Stone Company owner Curtis Wright, operated the company which furnished the exterior limestone for the Christian Church pictured below.

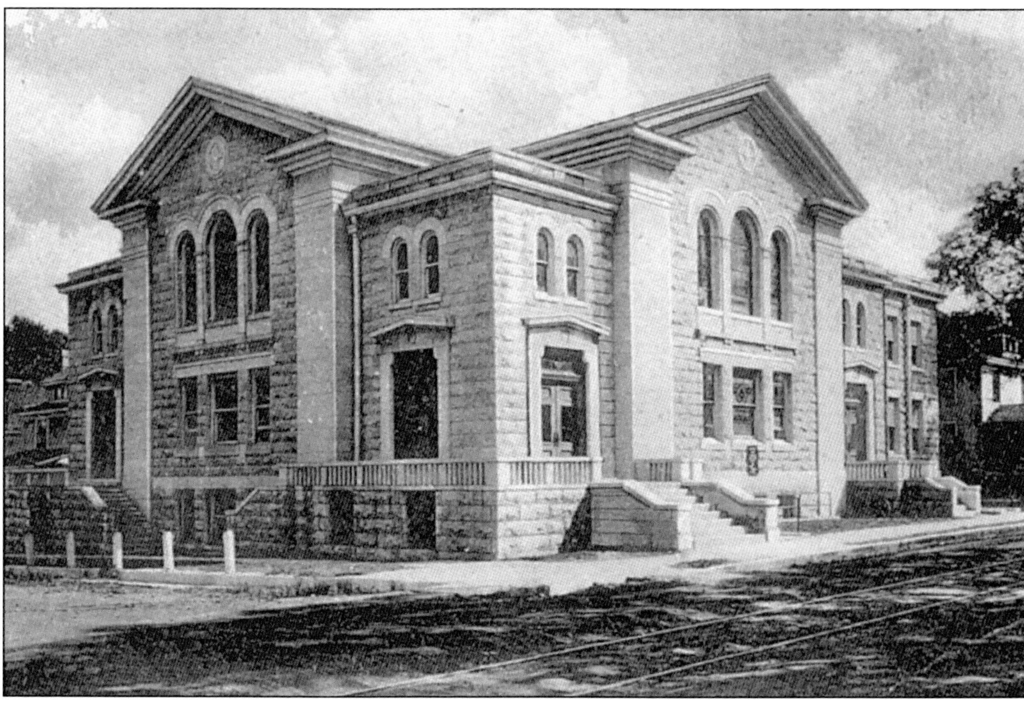

FIRST CHRISTIAN CHURCH, 800 SOUTH MAIN STREET, 1909–10. Replacing an older structure that was said never to have been completed, Joplin architect A.C. Michaels designed this place of worship.

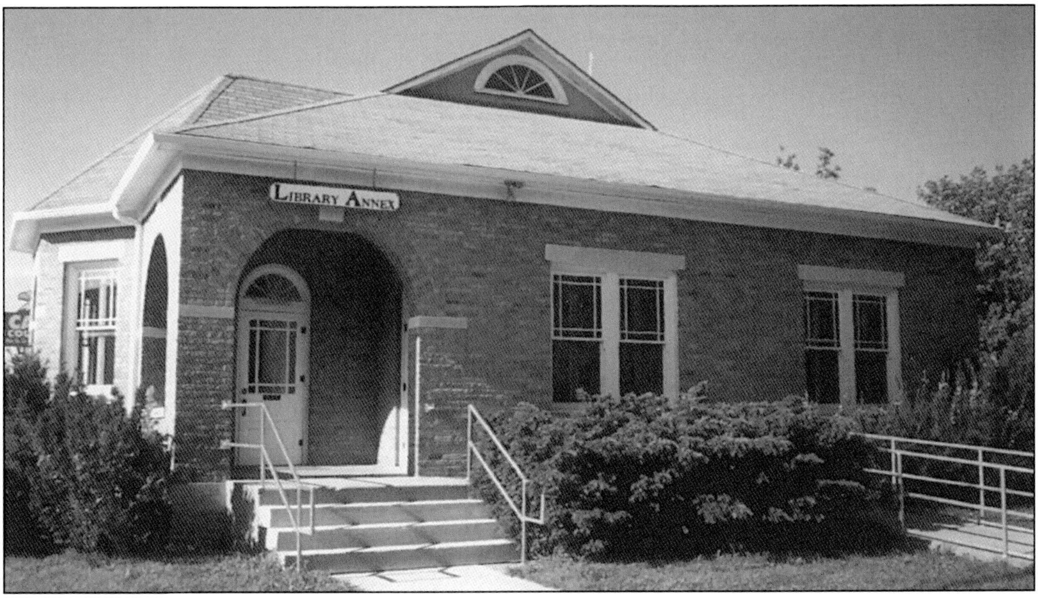

CHURCH OF CHRIST, SCIENTIST; 510 WEST GARRISON AVENUE, 1929. This brick and stone building housed the small Christian Science congregation that began in 1904. Prior to 1929, they met in various spots including the library and the former 1870–74 Congregational Chapel at 6th and Lyon Streets. When first constructed by G.W. Miller and W.E. Rice, a brass and copper crown and cross was fixed atop the roof. Today, it is the Library Annex.

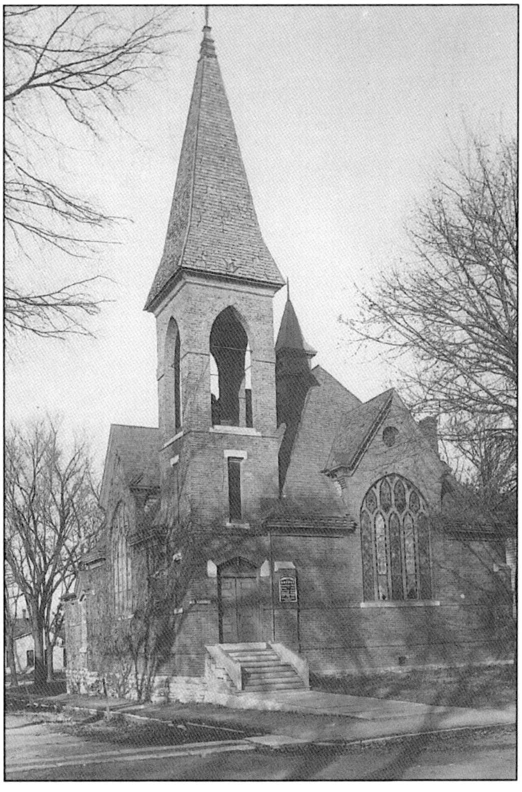

CONGREGATIONAL CHURCH, 215 WEST 7TH STREET, 1880–82. Every year industrialist Frank Hill asked for the amount of the church's previous year's debt and paid it, keeping the church solvent, but after his death the church was unable to meets its financial obligations and disbanded in 1919. The Carthage Masonic Lodge #197 purchased the building, removed the tower, and stuccoed the facade in the process of remodeling for lodge use in 1920. They continue to use the building today.

Four

Industry

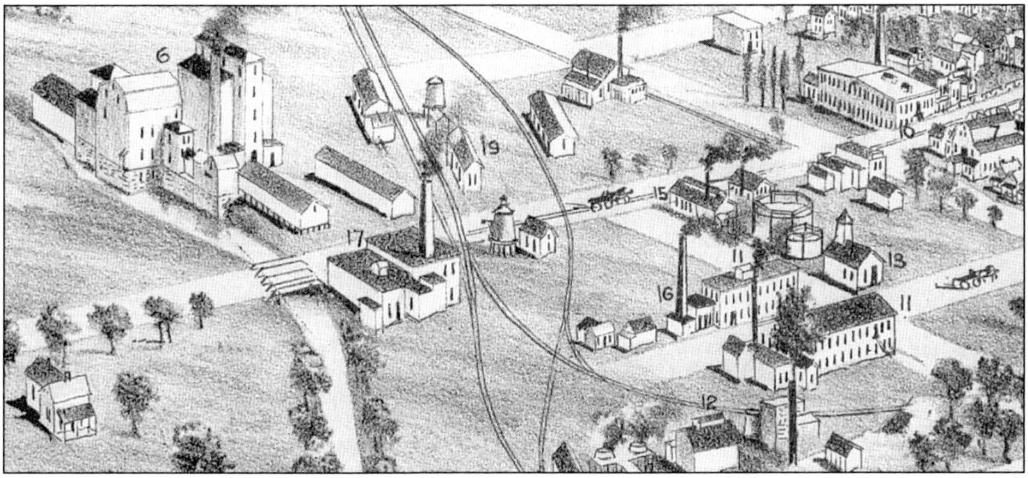

Detail of North Main Street from *Bird's-eye View of Carthage*, 1891. Carthage has always had a broad industrial base. Some of Carthage's factories in the 1890's included (left to right in view): #6—Cowgill and Hill's City Flour Mill, #17—Spring River Packing, #19—Frisco Railroad, #15—Gas Works, # 16—Electric Plant, #12—Missouri White Lime and Stone, #11—Missouri Woolen Mill, #13—Southwestern Light Fuel and Gas Works, #10—Carthage Woolen Mills, and #7—Carthage Springs Mill.

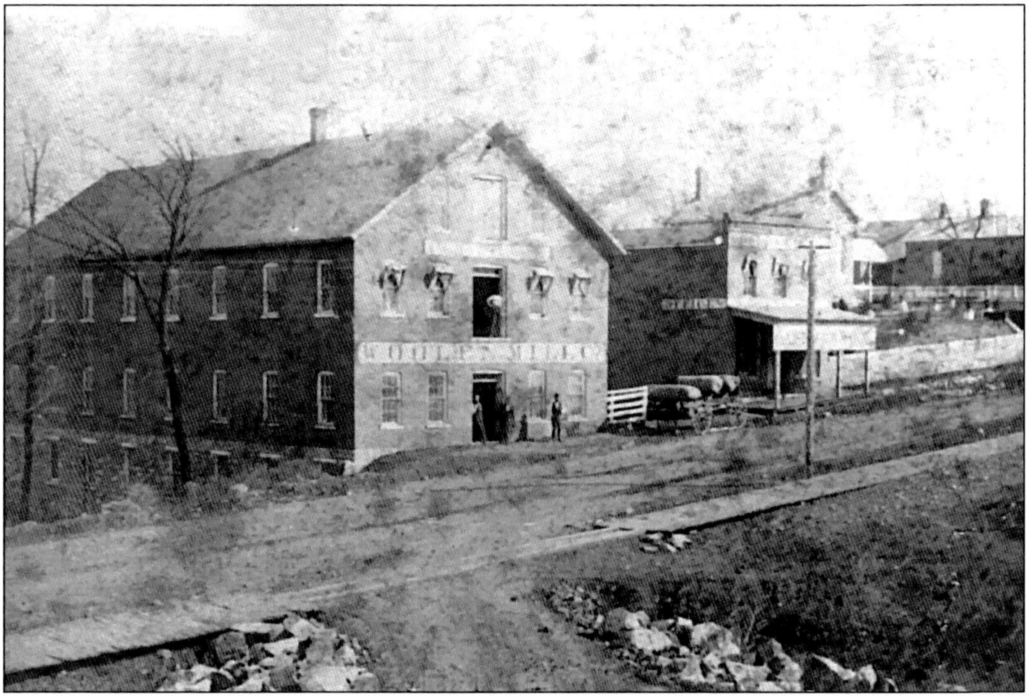

Carthage Woolen Mills, 310 North Main Street, c. 1870–71. Missouri's second largest woolen mill was built by William Myers, who later established the Missouri Woolen Mill nearby. Purchased by Frank Hill and H.C. Cowgill in the 1880s, up to 10,000 yards of "Kentucky Doe" jeans and other fabrics could be manufactured in a week. Carthage's largest employer in 1900, the mill employed 125 individuals, mostly women. Operations ceased around 1905. The mill building (one that had replaced this structure after a fire in 1882) was used by the Carthage Mattress and Manufacturing Company then the Keystone Driller (seller of mining equipment) before being destroyed shortly after World War I.

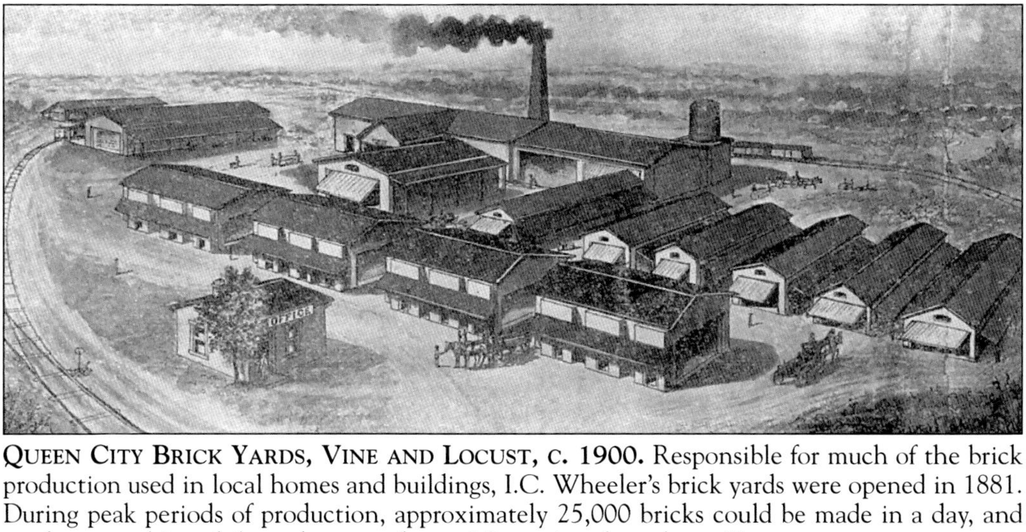

Queen City Brick Yards, Vine and Locust, c. 1900. Responsible for much of the brick production used in local homes and buildings, I.C. Wheeler's brick yards were opened in 1881. During peak periods of production, approximately 25,000 bricks could be made in a day, and product was shipped throughout southwest Missouri and southeast Kansas.

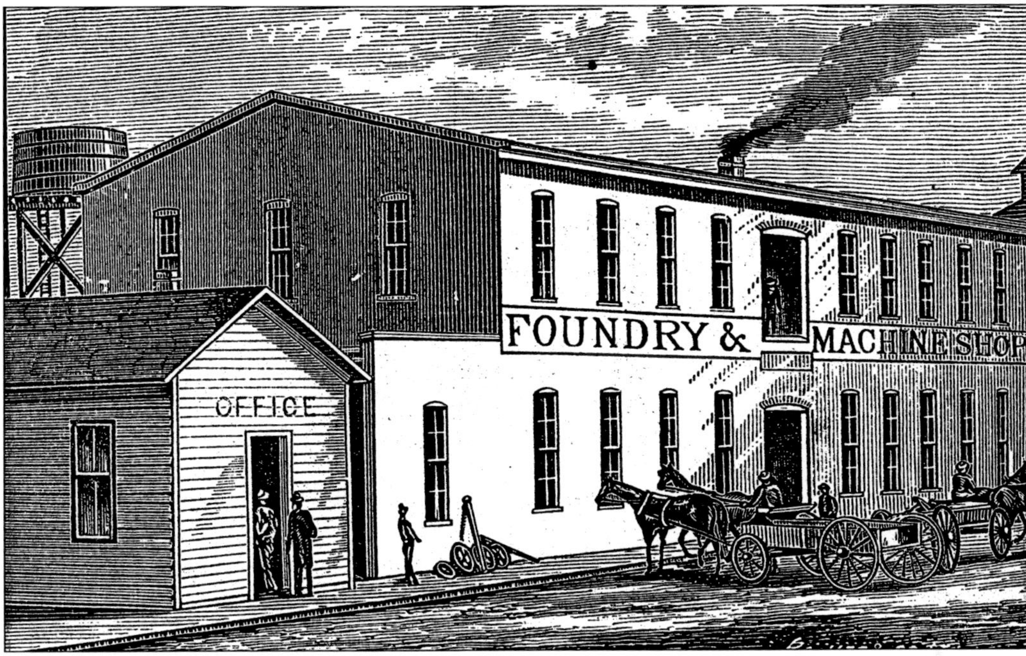

CARTHAGE FOUNDRY AND MACHINE SHOP, SOUTHWEST CORNER OAK AND GARRISON STREETS, 1875. Established by William McMillan and J.L. Moore, this firm produced an astonishing array of goods including quarry and mining machinery, iron railings, building fronts, and agricultural equipment including the Carthage corn planter, prairie sod cultivator, and rock and root grubber.

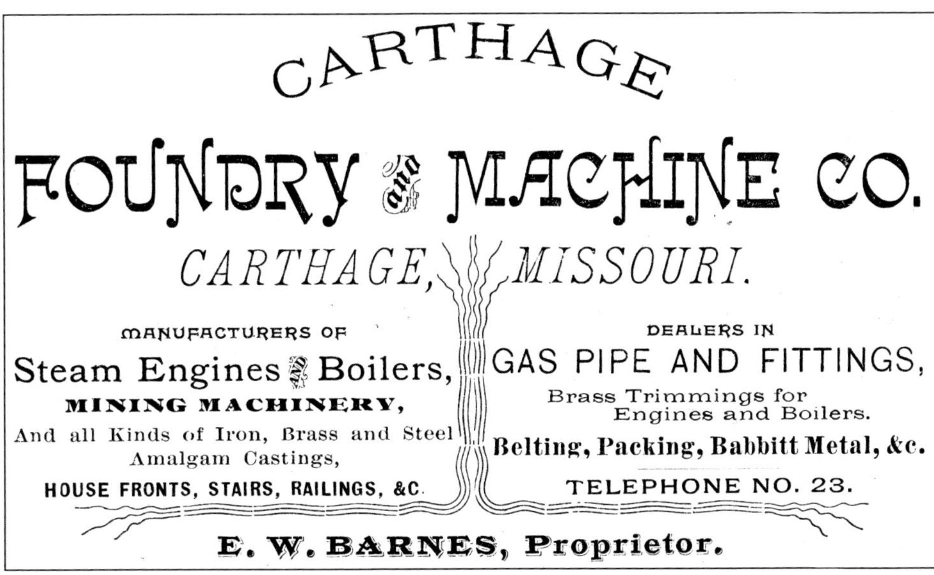

TRADE CARD, CARTHAGE FOUNDRY. House fronts are noted on this advertising card, but still visible today are numerous storefronts made by this firm in the 1880s. Among the more complete examples are those at 110 East 4th Street and the Polllard Building (see pg. 15). The iron porch at 631 South McGregor Street is said to be a product of this firm as well.

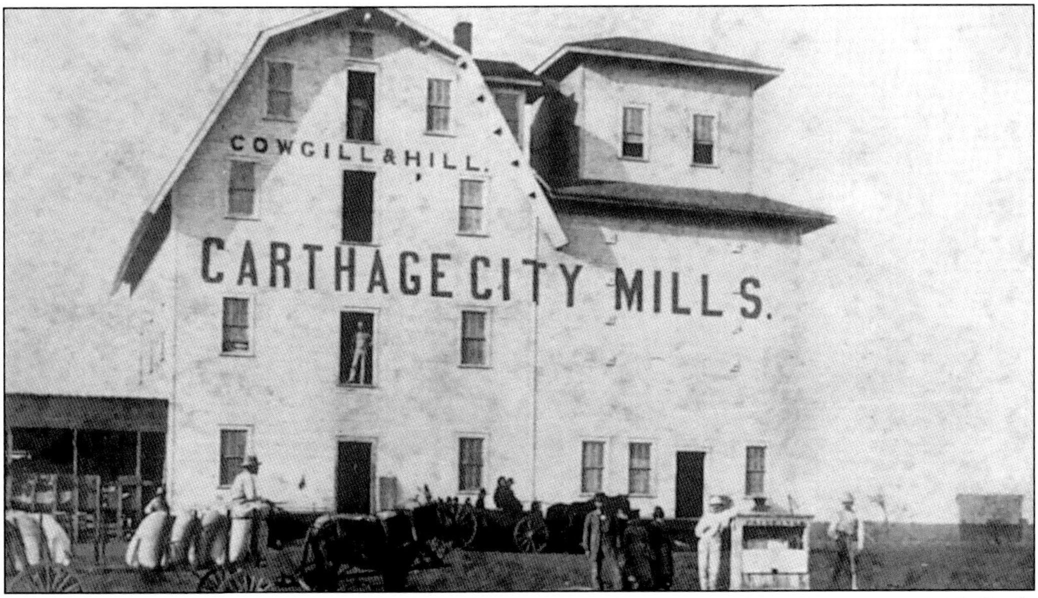

COWGILL AND HILL'S CARTHAGE CITY FLOUR MILLS, HIGH AND MAIN STREETS, 1875. Built at an expense of $40,000, H.C. Cowgill took Frank Hill as a partner when he opened his second mill (he began two years earlier with a mill on Center Creek), and they remained in partnership until other members of the Cowgill family bought out Hill's interest in 1901. Original capacity for this early mill was 150 bushels a day.

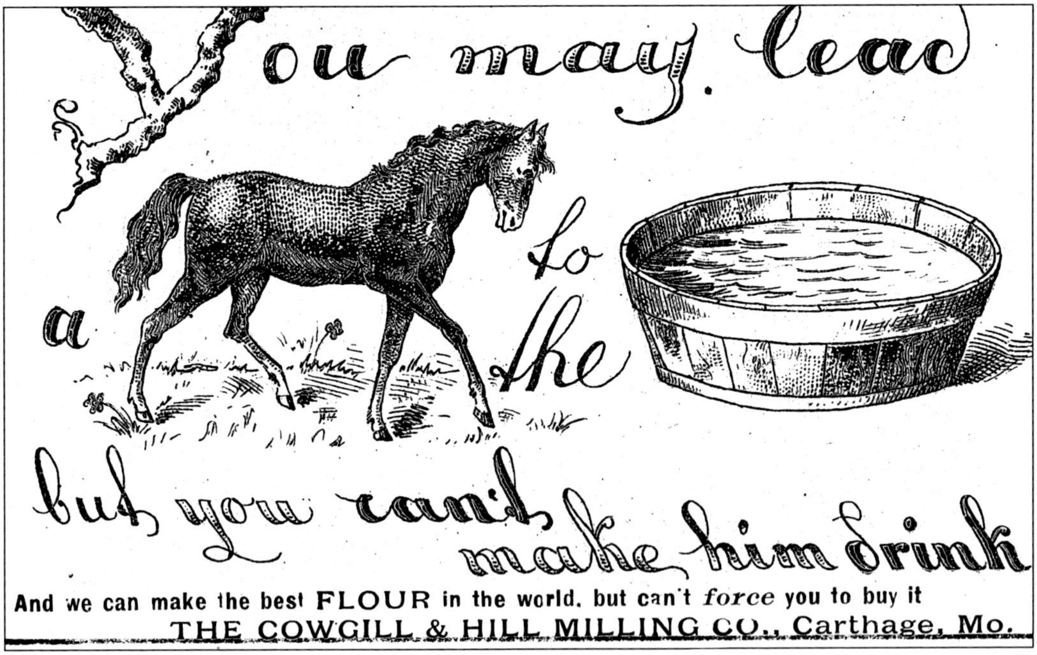

TRADE CARD OF COWGILL AND HILL MILLING COMPANY, c. 1890. Owners H.C. Cowgill, Frank Hill, W.H. Beckwith, and manager R. Finke are printed on the back with the advertisement that the mill produced 900 barrels of flour a day, making it the largest mill outside of Saint Louis, Missouri. The firm also operated the Globe Mill at the northwest corner of Oak and Garrison Streets.

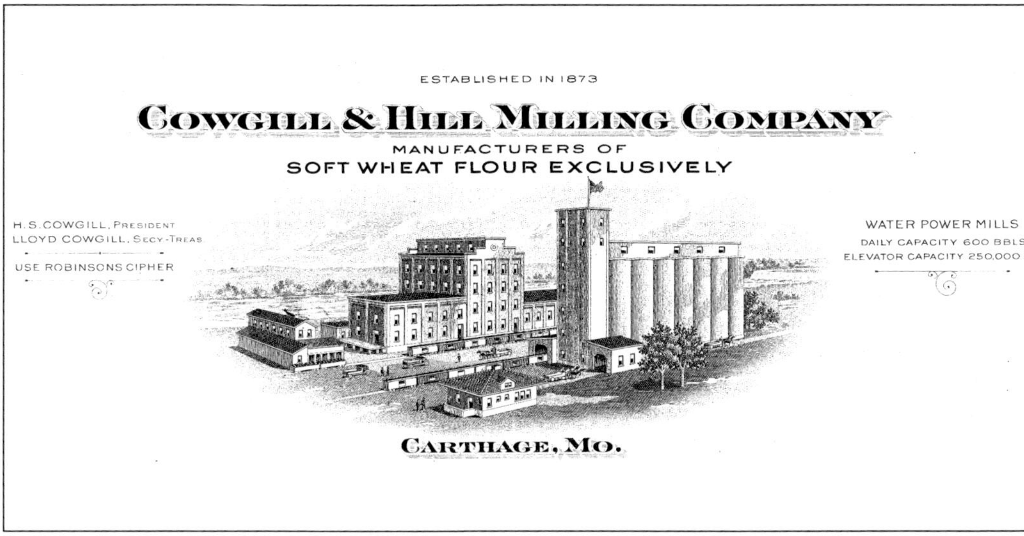

COWGILL AND HILL MILLING COMPANY. Taken from the company's letterhead, this image illustrates the growth of the company in the early 1900s, after rebuilding from the effects of two fires in 1902 and 1922. In addition to milling 100,000 barrels of flour a year, 75,000 bags of feed were produced, and 200,000 to 300,000 bushels of corn were stored or shipped in 1925.

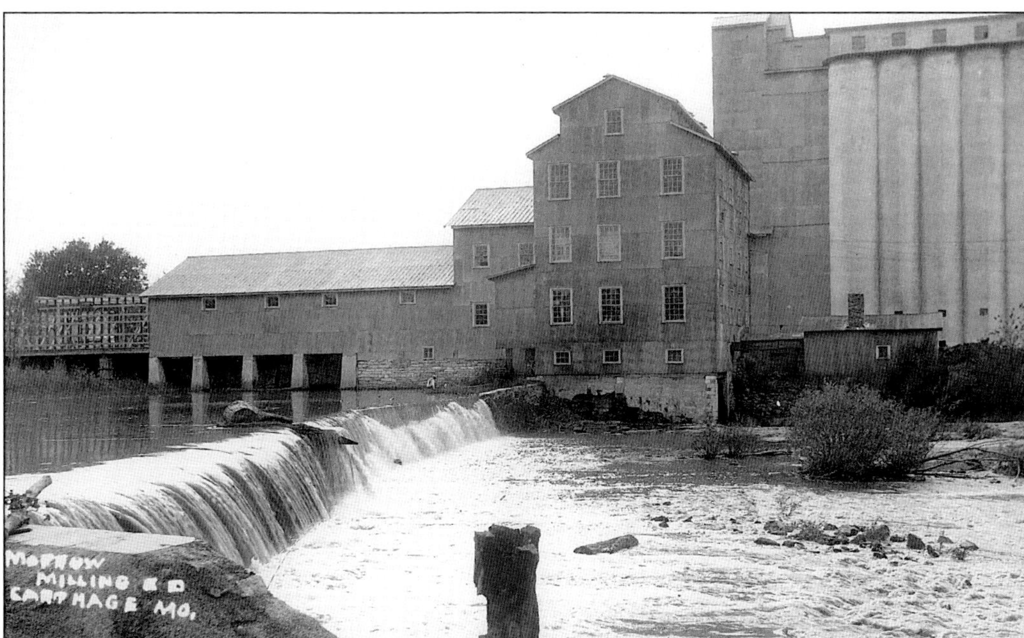

MORROW MILL, ON SPRING RIVER EAST OF CARTHAGE, C. 1930. Carthage was home to numerous other flour and grain mills in town and nearby, including the Pearl Mills owned by McDaniel and Ruffin. In 1884, S.O. Morrow purchased J.T. Ruffin's interest, and the named changed to McDaniel and Morrow until the Morrows acquired full interest in the twentieth century. Milling had taken place at this Spring River site since 1848.

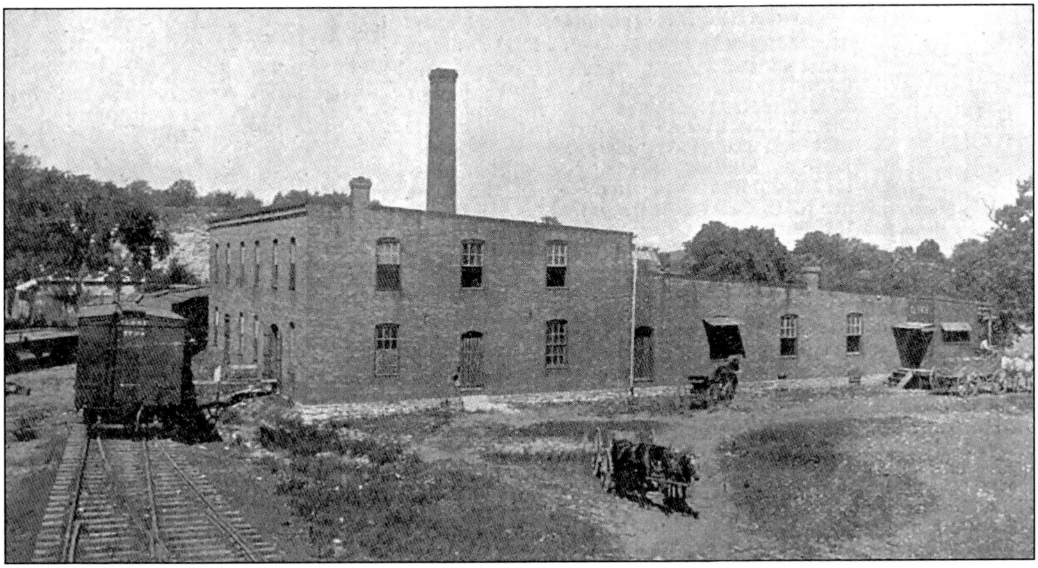

SPRING RIVER CANNING COMPANY, NORTH MAIN AND THE MILLRACE, C. 1900. Established in 1888 as McCannon and Fay Packing, J.H. Magee acquired part interest in the firm in 1897, and operated it as Spring River Canning after that date. According to the Sanborn Insurance maps, the factory had the means of processing 25,000 cans a day. Their product was sold from Missouri to Texas.

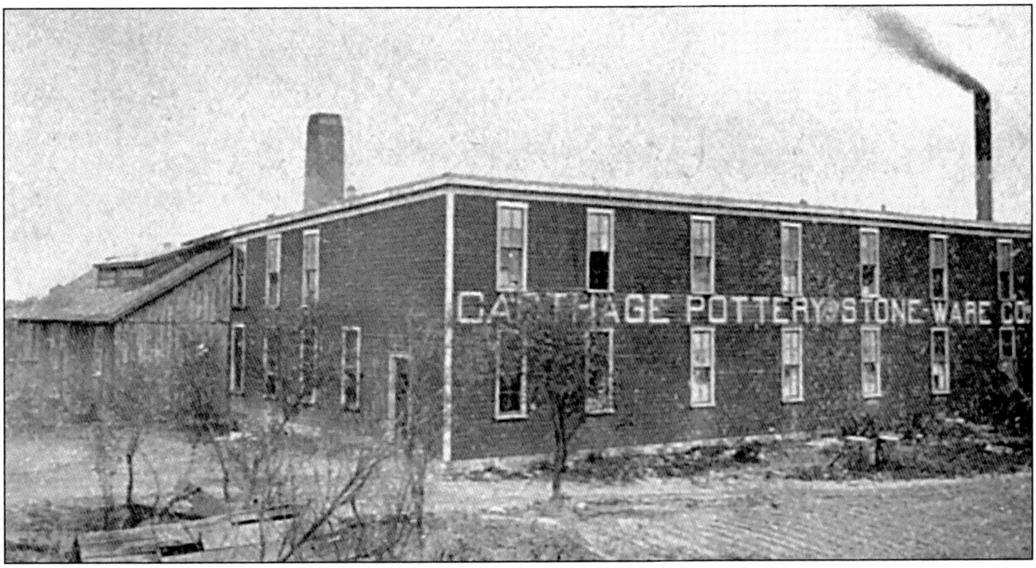

CARTHAGE POTTERY AND STONEWARE COMPANY, HIGH AND PARSONS STREETS, C. 1895. Coppock and Browne operated a pottery on site as early as 1888. By 1895, the capacity had been increased for the manufacture of double glaze black ware, which its makers claimed was far superior to light-colored or salt-glaze wares. Always battling financial difficulties, in 1899, 28 train cars of pottery were shipped despite being closed for reorganization part of that year.

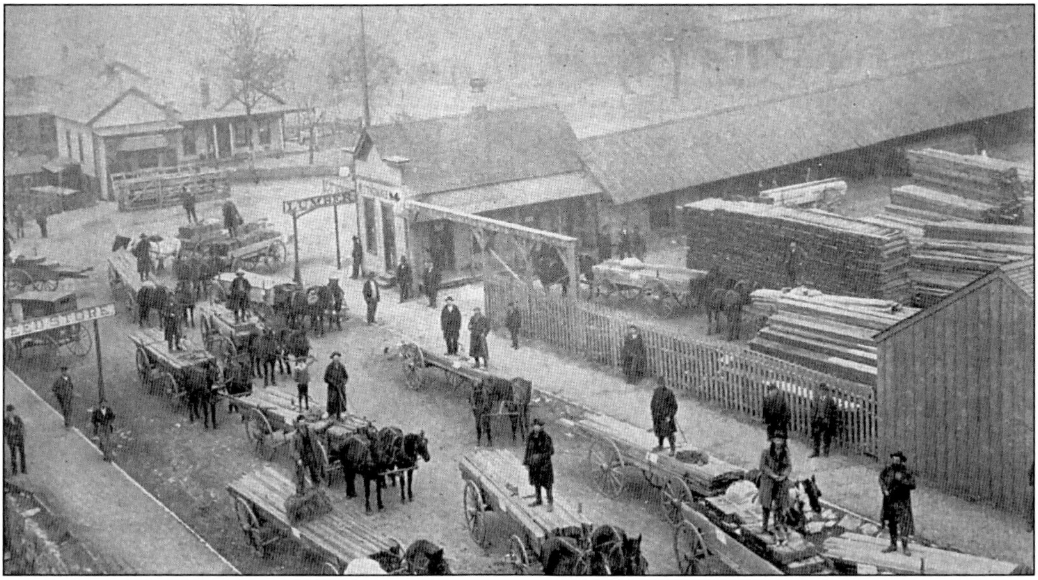

B.F. Thomas Lumberyard, Central and Grant Streets, 1890. Operated by Ben F. Thomas who, at various times, was also postmaster, mayor, and state senator, this business consolidated into Stanley-Thomas in the 1920s. Carthage had as many as six lumberyards in the 1880s–90s, which in expansion years like 1891, would have meant it was hard-pressed to keep up with five hundred construction projects as in that year.

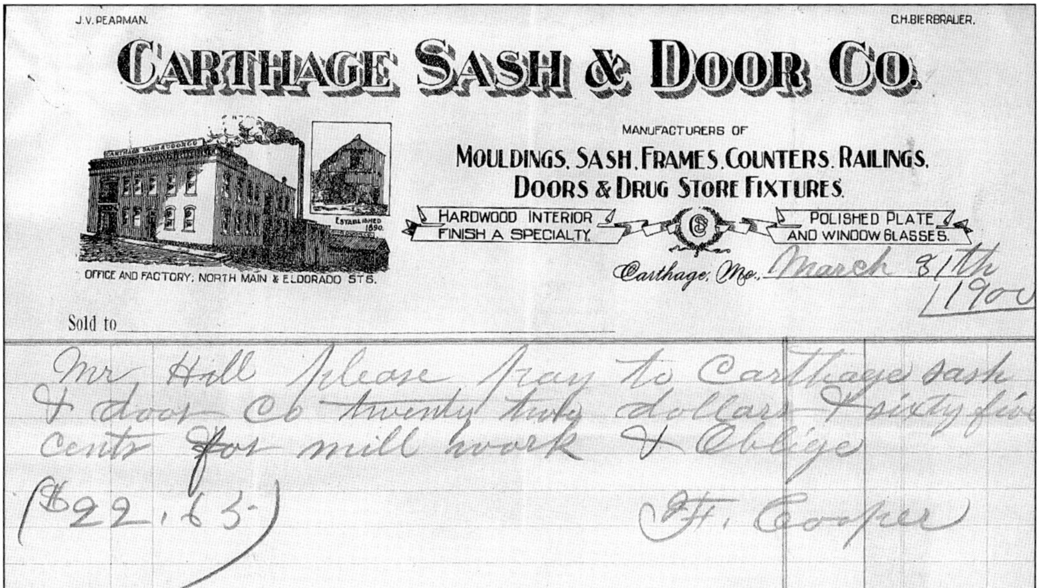

J.V. PEARMAN. C.H.BIERBRAUER.

CARTHAGE SASH & DOOR CO.

MANUFACTURERS OF
MOULDINGS, SASH, FRAMES, COUNTERS, RAILINGS, DOORS & DRUG STORE FIXTURES.

HARDWOOD INTERIOR FINISH A SPECIALTY. POLISHED PLATE AND WINDOW GLASSES.

OFFICE AND FACTORY: NORTH MAIN & ELDORADO STS.

Carthage, Mo., March 31th 1900

Sold to

Mr Hill please pay to Carthage sash & door Co twenty two dollars & sixty five cents for mill work & Oblige

($22.65)

F. Cooper

Letterhead of the Carthage Sash and Door Company, Main and Eldorado Streets, 1900. Owned by J.V. Pearman and C.H. Beirbrauer, this firm provided millwork including mouldings, sashes, doors, and other structural features. In 1900, the company sold 700 feet of lattice for $7.50 to be used in the remodeling of James F. Hill's home at 507 West Chestnut Street while this March 31, 1900 receipt is for $22.65 of millwork for the same project.

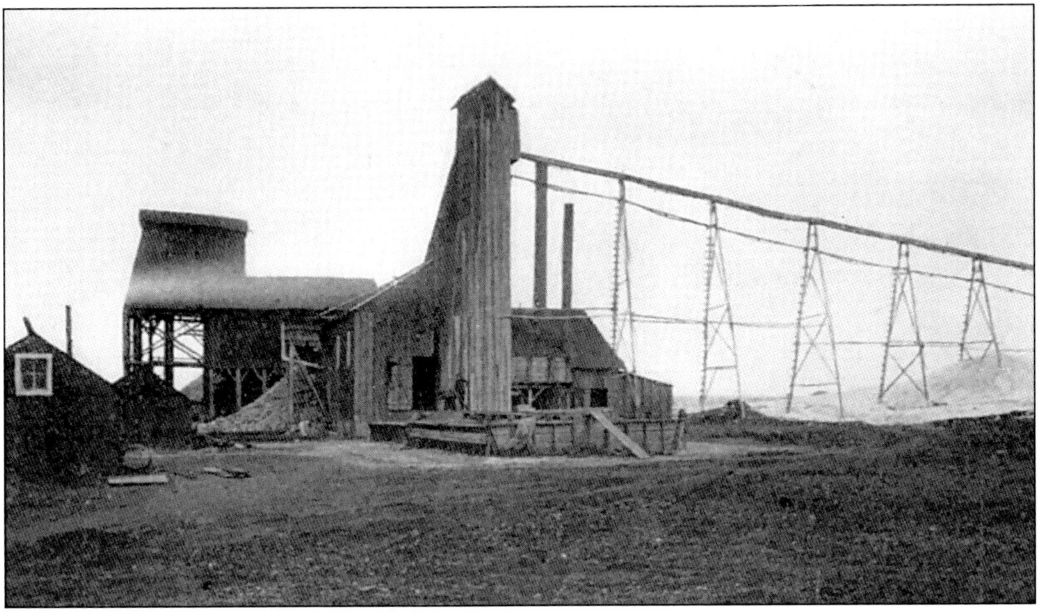

HUDSON MINE, WEST OF CARTHAGE, C. 1904. Lead was mined in Jasper County as early as 1848, but it was not until the 1870–80s that zinc was mined with commercial success. Most efforts focused west of Carthage near Joplin, but in the late 1880s, investors began to open mines around Carthage and worked them according to the rise and fall of the mineral markets into the early decades of the twentieth century.

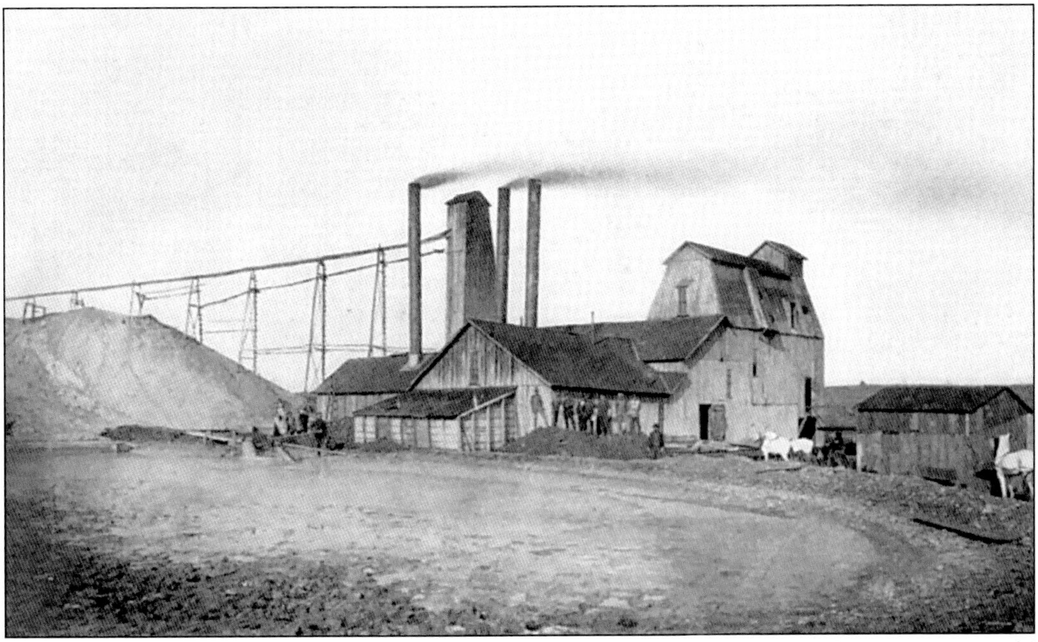

TROUP LEAD AND ZINC MINE, NEAR PROSPERITY, C. 1904. In 1892, this mine was sold to Indiana investors for $150,000, marking the largest mine sale of its time in the region. Local sellers who benefited included Curtis Wright (who invested in the stone business), T.J. Rittenhouse, B.B. Allen, J.W. Ground, V.A. Wallace, and Mrs. M.B. Parke. Organized in 1888, Troup was the first mining operation in the Prosperity area.

UNIDENTIFIED MINER AT UNKNOWN MINE, C. 1910–20. In 1900, there were at least 20 mines within 3 miles of Carthage and, it was remarked that "there was no telling anymore when you are going to strike mineral in Jasper County. The whole territory is underlaid with it and every day brings its reports of new mines being opened up." But it was a dangerous business with reports of injury and death happening almost as frequently as strikes.

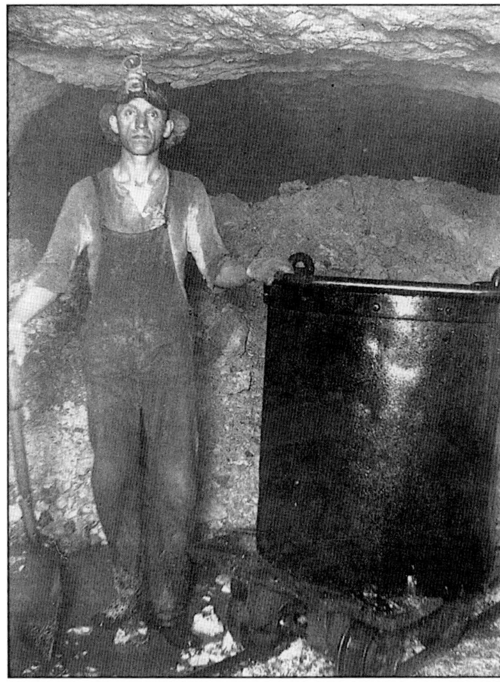

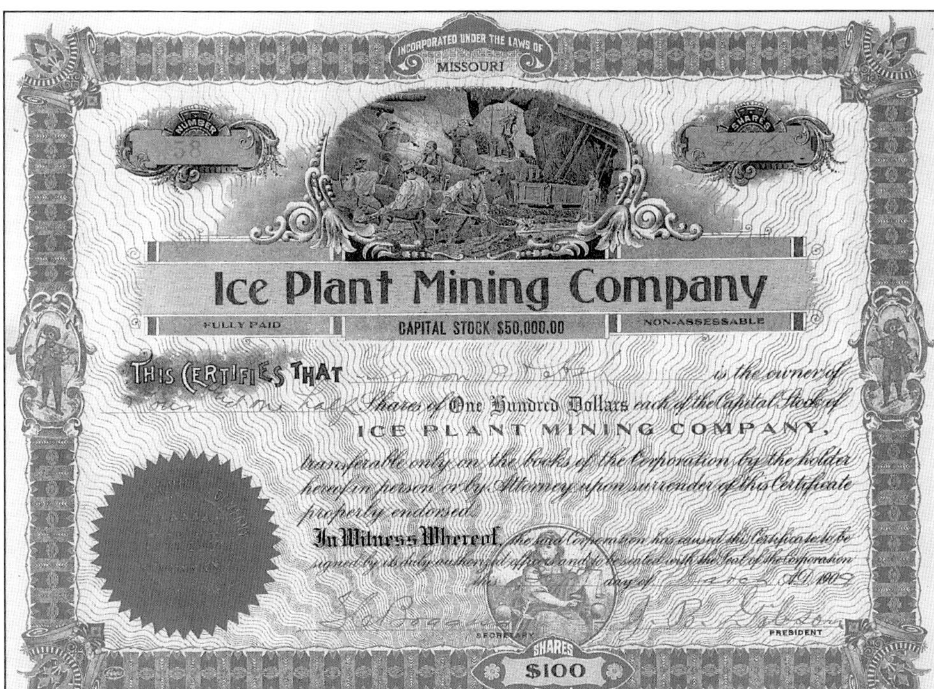

MINING STOCK OF ICE PLANT MINE, 1909. While ore prices were followed in the newspapers, the names of new mines were almost as interesting to watch. These names included New Hope, Black Eagle, Hayseed, Blue Herring, Hazel Dell, Buzzard, Wise Guy, Vesuvius, and from the Neck City, Missouri, 1897 strike known as the "Klondike of the Southwest," came Little Em, Big Kate, Close Call, and Sphinx.

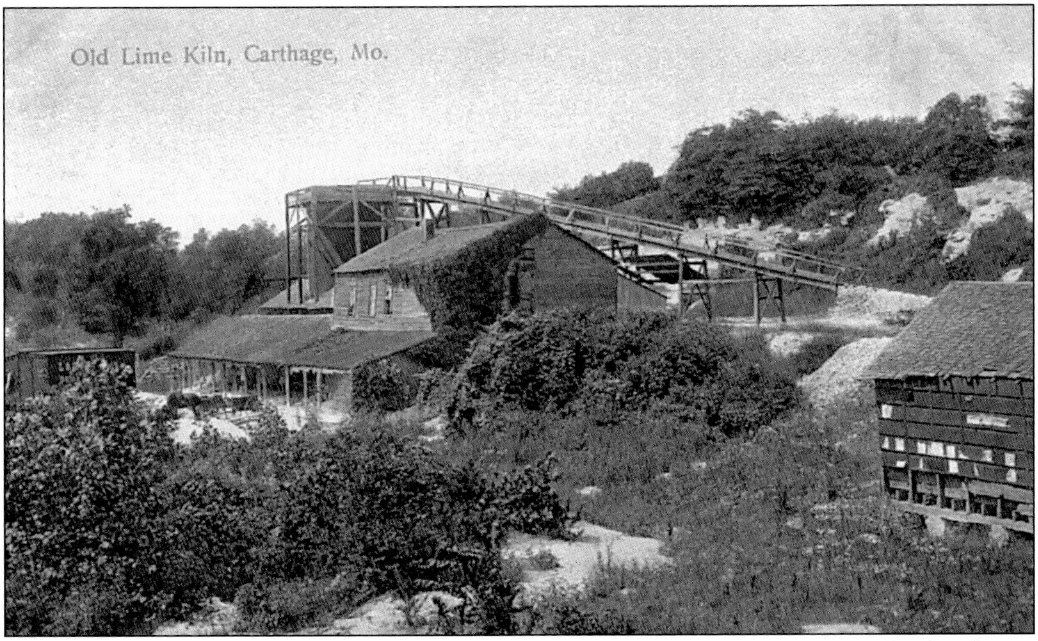

OLD LIME KILN, NORTH OF CARTHAGE NEAR KENDRICKTOWN, C. 1900–10. The first large-scale quarry and dressing plant was opened in 1874 by Isaac Garner on the Kendrick farm, which in 1883, was being managed by Gilfillan Stone Company of Fort Scott, Kansas. Other early 1880s quarries were operated by J. McNamara, Gates and Merton, and a Mr. McDanavin.

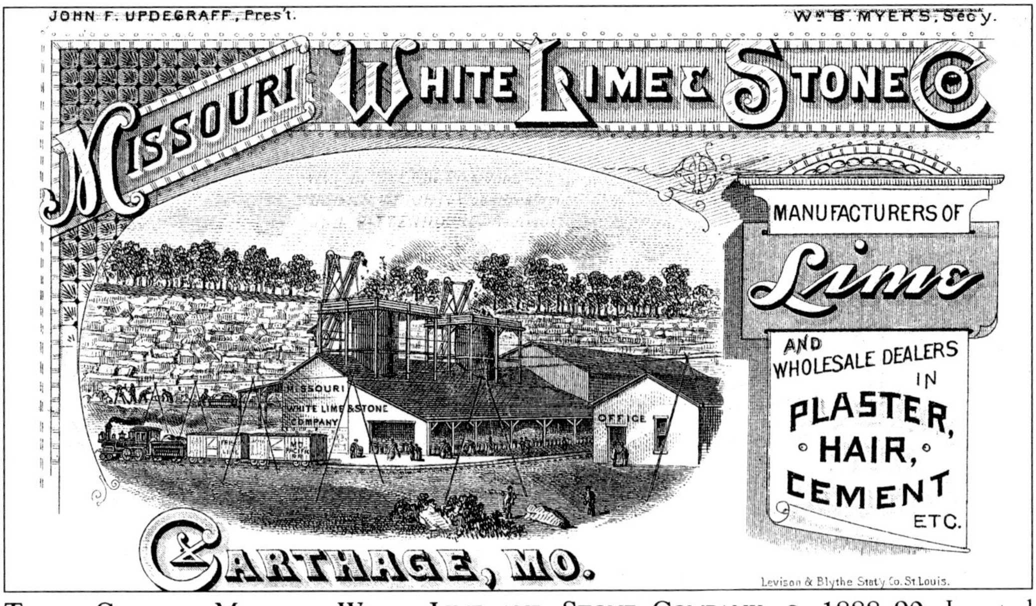

TRADE CARD OF MISSOURI WHITE LIME AND STONE COMPANY, C. 1888–90. Located northwest of Carthage near the Star White Lime Works operated by Charles Hubbs, T.J. Rittenhouse and Curtis Wright bought out fellow Hoosier John F. Updegraff's interest in this quarry shortly upon arrival in Carthage. Production included lime for agricultural and construction purposes, as well as a small amount of building stone.

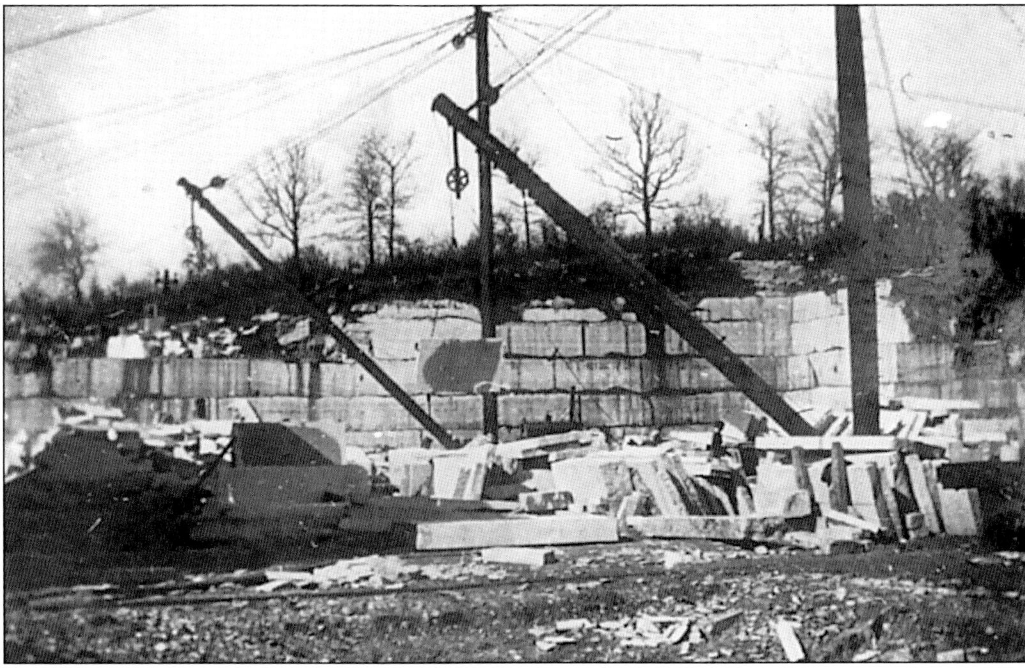

Carthage Stone Company Quarry View, c 1895–1898. Taken by son Nat, this view of Curtis Wright's second quarry (owned with W.R. Logan and B.B. Allen) shows the derricks used to lift and haul stone. Organized in 1892, offices were maintained in Kansas City and Saint Louis. The Cole County Courthouse in Jefferson City, Missouri, and the old public library in Kansas City, Missouri, are examples of this quarry's product.

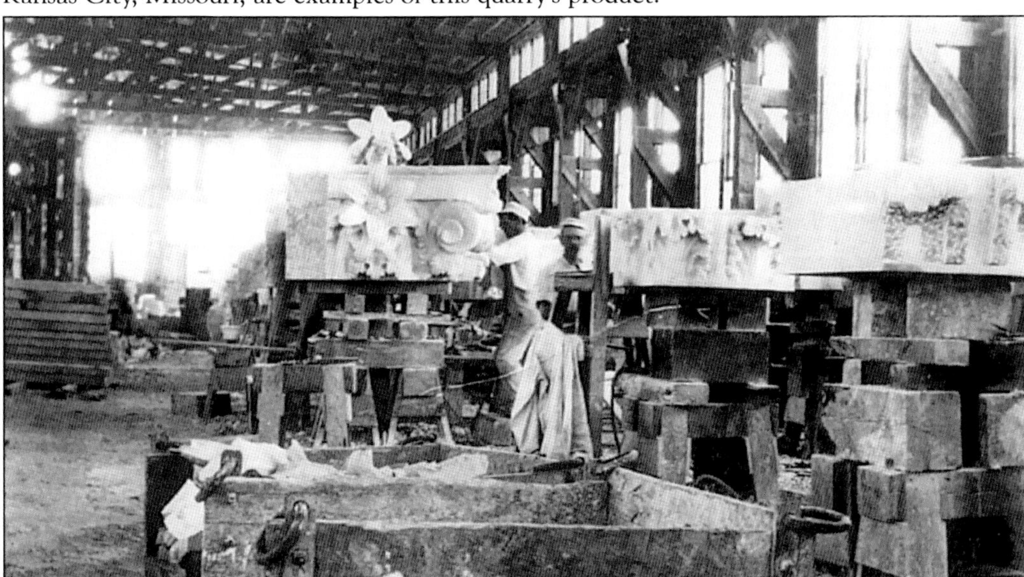

Stone Carvers at Unidentified Quarry, c. 1914–15. These two carvers are working on enormous Corinthian capitals, possibly at the processing warehouse of Lautz-McNerney Stone Company, or F.W. Steadley and Company. This photograph was taken by Jewell and Justin Brown on an outing to the quarries located northeast of town, a popular pastime for residents and tourists.

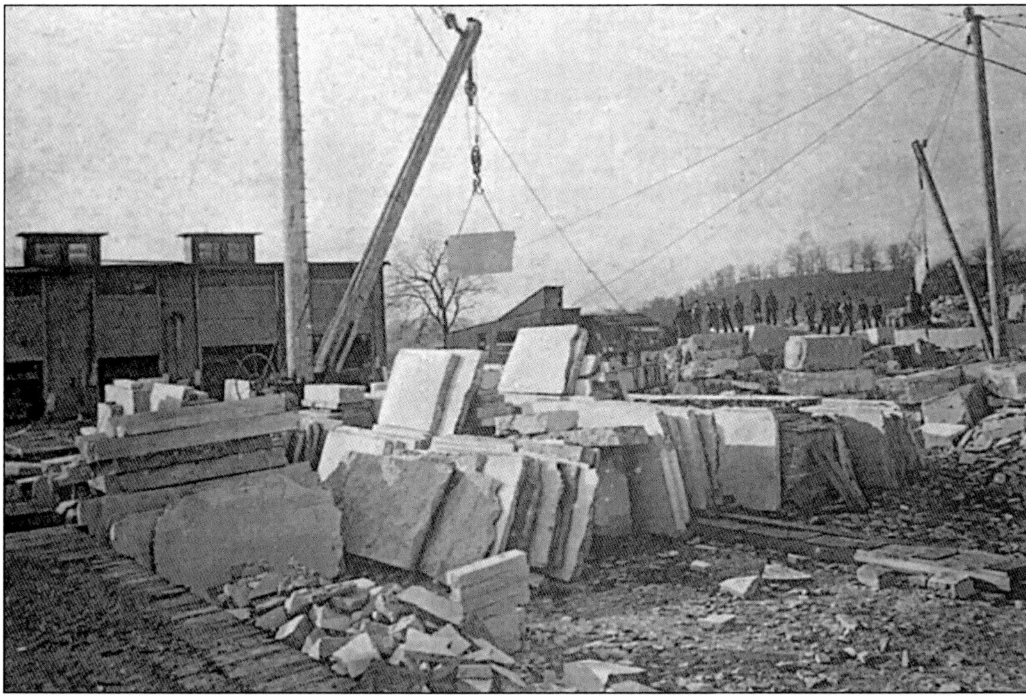

Carthage Quarry Company, c. 1910. Owned by Eugene O'Keefe and F.W. Steadley, and managed by Martin McNerney, this company worked 9 acres and could produce 1,000 cubic feet of stone a day. It employed 25 men in 1900.

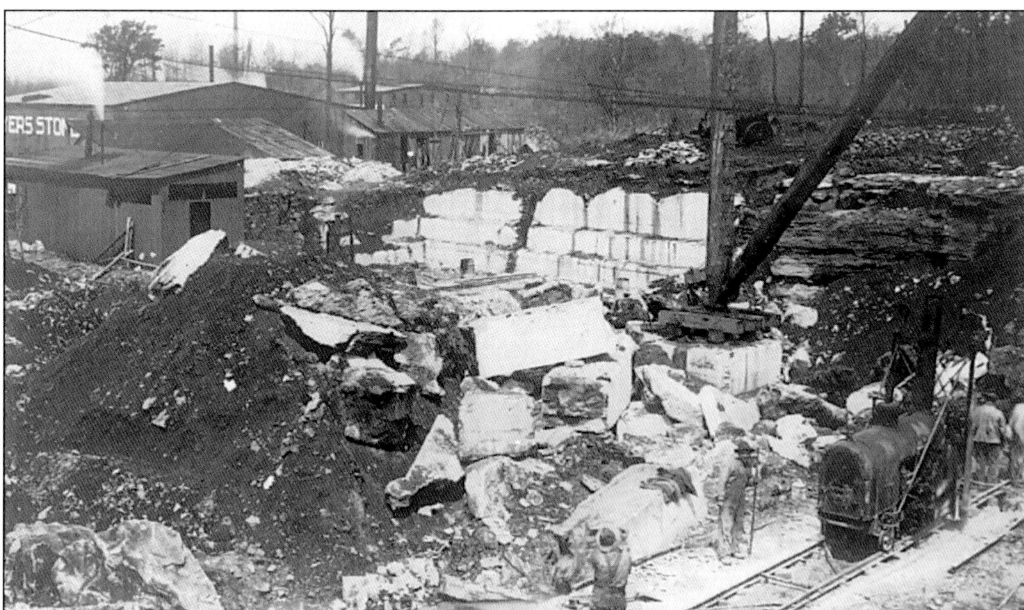

Myers Stone Company, c. 1910. Located about 4 miles southwest of Carthage, this company was owned by Frank Myers, George Lawrence, G.C. Kellogg, and George Beimdiek at the time of this postcard, which depicts the processing plant, derricks in the quarry, and in the lower right corner, a channeler that cuts the stone.

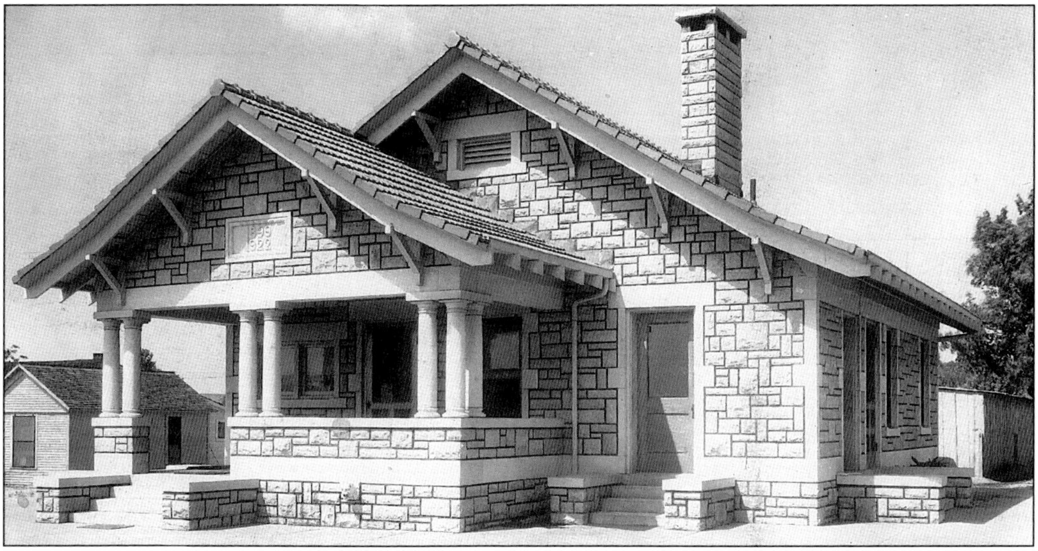

Office and Drafting Department of F.W. Steadley and Company, c. 1922. The office for "The Big Quarry" was built to demonstrate the exterior and interior use of the company's "Colonial Grey Marble," which it sold. National examples of the quarry's product include Union Station in Chicago, Republic Building in Denver, Jewish Hospital in Saint Louis, and the Mid-Continent Building in Tulsa. Steadley was the largest quarry prior to consolidation, employing two hundred people.

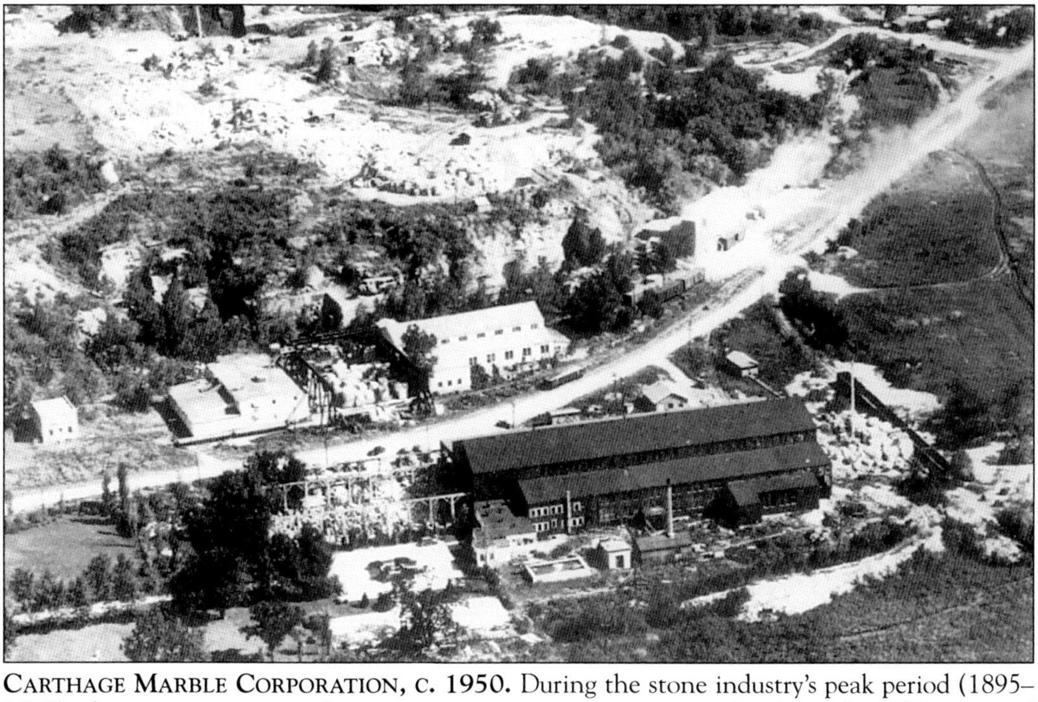

Carthage Marble Corporation, c. 1950. During the stone industry's peak period (1895–1925), there were over two dozen stone companies operating in Carthage. In 1927, seven of these companies merged into one corporation, which continued quarrying to the 1980s while diversifying into underground storage at the former quarry sites. The vast complex, now owned by Americold Logistics, can still be seen from North Francis Street and Civil War Road.

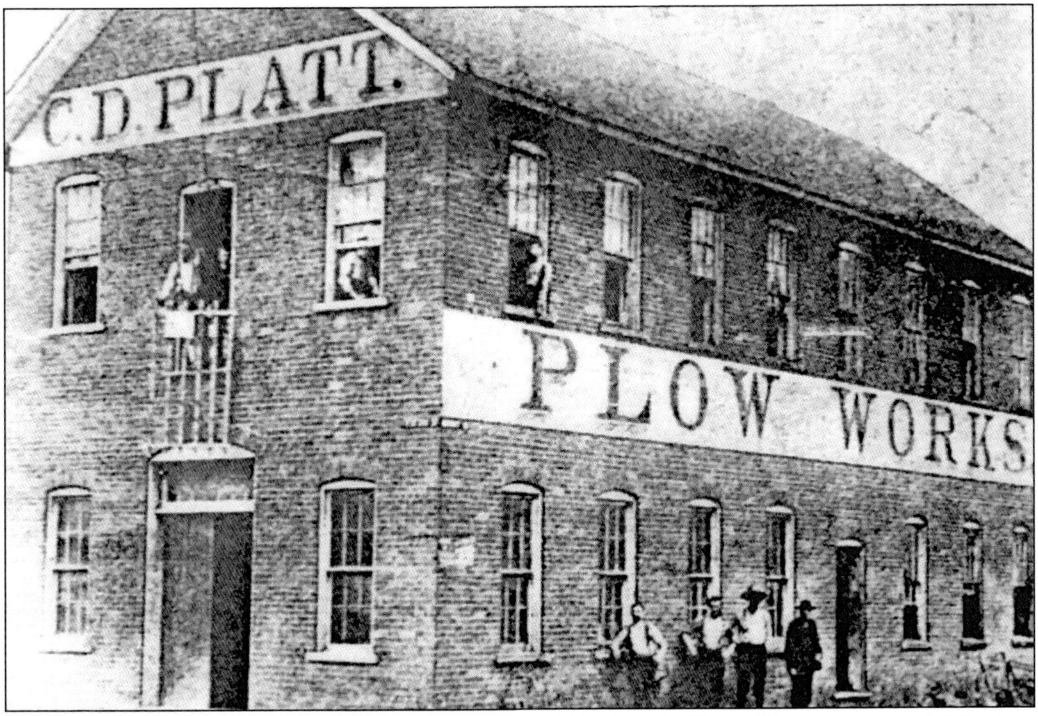

C.D. Plow Works, 500 Grant Street, c. 1885. Platt's Plow Works was established in 1873. Under the operation of son C.B. Platt, two hundred plows a day were made in the early 1880s, when Platt was approached by his brother-in-law Joseph P. Leggett with a new type of bedspring he had patented. The two perfected the invention and the equipment to make them at the plow factory, and then began producing the bed springs there as well.

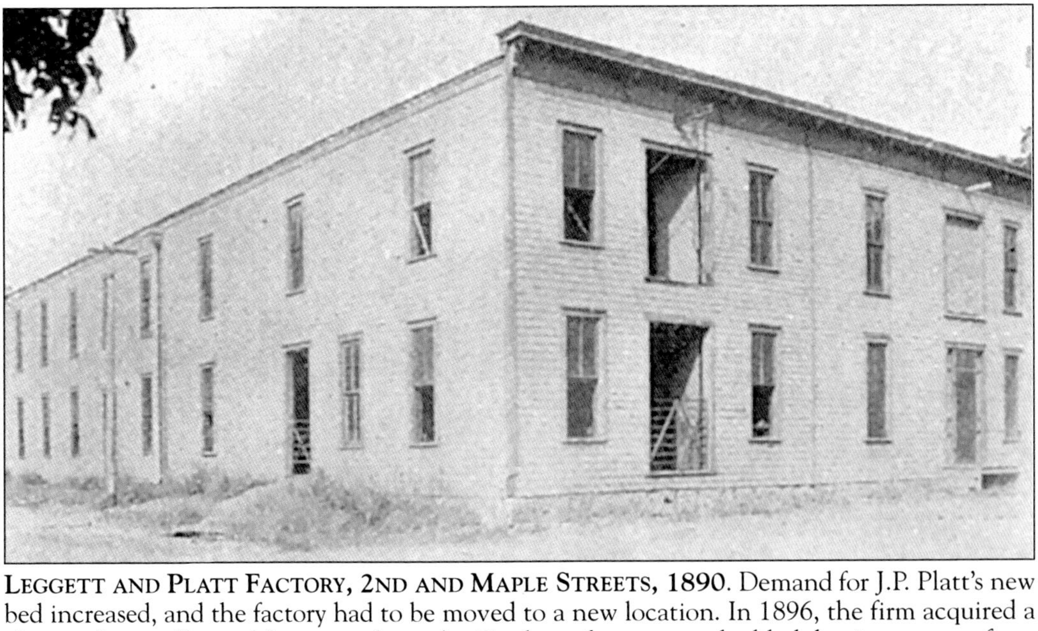

Leggett and Platt Factory, 2nd and Maple Streets, 1890. Demand for J.P. Platt's new bed increased, and the factory had to be moved to a new location. In 1896, the firm acquired a plant in Louisville, and four years later the Carthage factory was doubled despite protests from neighbors. In 1901, Leggett and Platt Bed Spring Manufacturing Company was incorporated.

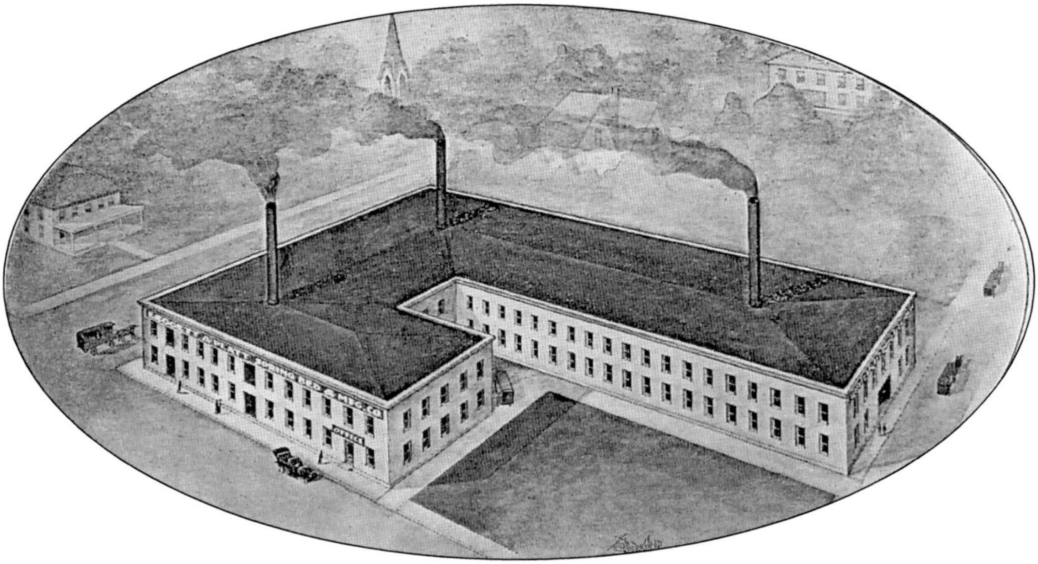

LEGGETT AND PLATT FACTORY, 2ND AND MAPLE STREETS, C. 1910. A promotional booklet touted that "in this section we have some progressive industrial organizations engaged in the manufacture of different products, but none have been more prominent in advancing the enviable position which Carthage now holds than the above–named firm."

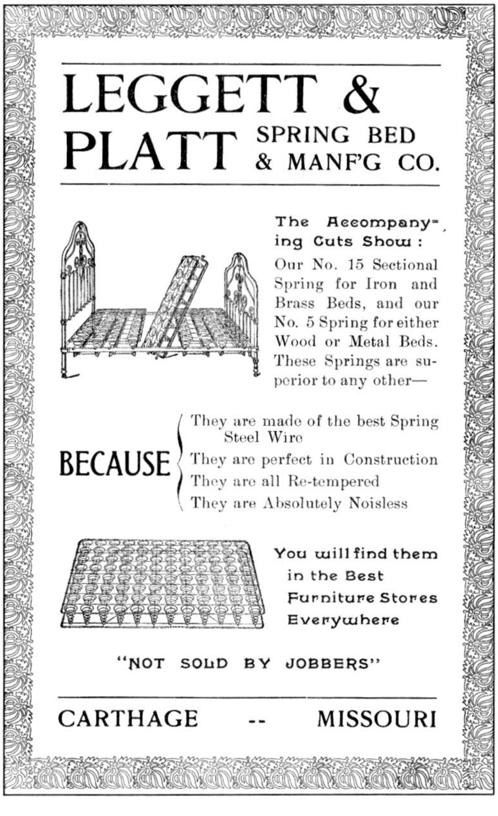

LEGGETT AND PLATT ADVERTISEMENT. Advertising in the 1905 Carthage High School *Herald*, the #15 sectional bedsprings set is illustrated here, as well as the #5 full bed unit. Springs were replaced free if found to sag or break within ten years of purchase. Demand for bed springs continued to increase and in 1925, a new factory at Vine and Orner Streets was built.

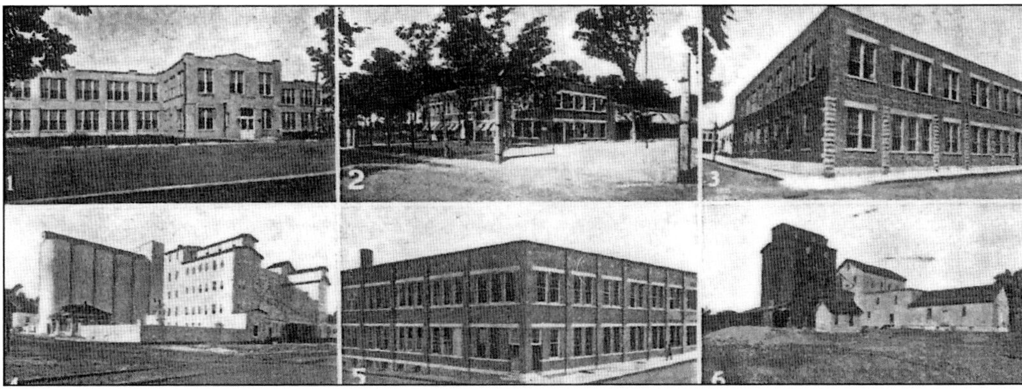

CARTHAGE FACTORIES, C. 1920. Pictured from the top, left to right, are: Kaut Footwear Company at Oak Street and Garrison Avenue (later Carmo Shoe), Juvenile Shoe Corporation at 200 River Street, Howard-Hume-Dittrick Shoe Company at Fourth and Maple Streets, (bottom row) McDaniel Mill at Meridian and El Dorado Streets, Carthage Shoe Manufacturing at Main Street and Central Avenue, and Morrow Mill. The shoe industry began in Carthage during World War I and continued for several decades with many of these companies occupying competing factory buildings at a later date.

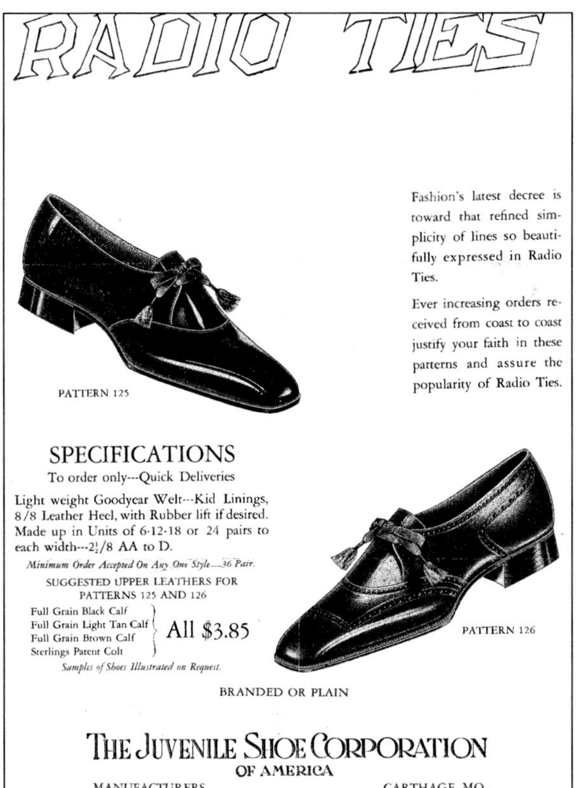

A JUVENILE SHOE CORPORATION ADVERTISEMENT, 1922. Juvenile Shoe continued to operate in Carthage until 1929–30 although it retained its facilities in nearby Aurora, Missouri. It manufactured men's, women's, and children's footwear including a line called "National Park Hiking Boots" that is represented in the Powers Museum's collections. Juvenile Shoe returned to Carthage in 1971 but closed again in 1990.

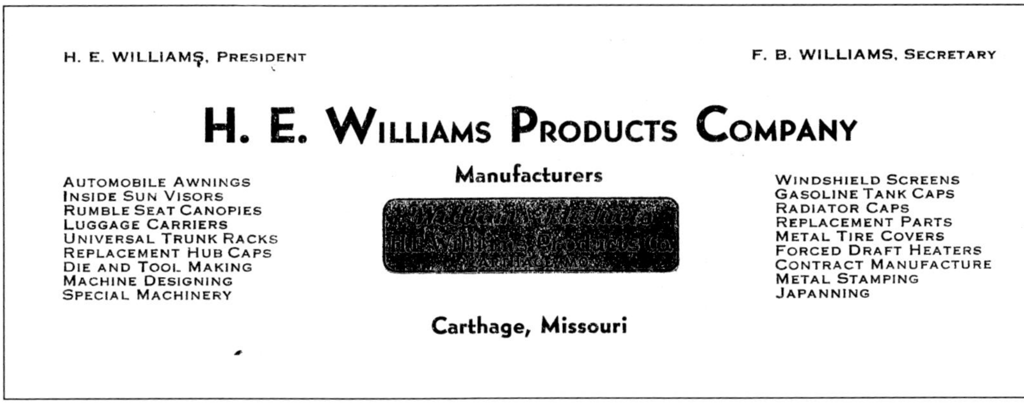

H. E. WILLIAMS, PRESIDENT

F. B. WILLIAMS, SECRETARY

H. E. WILLIAMS PRODUCTS COMPANY

Manufacturers

AUTOMOBILE AWNINGS
INSIDE SUN VISORS
RUMBLE SEAT CANOPIES
LUGGAGE CARRIERS
UNIVERSAL TRUNK RACKS
REPLACEMENT HUB CAPS
DIE AND TOOL MAKING
MACHINE DESIGNING
SPECIAL MACHINERY

WINDSHIELD SCREENS
GASOLINE TANK CAPS
RADIATOR CAPS
REPLACEMENT PARTS
METAL TIRE COVERS
FORCED DRAFT HEATERS
CONTRACT MANUFACTURE
METAL STAMPING
JAPANNING

Carthage, Missouri

LETTERHEAD OF H.E. WILLIAMS COMPANY, C.1930. While today this firm specializes in electrical light fixtures, during the company's early years, the product focus was automobile accessories, beginning with window awnings and expanding to the items listed on the company's stationery. One factory, located at 116 North Main had previously been the Carthage Planing Mill. Established in 1920, Williams moved to the old shoe plant at 100 South Main in the early 1930s and introduced light fixtures to its product line. By 1940, production focused entirely on lighting.

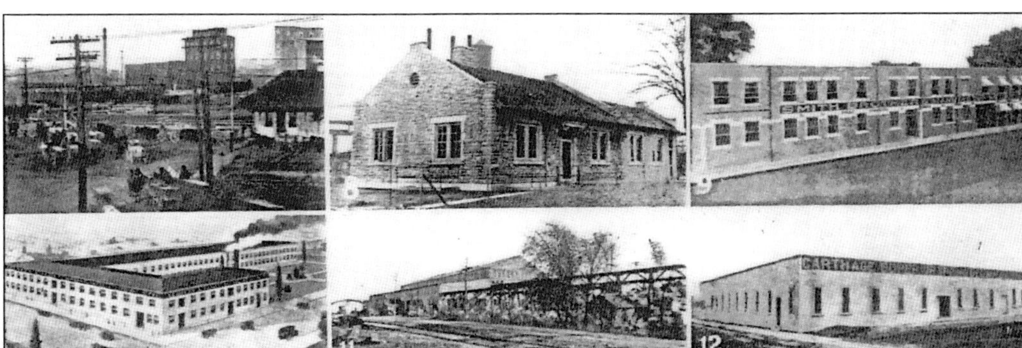

CARTHAGE FACTORIES, C. 1920. Pictured from the top, left to right, are: Cowgill and Hill Mill, Hercules Powder Plant west of Carthage, Smith Brothers Manufacturing Company at 5th and Grant Streets, Leggett and Platt Bed Spring Manufacturing, Lautz-Missouri Marble Company, north-west of the city, and Carthage Superior Spring Bed Factory at 408 North Main Street. The Chamber of Commerce was able to attract new industries during the Depression years (most notably the poultry industry) and to boast that Carthage did not have a single plant close during that time. Many industries worked reduced hours or shifts but no factory went idle long before the Chamber found a new occupant.

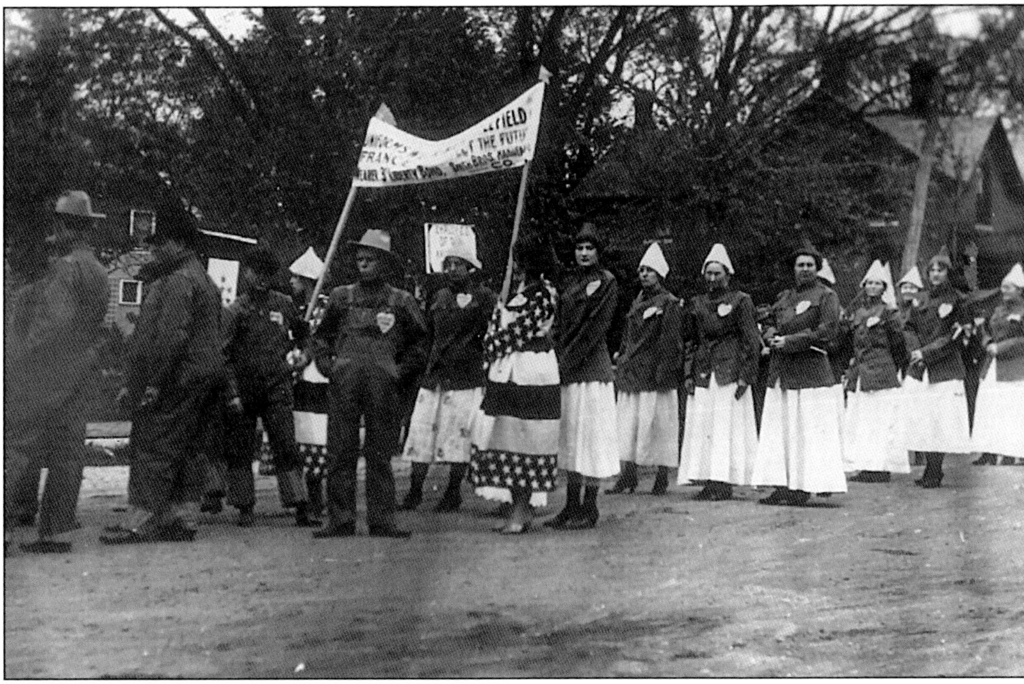

SMITH BROTHERS MANUFACTURING COMPANY WORKERS IN PATRIOTIC PARADE, 1918. Workers model army jackets and overalls made during World War I. Just two years before, brothers Clayton and E.O. Smith moved their business from Sedalia, Missouri, to Carthage, where the company operated until 2000. Many recognize the *Big Smith* label, but another trademark was registered—*Corn Belt Guaranteed Garments*—and used when first established.

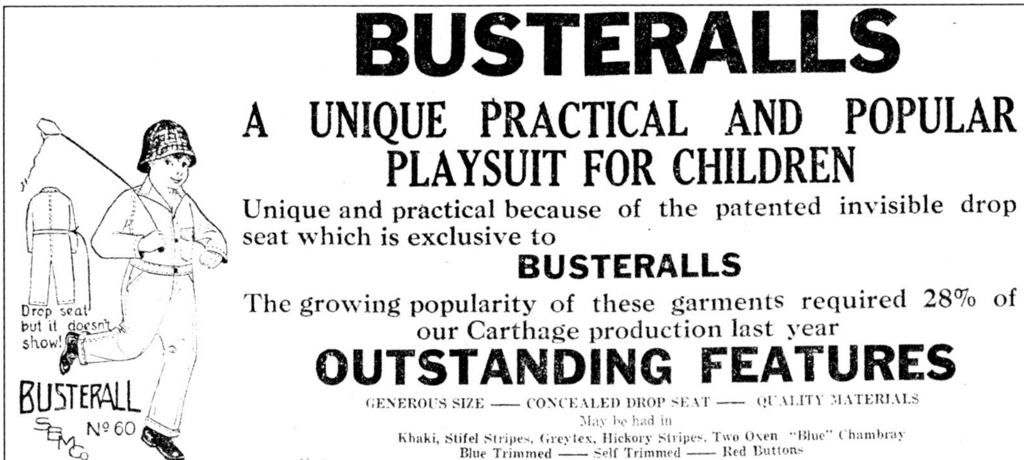

SMITH BROTHERS *BUSTERALLS* ADVERTISEMENT, 1926. *Big Smith* overalls and playsuits, such as *Busteralls*, were manufactured in Carthage while the Neosho, Missouri, plant made corduroy suits, riding breeches, pants, shirts, and other articles. Eventually facilities were built elsewhere in Missouri (Webb City, Lamar, and St. Joseph), but at least until the 1930s all garments were shipped from Carthage.

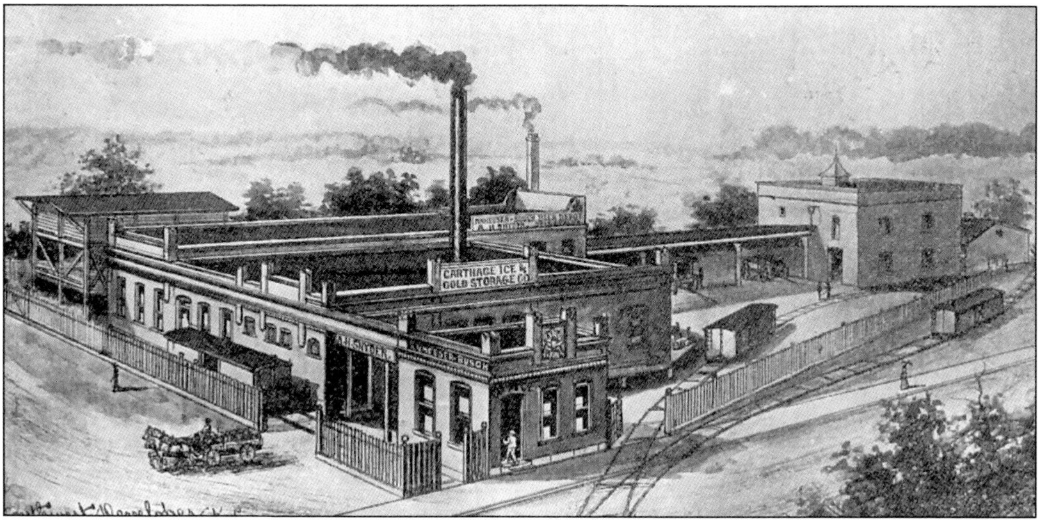

Carthage Ice and Cold Storage Company, Limestone and Main Streets, c. 1900. Carthage supported several ice plants over the years, including one located on the northeast corner of Central and Main Streets in a former apple packing plant. However, the plant pictured here was located at Main and Limestone Streets and also served as the "beer depot" for Anheuser Busch. Managed by A.H. Synder in 1900, the firm had come under the ownership of H.A. Spradling and C.K. Rowland by 1927.

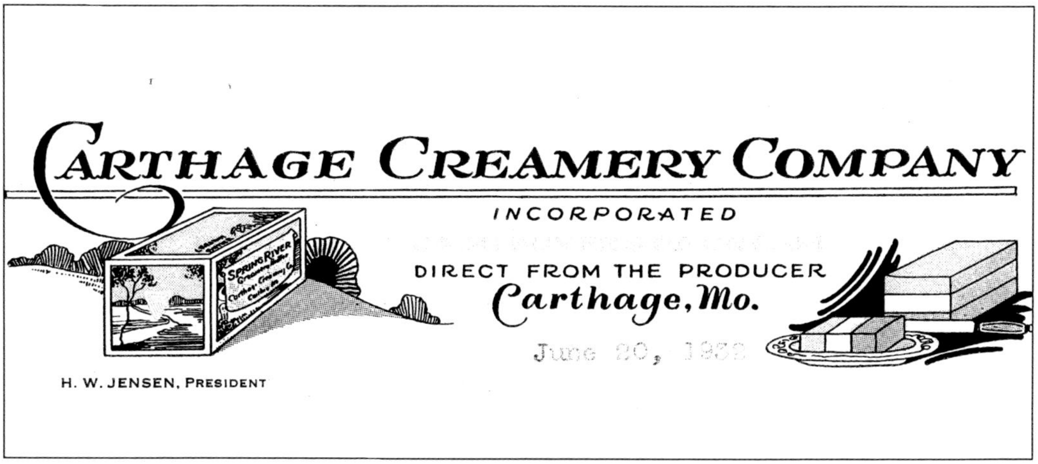

Letterhead of Carthage Creamery Company, c. 1930. Although an earlier creamery establishment was located at Vine and Willow Streets in the 1880s and 1890s, the Carthage Creamery Company business started in 1915 and was located on North Meridian Street. Among its products were *Land O' Smiles* ice cream and *Spring River* butter in 1937. Known as the "farmer's friend," the creamery purchased over $1,250,000 of milk and cream from area farmers through the four-state area during peak production years.

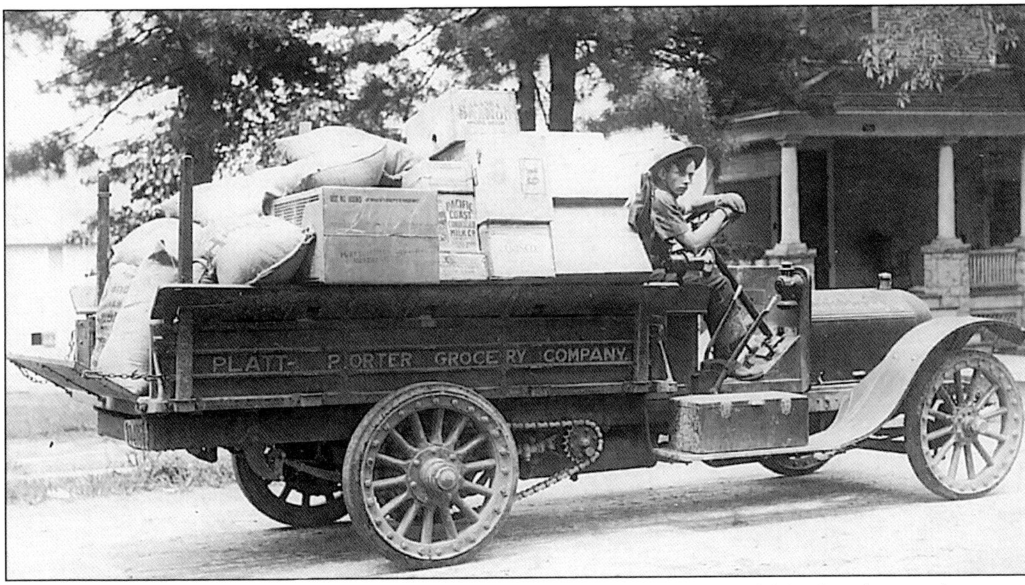

DELIVERY TRUCK OF PLATT-PORTER GROCERY COMPANY, C. 1920. In the tradition of Carthage's older groceries Griswold and Wells-Woodward (wholesalers it bought out), Platt-Porter serviced the retail groceries of this area with wholesale goods including their private label condiments and coffee. Originally located at 609 South Main Street, a new office and warehouse was built in 1926 at 527 South Main Street, now the Carthage Press Building.

"Particular People Prefer Platt-Porter's Coffee"

Coffee is but the container of volatile oils, which boiling water instantly extracts---age gradually extracts these oils by evaporation---leaving only bitterness.

PLATT-PORTER'S COFFEES

TROPIC BLEND | PP — PARTICULAR PEOPLE PREFER PLATT-PORTER'S COFFEE | GOLDEN ROD

Comes from Your Grocer Freshly Roasted, Freshly Ground, Freshly Packed

PLATT-PORTER GROCERY COMPANY

OFFICE: SIXTH AND MAIN — CARTHAGE, MISSOURI

PLATT-PORTER COFFEE ADVERTISEMENT, 1926. According to the advertisement, "particular people prefer Platt-Porter's Coffee," and it was offered in five varieties. Roasted on the second floor of the company's building, in the late 1920s Platt-Porter sold 165,000 pounds of coffee a year.

Five

LEISURE

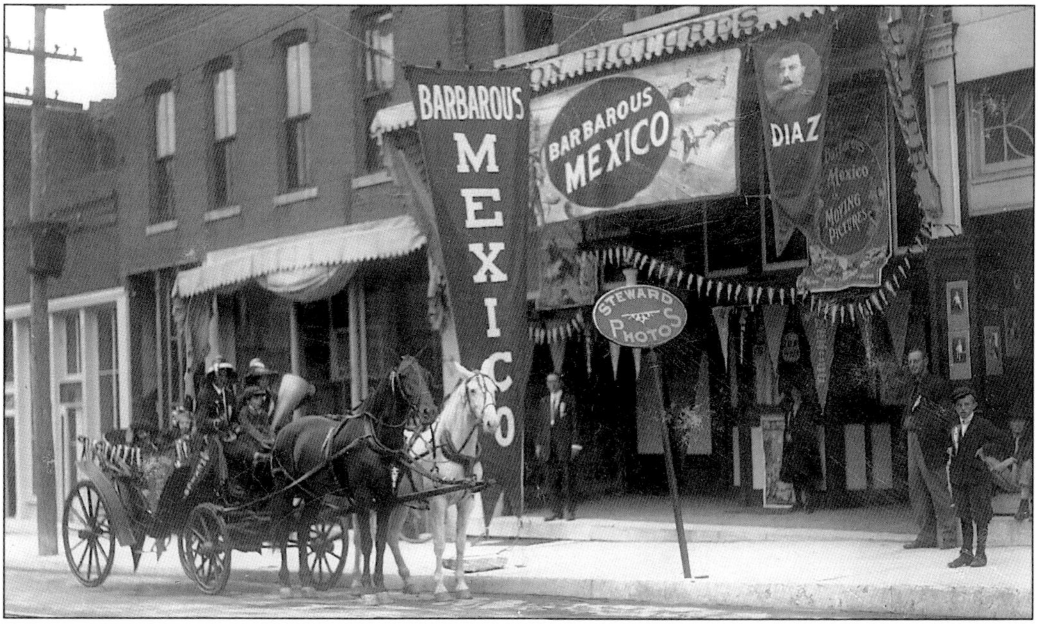

SHO-TO-ALL THEATRE, 403 SOUTH MAIN STREET, 1914. The movie *Barbarous Mexico*, a "thrilling, exciting, and beautiful visualization of picturesque Mexico" was presented April 20 and 21. Promotion included a carriage driven through town announcing the movie, and one of its passengers was Marian Louisa Powers. The entrance for Steward's Photography Studio is at the far right.

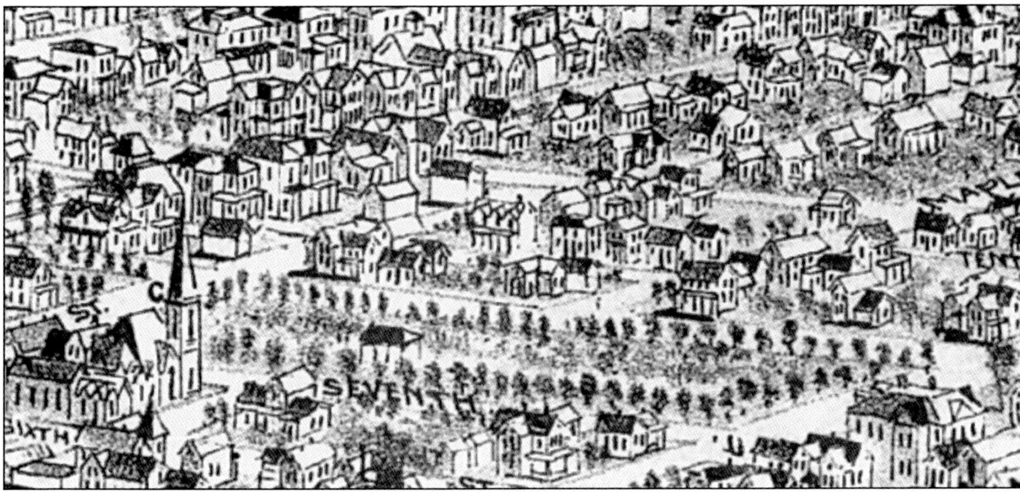

CENTRAL PARK DETAIL FROM *BIRD'S-EYE VIEW OF CARTHAGE, 1891*. Originally a burial ground for the casualties of the Battle of Carthage, in 1861, the city acquired this property in 1869 and eventually developed a park on the site after the soldiers were reburied. Formally landscaped in the 1890s with a plan created by George Kessler of Kansas City, Missouri, the park was situated near downtown, surrounded by homes and the Congregational Church (#C).

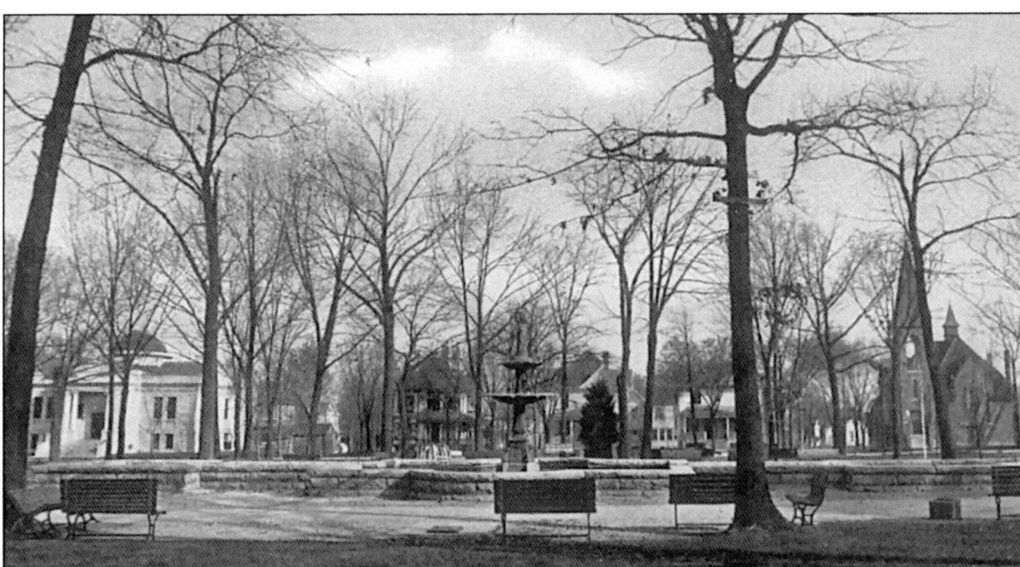

CENTRAL PARK, C. 1905. With the buildings of West 7th Street showing through the trees, the park's landscape was enhanced frequently. In 1917, hundreds of bushes and flowers, as well as 50 maple and oak trees were planted. Much of the stock came from the Curtis Wright farm, which had been part of Wild's Nursery in Sarcoxie, Missouri.

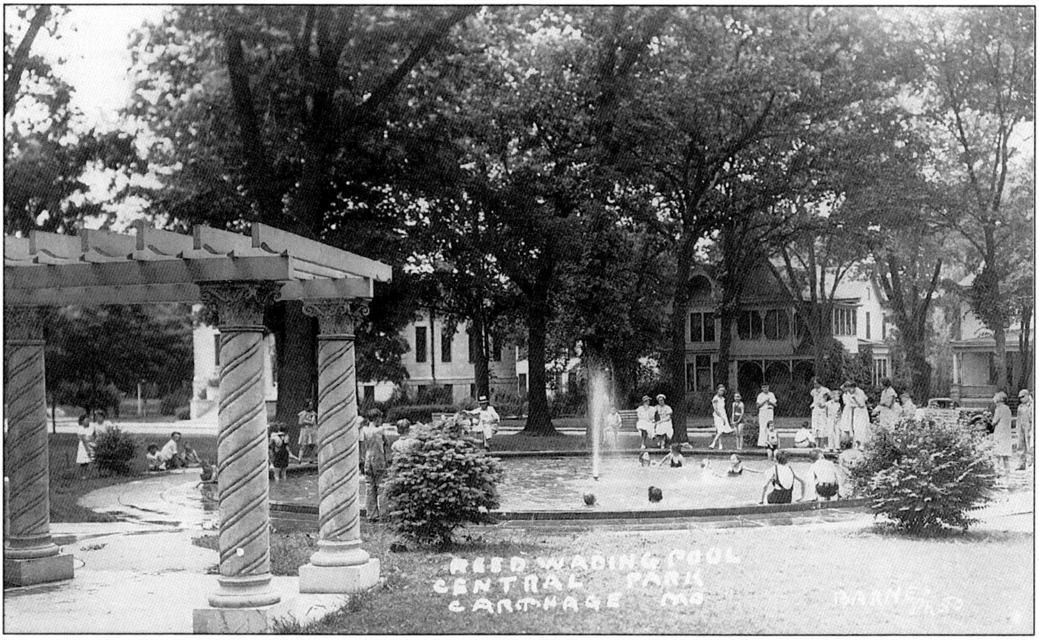

REED WADING POOL, CENTRAL PARK, c. 1935. The Carthage stone bathhouse with pergola and adjoining wading pool was a gift to the city from the Reed family of Neosho, Missouri. It serves today as it did in this view. The Whitney house, visible in the background, has been moved recently to the Precious Moments complex for future development.

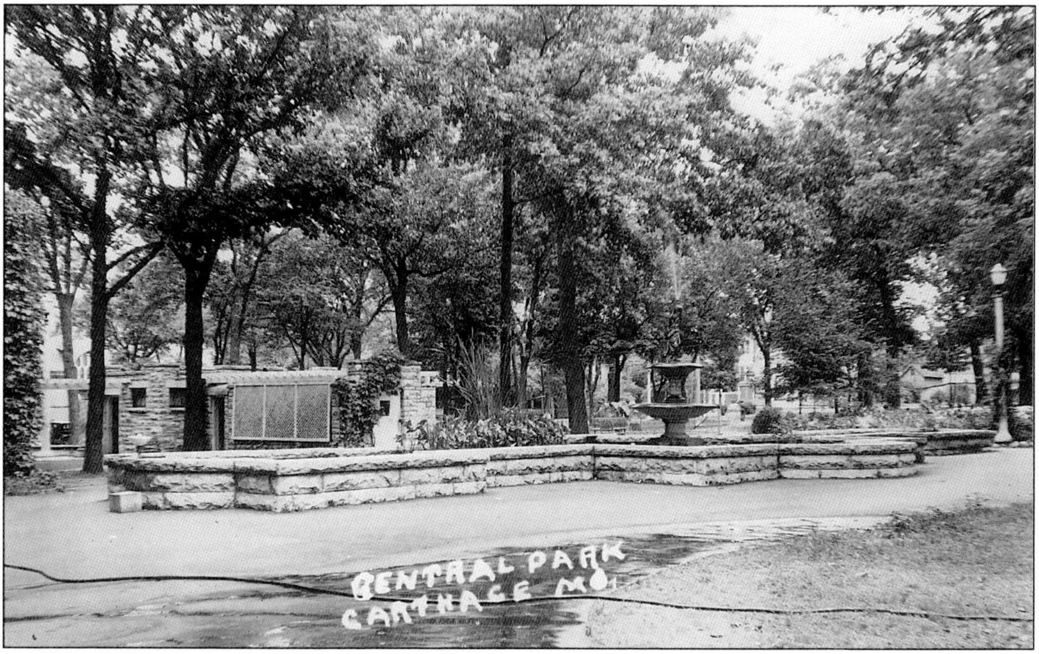

CENTRAL PARK FOUNTAIN AND FISH BASIN, c. 1935. A Victorian fountain in the center of the pond was placed in this park in 1900 by the ladies of the Carthage Federation of Clubs. Other additions have included a bandstand and a statue of Carthage High School graduate (Class of 1923) Marlin Perkins, as well as Missouri's Vietnam Memorial.

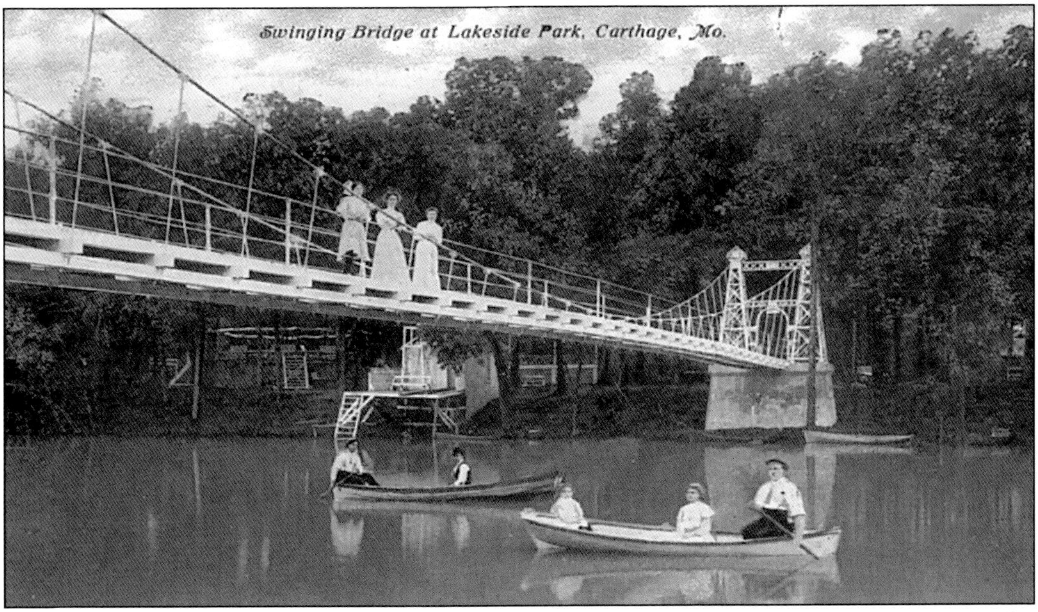

SWINGING BRIDGE, LAKESIDE PARK, WEST OF CARTHAGE, C. 1905–10. Traveling on the Southwest Missouri Electric Railway, Carthaginians, as well as fellow residents of the tri-state mining district, could enjoy the nearby resort park of Lakeside located between Carthage and Carterville. Owned and developed by A.H. Rogers, the swinging bridge connected the two land areas of the park that were separated by a lake created by damming up Center Creek.

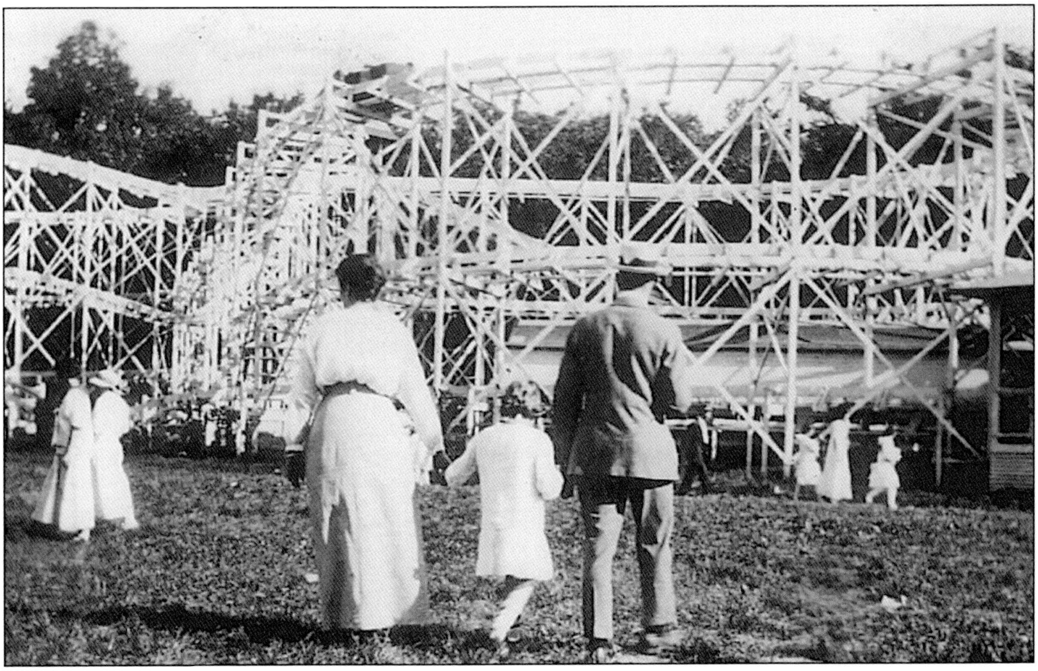

ROLLERCOASTER AT LAKESIDE PARK, 1915. In addition to the rollercoaster and water activities, other attractions at Lakeside included a midway, dance pavilion, 2,000-seat movie and vaudeville theater (1902), children's playground and mother's restroom with nurse supervision (1909), cafe, hotel, and Sunday band concerts.

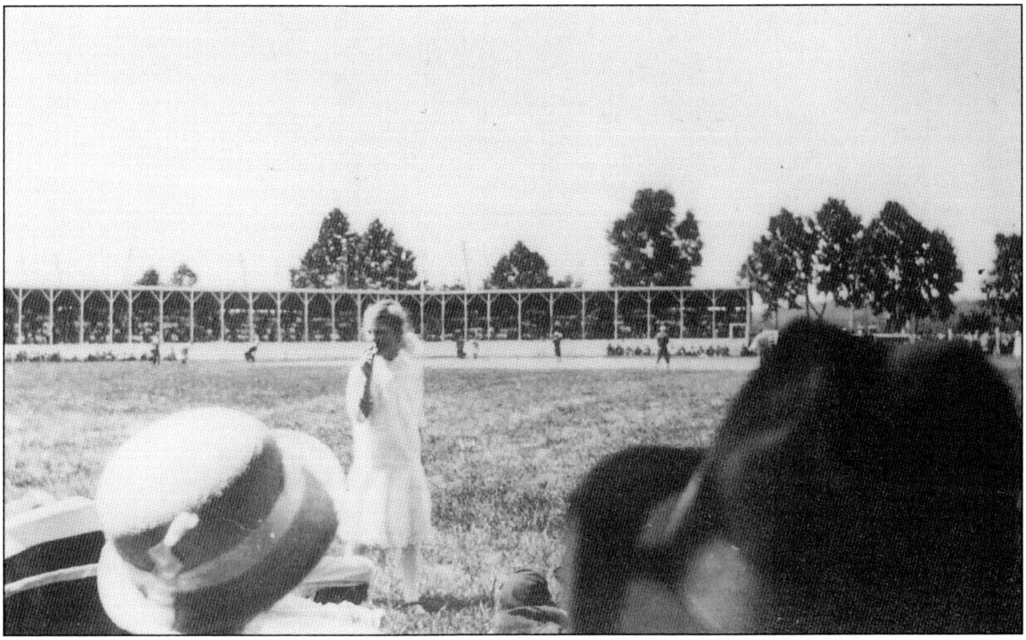

LAKESIDE PARK BASEBALL FIELD AND GRANDSTAND, 1914. Ball teams from all over the tri-state district "trolley league" played at the ball park, which was built in 1909. The day Justin and Jewel Brown took this photograph, teams from Webb City, Joplin, Carterville, and Oronogo were entertaining July 5th crowds. Other activities included a balloon ascension, all-day dance, and three concerts by the Carthage Light Guard Band.

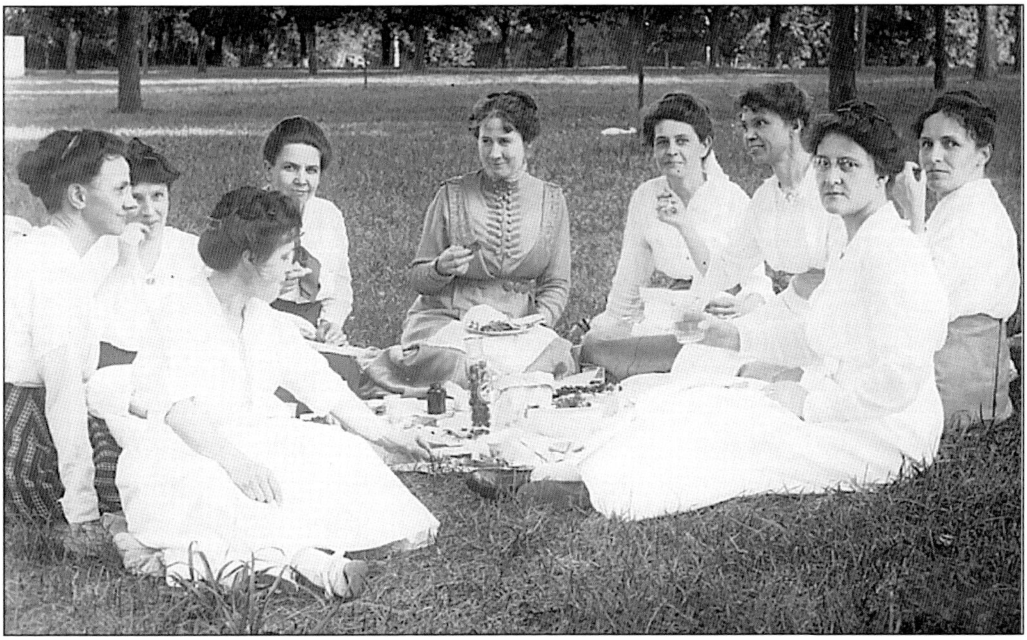

PICNIC GROUP AT LAKESIDE PARK, 1915. Pictured in this group (although order is not known) are: Laura Wood, Minnie Gladden Jane, Edith Harker, Elizabeth Luscombe Post, Hester Ornduff Bailey, Augusta "Gussie" Knight, Alice Gladden, Ella Knight, and Jennie Robertson. Lakeside was a favorite place for small outings as well as large conventions.

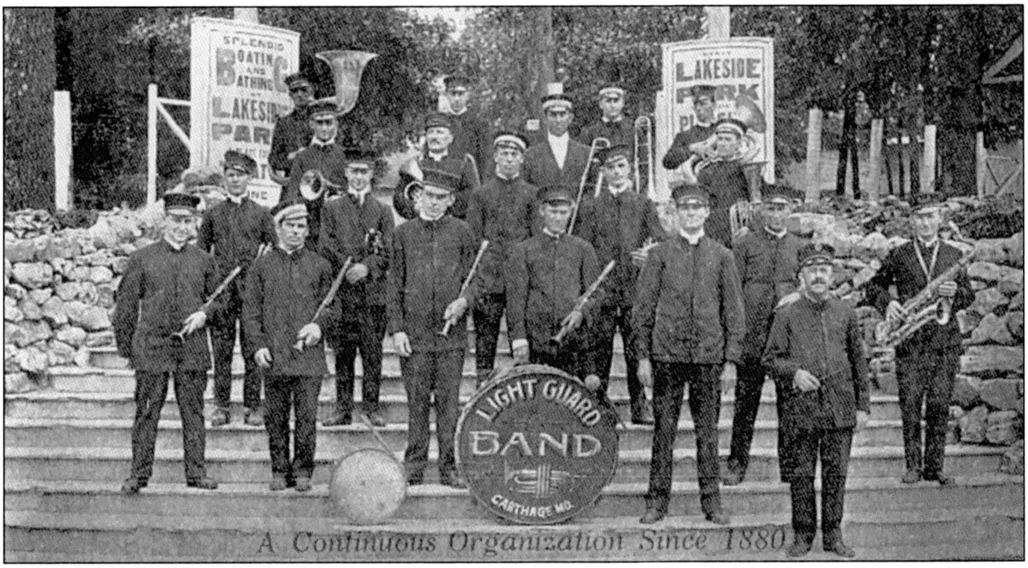

CARTHAGE LIGHT GUARD BAND, C. 1910. Poster marquees of Lakeside are behind the band and its director Charles Dumars (front right). Established in 1880, CLGB gave concerts on the square and participated in parades and band competitions across the country. Playing music that most people today associate with John Phillip Sousa and his band (who performed in Carthage in 1911), the GLGB was one of the most honored community bands in America.

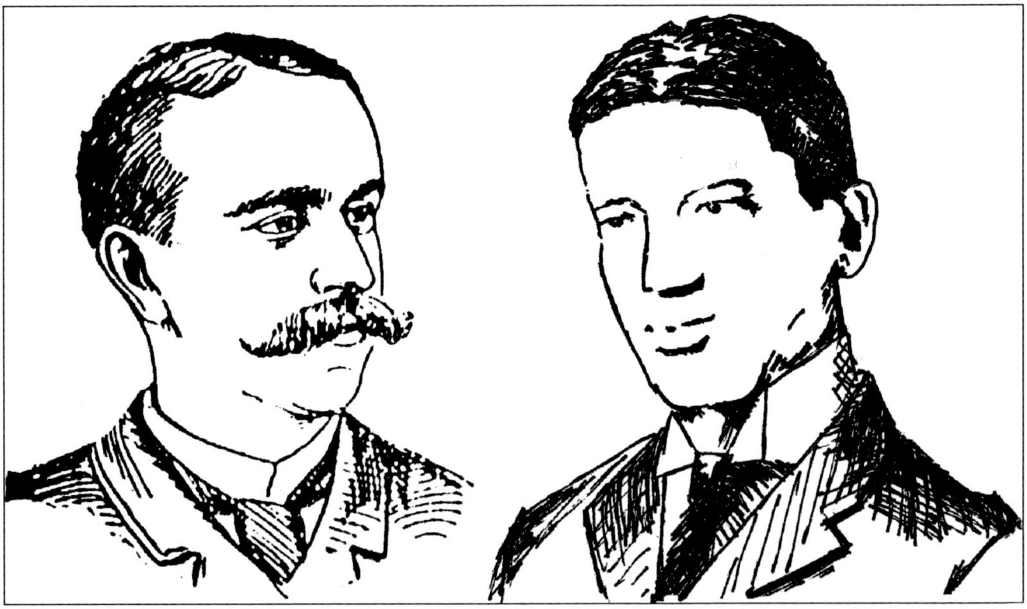

CHARLES R. DUMARS AND JAMES C. SCOTT. Dumars had a music shop downtown and employed James C. Scott to demonstrate pianos and frame artwork. A gifted pianist, Scott composed ragtime music that Dumars published. Scott organized concerts and dances at Lakeside for the African-American residents of the area, and was eventually so well-known for his compositions that he gained the title of "Crown Prince of Ragtime" and is considered second to Scott Joplin.

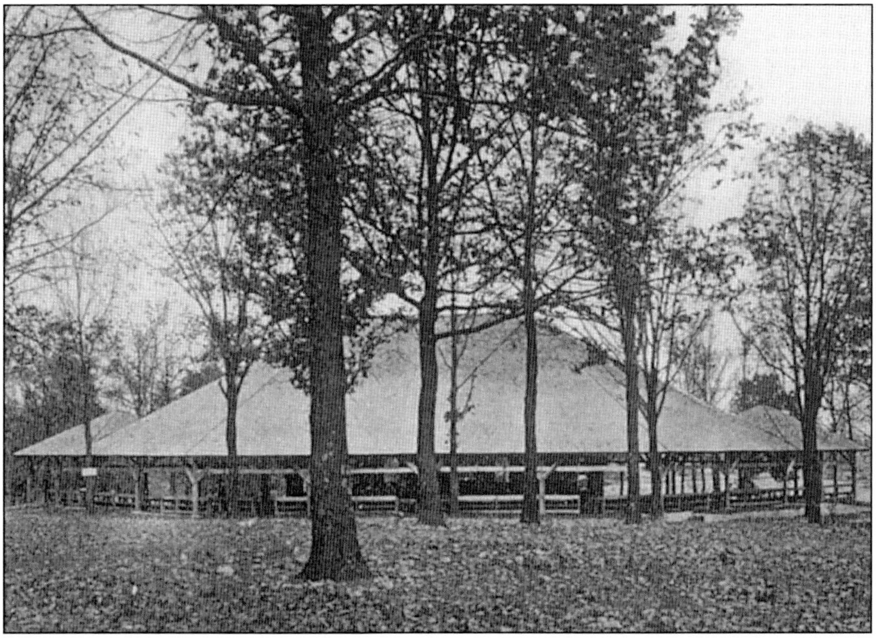

CHAUTAUQUA AUDITORIUM, WEST VINE STREET, C. 1900–5. Located near the Missouri Pacific Railroad, Carthage's second Chautauqua location hosted week-long encampments that featured lectures by famous orators like Jane Addams, Carrie Nation, William Jennings Bryan, and Warren Harding as well as other religious and social leaders, politicians, educators, and musicians, until Chautauquas ceased in Carthage about 1912.

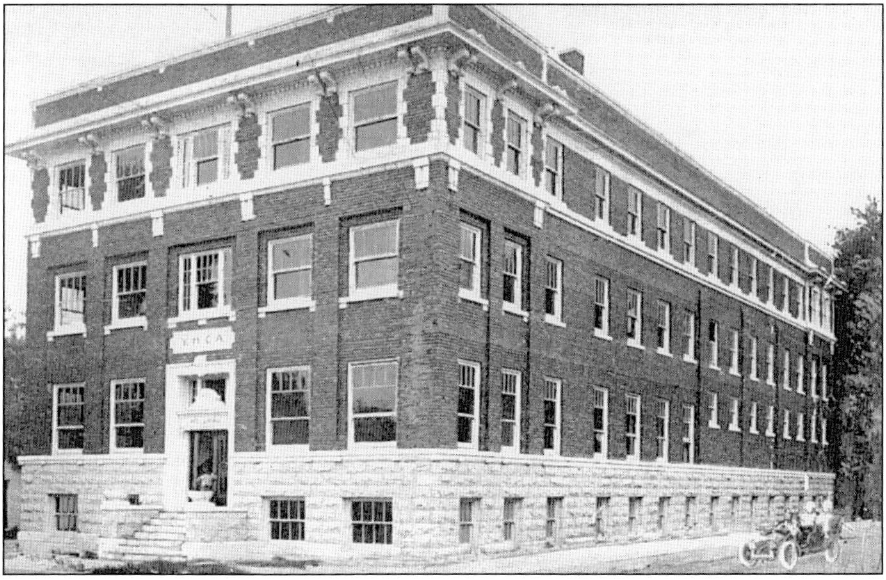

YMCA BUILDING, 6TH AND MAIN STREETS, 1909. Carthage had a YMCA organization in the 1890s situated on the second floor of 103 East 3rd Street, but this building opened in 1909. Built by Howard and Brown of Joplin, it contained an indoor pool, bowling alley, gymnasium, game areas, dorm rooms, and a dining hall. In the 1910–20s, it was used by Carthage schools for athletic events, and a YWCA program for girls was developed in the mid-1920s. The Y closed in 1967.

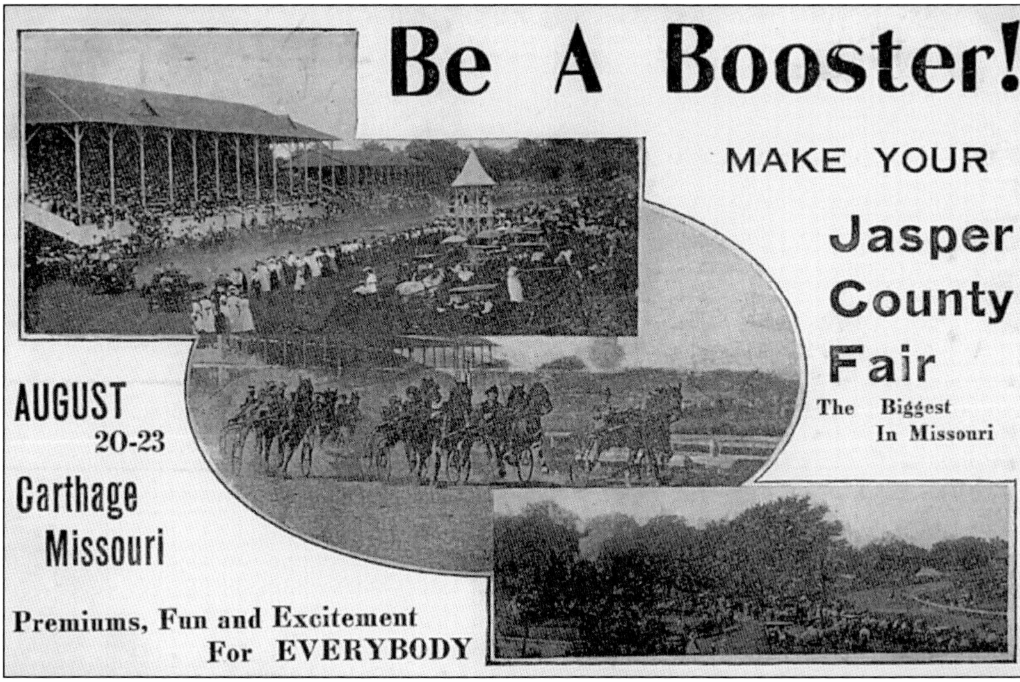

ADVERTISEMENT FOR JASPER COUNTY FAIR, C. 1910. Located at the Knell fairground or driving park west of Carthage, this event sponsored horse races (later car races) as well as agricultural and domestic expositions, awarding prizes up to $10,000 annually. Emma Knell, the fair's secretary for 25 years, was thought to be the only female in America in such a capacity.

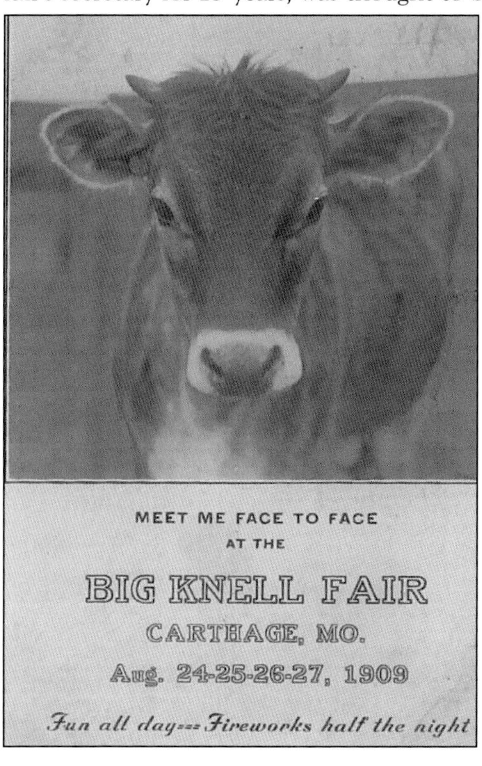

PROMOTIONAL CARD FOR THE KNELL FAIR, 1909. Established in 1902 by Edward Knell and also called the Knell or Southwest Missouri Fair, the Jasper County Fair was famous for its stock shows and competitions, due in part to the interests of the Knell family in raising jersey cattle and other pure-bred livestock. Besides the animals, as the card announced, the fair was "fun all day—fireworks half the night."

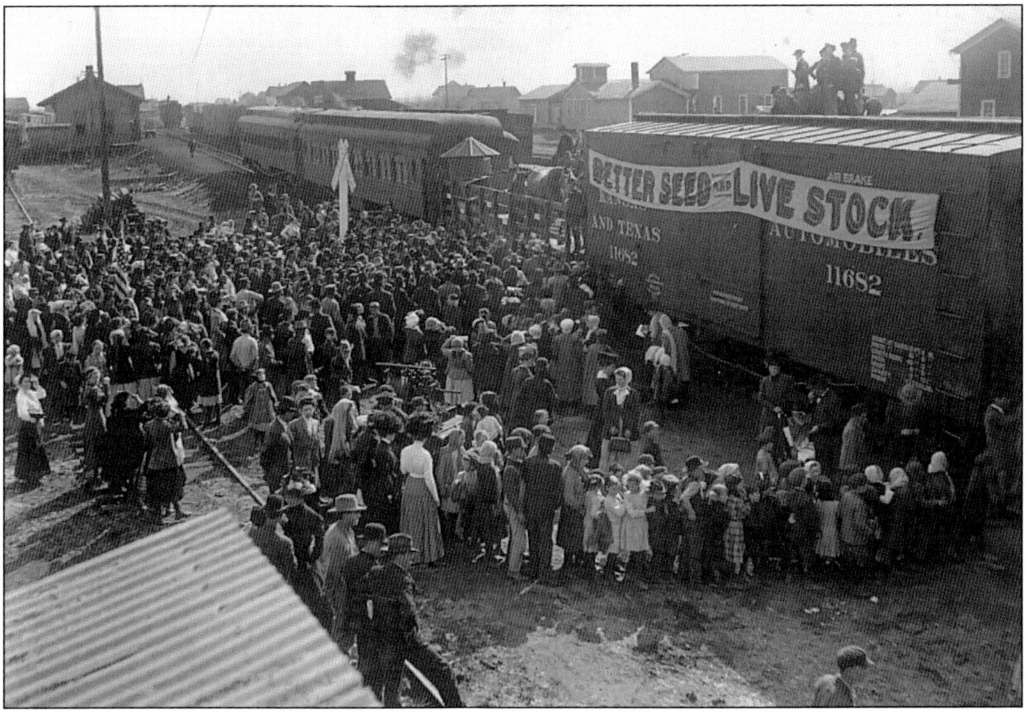

TRAIN LOADING FOR JASPER COUNTY FAIR, 1914. The agricultural emphasis of the Carthage-based fair is depicted on the banner on this Missouri, Kansas, and Texas rail car that reads "Better Seed and Livestock." Horticultural and agricultural expositions and fairs had been held in Carthage ever since 1869.

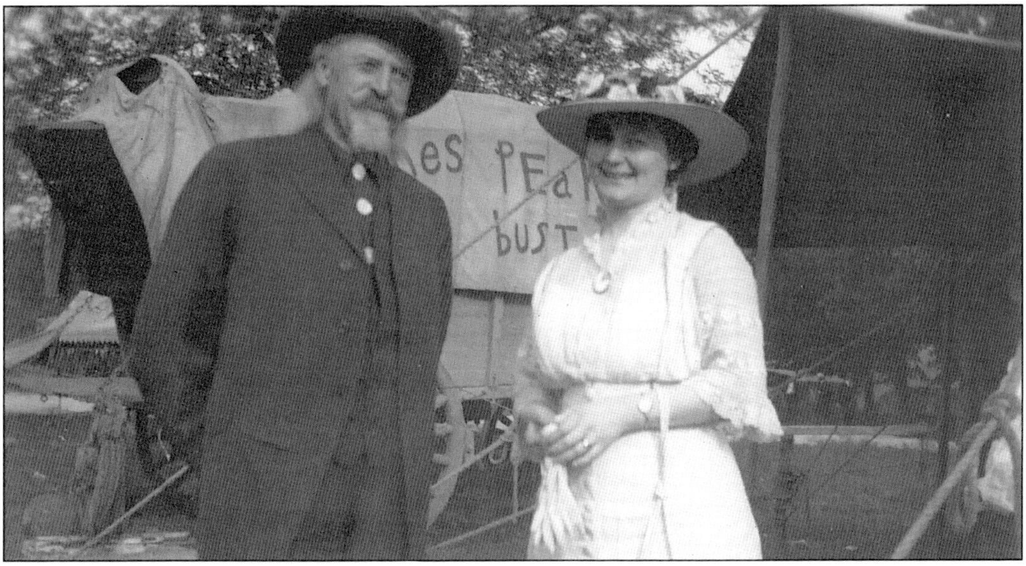

WILLIAM F. CODY AND MARIAN WRIGHT POWERS, 1915. Thacker's Park, located at Wooster and Forest Streets, was another local site for large outdoor events, including the Sells-Floto Circus and Buffalo Bill's Original Wild West Show on August 27. Advertisements promised 450 horses, 40 clowns, 11 acres of tents, and seats for 10,000, besides the appearance from "Buffalo Bill" and his Wild West Show.

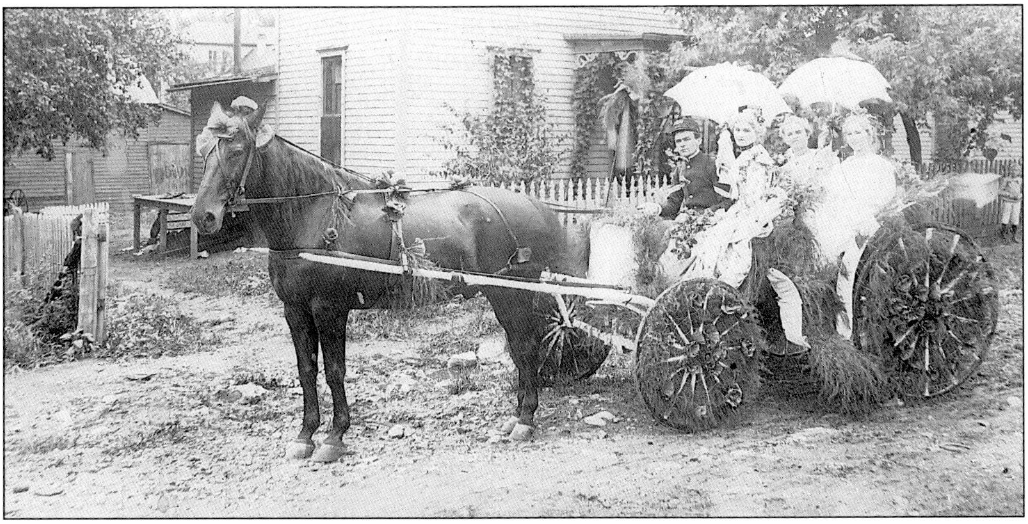

FLOWER PARADE CARRIAGE, JULY 4, 1898. Parades have always been popular pastimes in Carthage. This unit contained Westley Haliburton, Marian Wright, Armilda McReynolds, and Belle Perkins and was decorated with red poppies and asparagus ferns. Competitions were held for float decorating, and units were often pulled to the fairgrounds so they could be inspected after the parade.

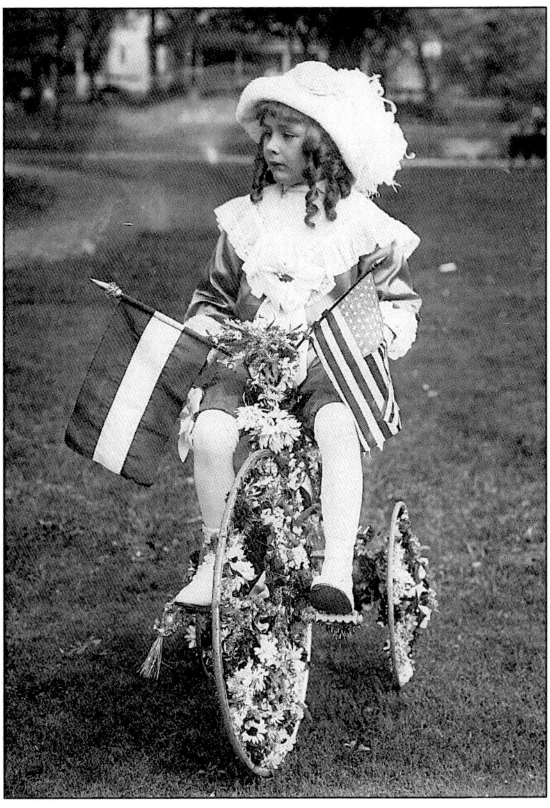

MAY FETE, 1913. Carthage's free kindergarten was financed in part by the May Fete event held in Central Park. In 1913, Tom Korn took first prize for a boy with a decorated play vehicle. He won a watch donated by jeweler H.P. Hall. The fund-raising concept was publicized by Carthage writer Emily Newell Blair in *Woman's Home Companion*, May 1911.

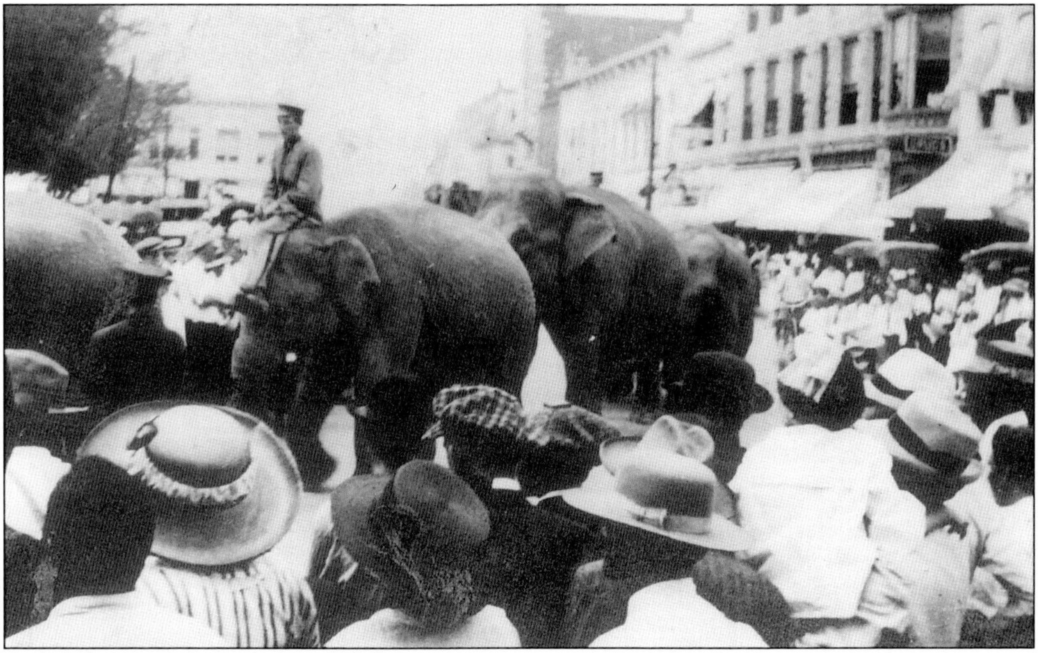

CIRCUS PARADE ON SQUARE, C. 1914–5. Onlookers are lined up at the southeast corner of the square to see a circus parade. Other photos in the series show "charioteers," polar bears, Gentry's Band, and other circus acts, although no specific circus can be identified. It may represent the Gentry Brothers Circus or the promotional parade for the Sells-Floto Circus of August 1915.

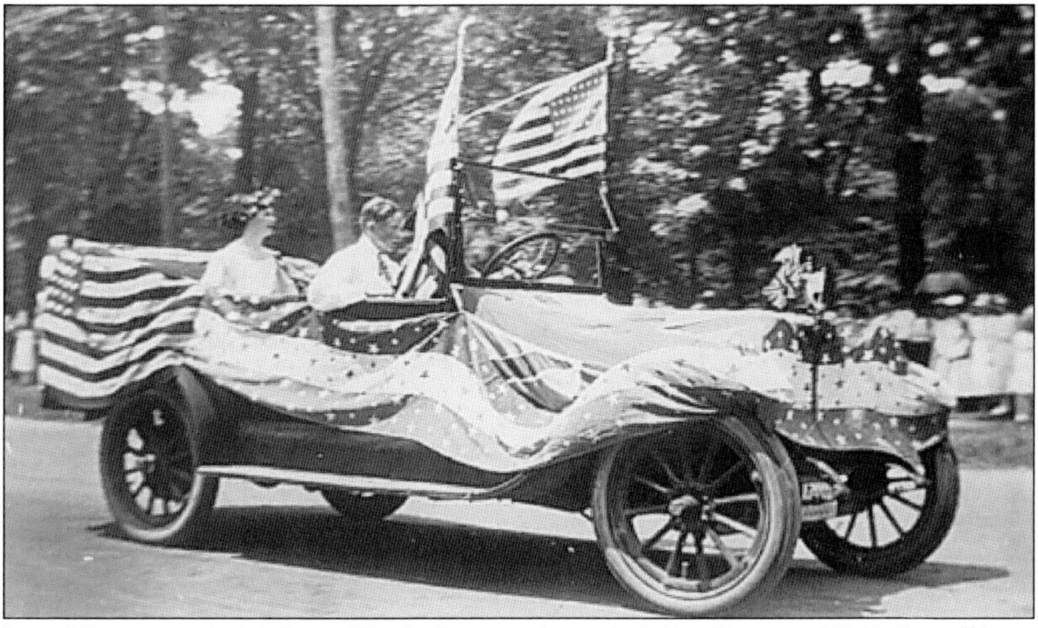

JULY 4 PARADE, 1918. Marian Wright Powers rides with Cullen Briggs and H.C. Cowgill Jr. in a parade that ended in a pageant in which she was the Goddess of Liberty. This and two other parades were sponsored by the Carthage Red Cross in 1918 in order to encourage patriotism, sell bonds, and celebrate the end of World War I.

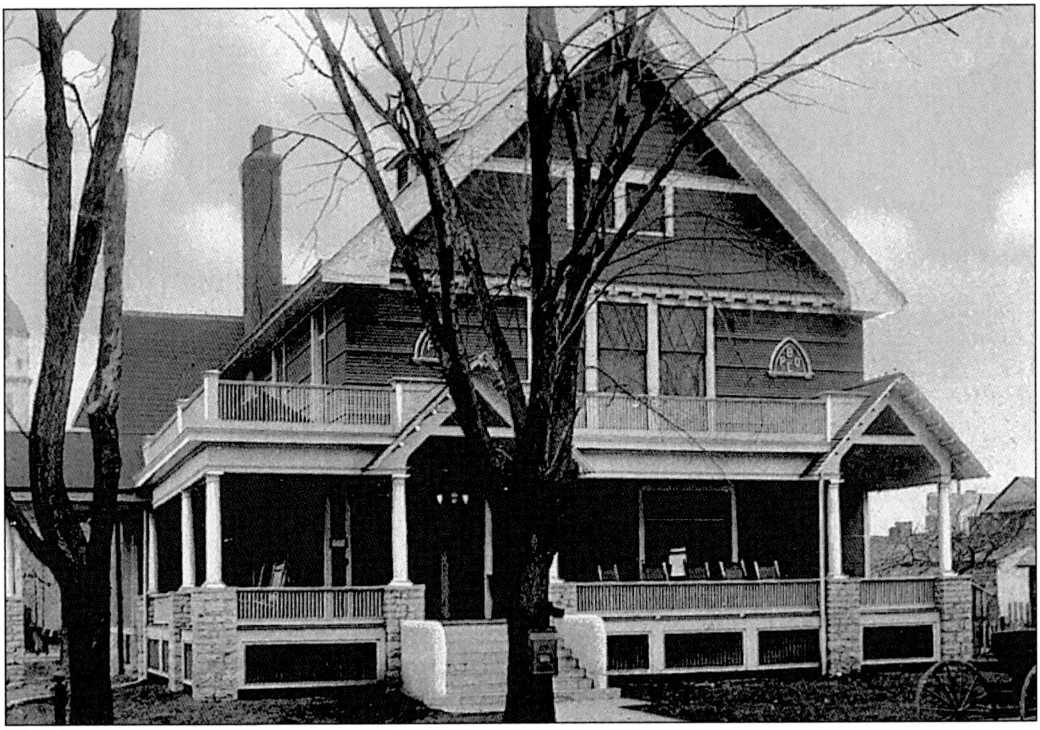

ELK'S CLUBHOUSE, 105 EAST 6TH STREET, 1900. Started in 1900, this building was constructed on land—like the YMCA next door—that was donated by G.A. Cassil.

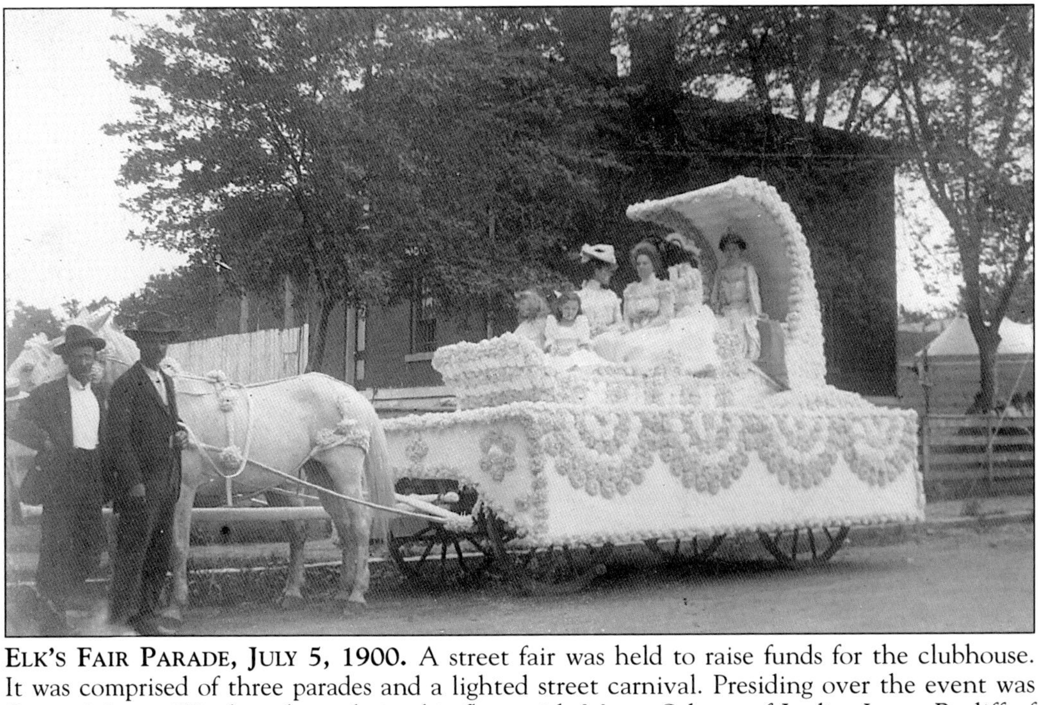

ELK'S FAIR PARADE, JULY 5, 1900. A street fair was held to raise funds for the clubhouse. It was comprised of three parades and a lighted street carnival. Presiding over the event was Queen Marian Wright, who rode in this float with Mame Schnur of Joplin, Laura Ratliff of Parsons, Kansas, and Julia McElroy and Brice McMillian of Carthage.

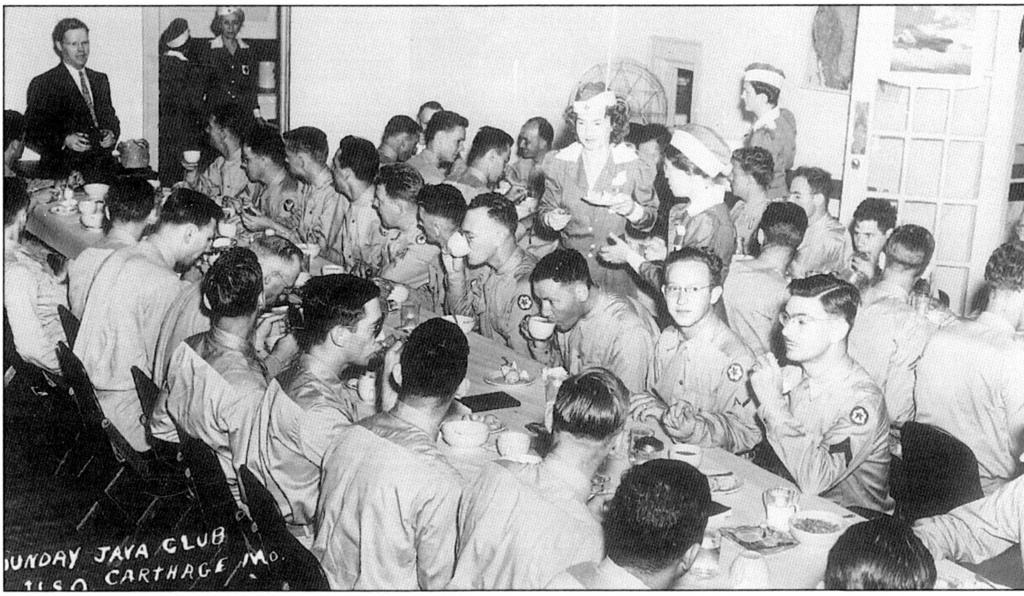

JAVA CLUB, CARTHAGE USO, c. 1943–46. Converted to the USO Center during World War II, the Elks Club became a social club for visiting service men. Carthage Red Cross Secretary Marian Louisa Powers (in the center, facing camera) is serving coffee to the Sunday bunch.

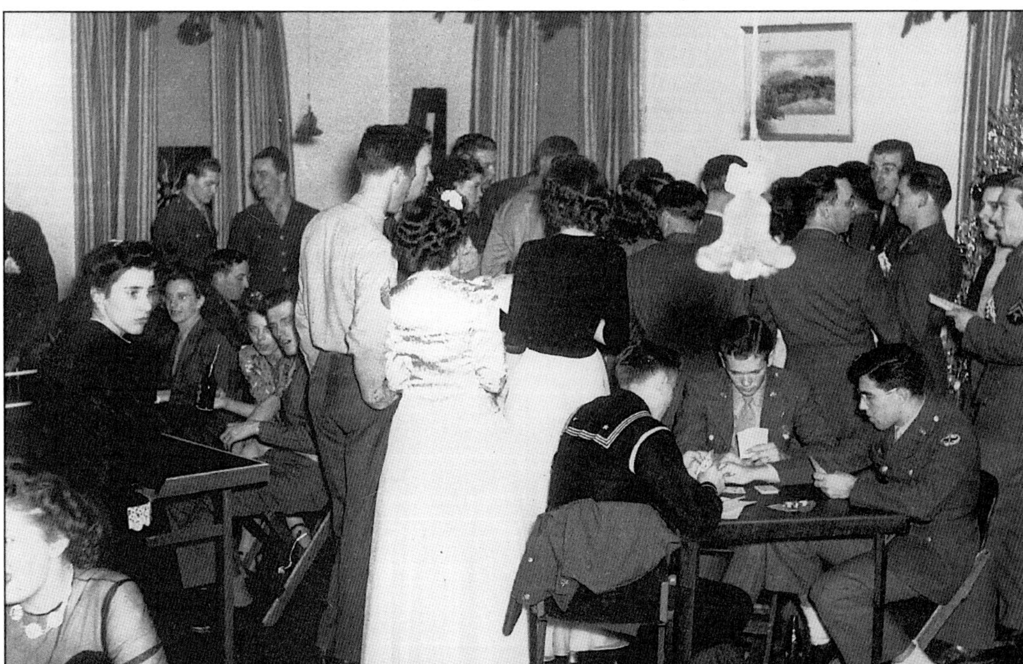

GAME ROOM, CARTHAGE USO, 1943. Service men, including many from Camp Crowder in Neosho, Missouri, participated in the holiday events, such as this Christmas party, dances, musical concerts, film programs, and field trips to the local quarries and mines that were organized by USO volunteers.

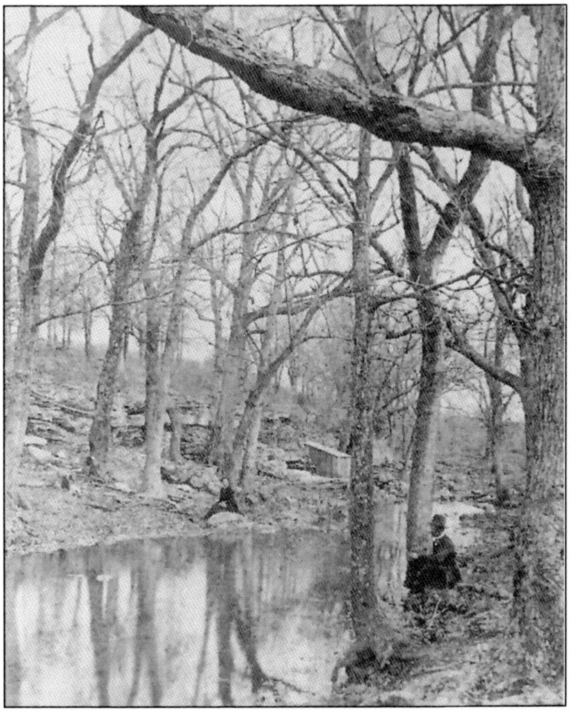

SPRING RIVER, C. 1868–72. Identified as Spring River, this image comes from an unknown photographer's stereopticon card and may have been taken at Carter's Spring instead. Regardless, it represents one of the earliest views of the Carthage area and its natural beauty.

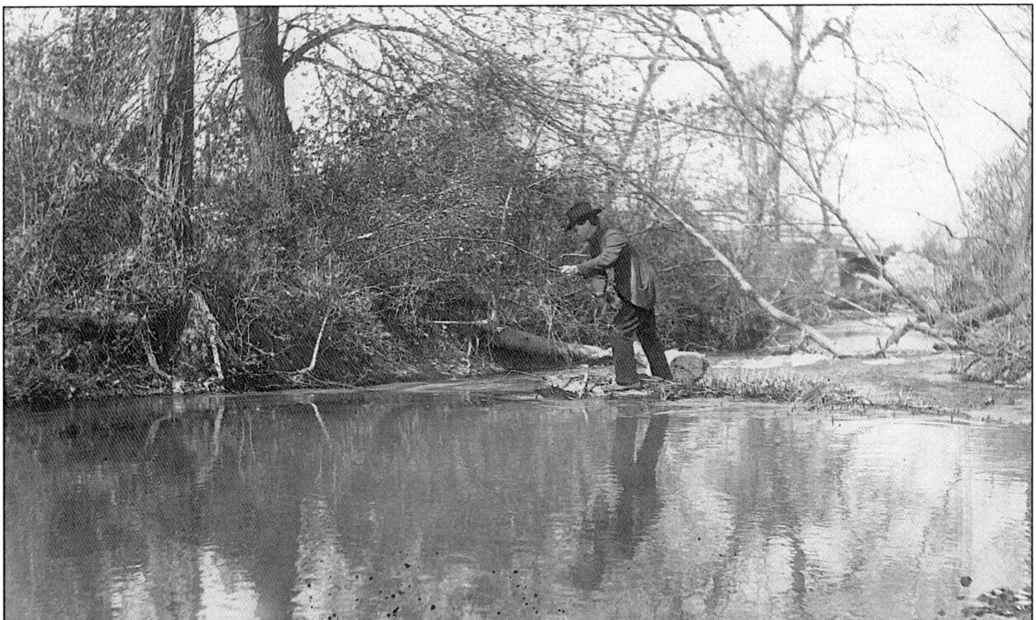

CURTIS WRIGHT JR. FISHING ON SPRING RIVER, C. 1895–98. Avid outdoors people, the Wright family, like many others, enjoyed the opportunities that Carthage's natural setting afforded for fishing, hunting, hiking, and other sporting activities. The Wrights also pursued these activities around their slate mines in Mena, Arkansas, and frequented the nearby Eureka Springs, Arkansas, resorts on a regular basis.

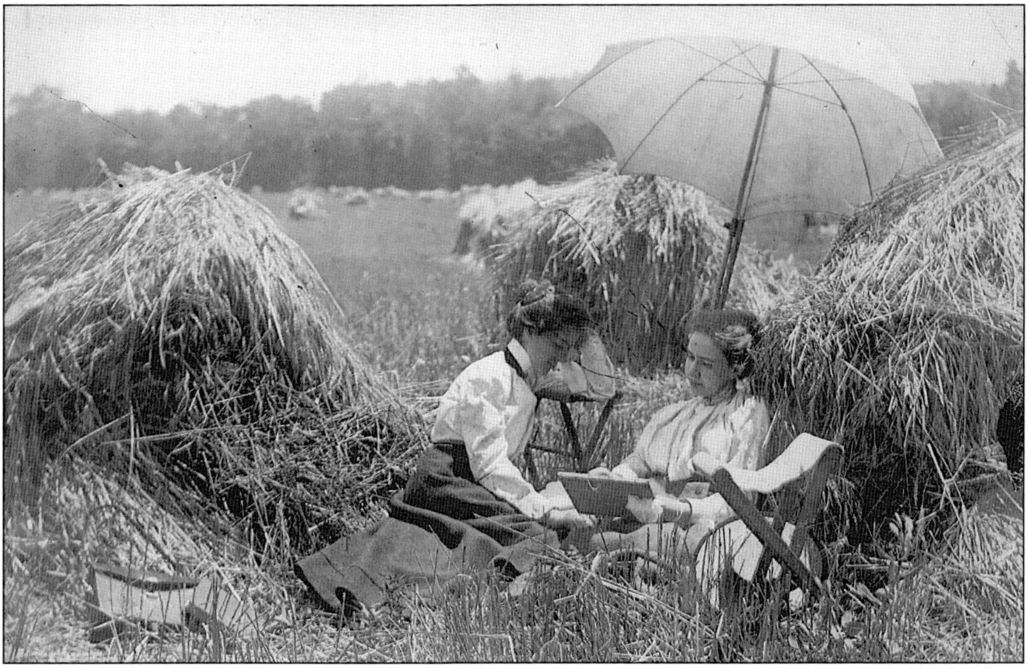

GERTRUDE WOOD AND AUGUSTA KNIGHT ON SPRING RIVER ISLAND, 1900. Amid haystacks, these ladies are drawing, an appropriate activity—especially for Miss Knight (thought to be on the left) who was an art instructor at Carthage Collegiate Institute, and who also taught many upper-middle-class young ladies such as Marian Wright the popular pastime of china painting.

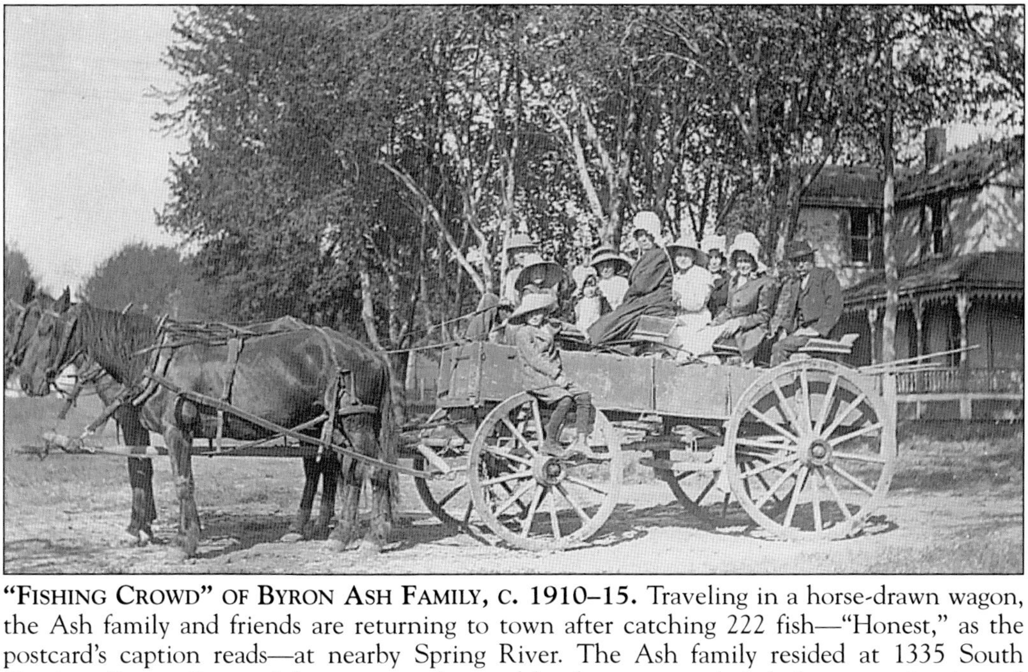

"FISHING CROWD" OF BYRON ASH FAMILY, C. 1910–15. Traveling in a horse-drawn wagon, the Ash family and friends are returning to town after catching 222 fish—"Honest," as the postcard's caption reads—at nearby Spring River. The Ash family resided at 1335 South Garrison Street. Byron Ash was a teacher and hardware store clerk before engaging in real estate and mining, including the Ice Plant Mine (see page 61).

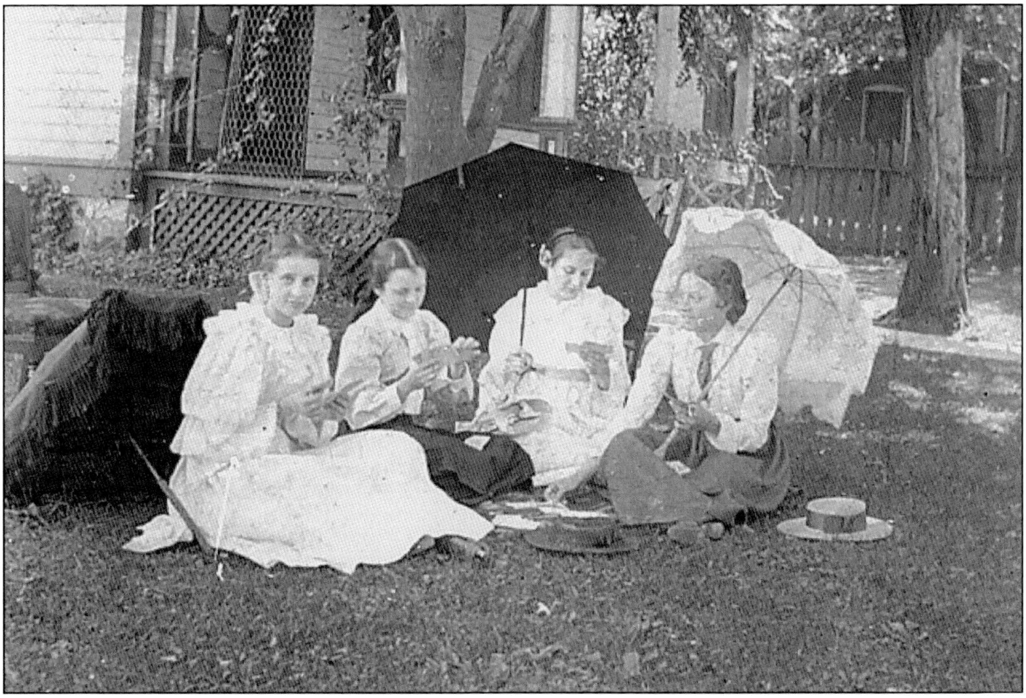

Girls Playing Cards at Unidentified Home, 1894. Although the exact order is not known, pictured here are Zula Crenshaw, Mame Morgan, Winifred Whitsett, and Marian Wright (under black parasol).

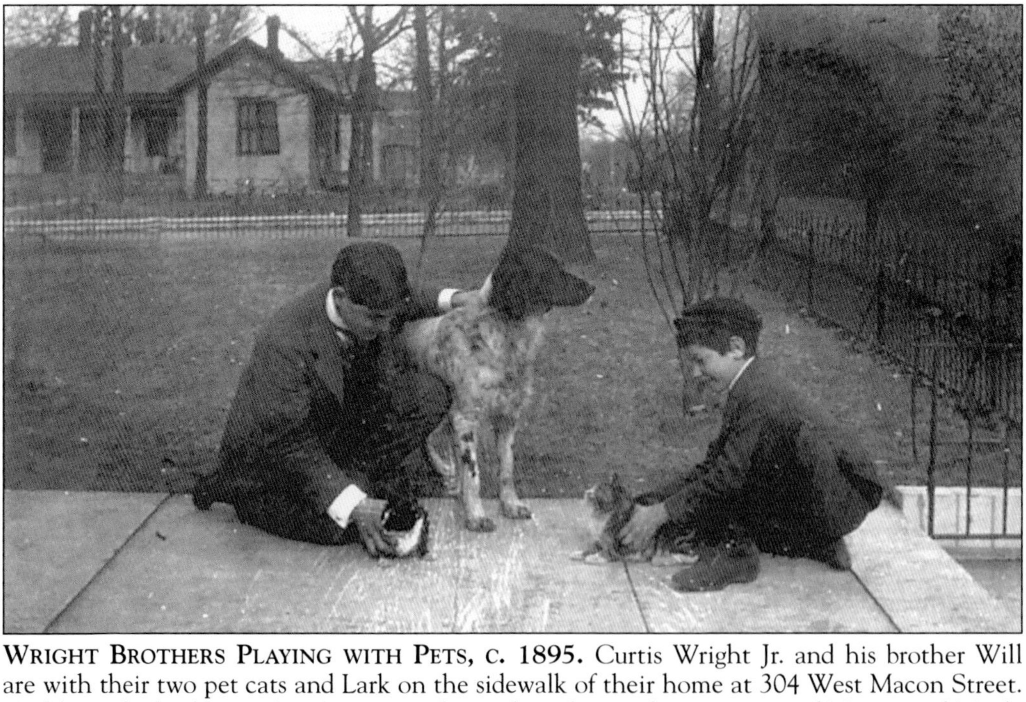

Wright Brothers Playing with Pets, c. 1895. Curtis Wright Jr. and his brother Will are with their two pet cats and Lark on the sidewalk of their home at 304 West Macon Street. Visible in the background is the cottage located on the northwest corner of Macon and Maple Streets.

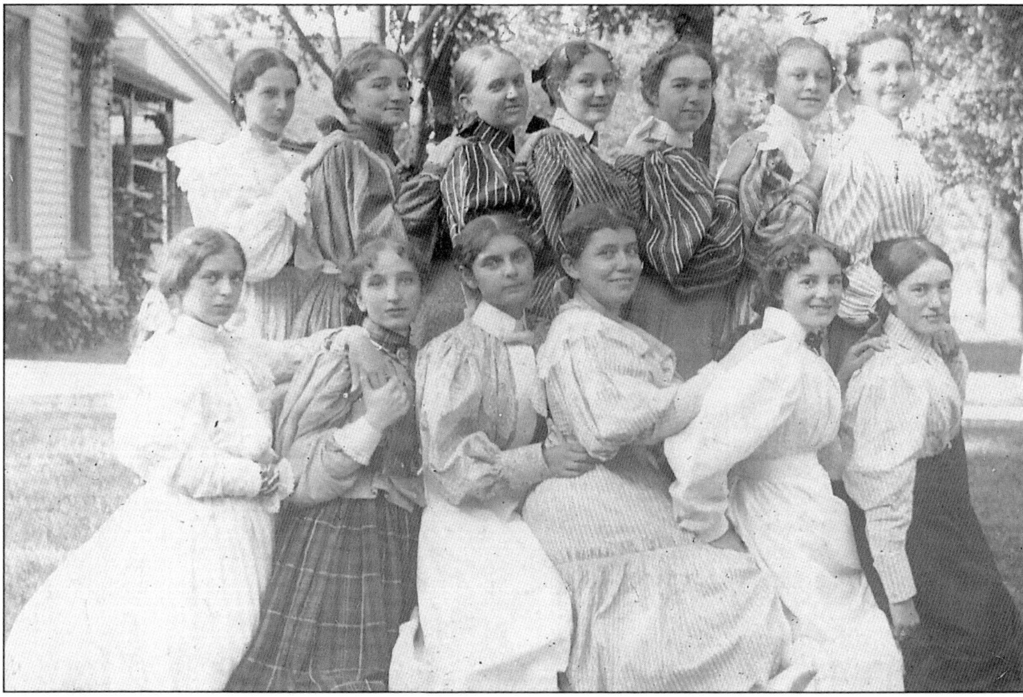

"BAKER'S DOZEN," 1898. Pictured from the back, left to right, are: Verna Brinkley, Lila Oldham, Armilda McReynolds, Marian Wright, Belle Perkins, Winifred Whitsett, and Blanche Moore; (front row) Pauline Bolanz, Kittie Herrin, Alta Jacobs, Eva Meyers, Mayme St. John, and Pearle Clarkson. These were the school chums of Marian Wright, with whom she socialized and learned sewing and china painting.

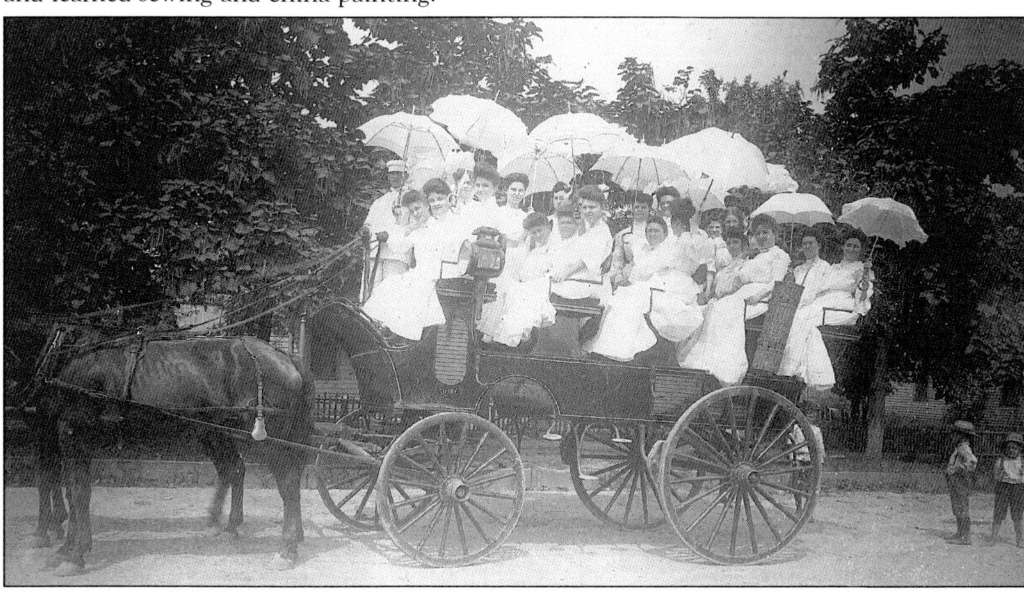

LADIES IN LIVERY VEHICLE, C. 1910. Unfortunately, these 21 ladies in their "lingerie" dresses sitting under parasols, are unidentified, but they have all piled into one of Carthage's finer livery hacks and must be headed to the Carthage Fair or some other event. Special excursion trains and vehicles always ran to the fair, Lakeside Park, or other nearby attractions.

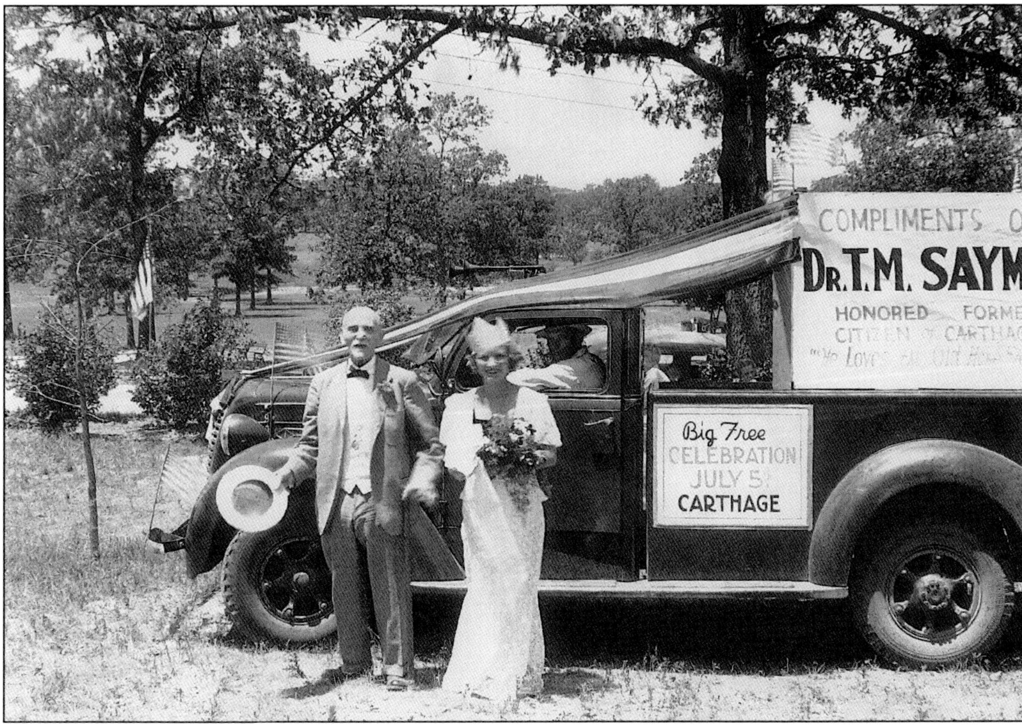

MUNICIPAL PARK DEDICATION, JULY 5, 1937. Thomas Sayman, who began his career as a soap manufacturer in Carthage, eventually moved to St. Louis, where his product made him a millionaire. Shortly before his death in 1937, he returned to dedicate Municipal Park. With him is "Miss Carthage, Fourth of July Queen," Grace Preston.

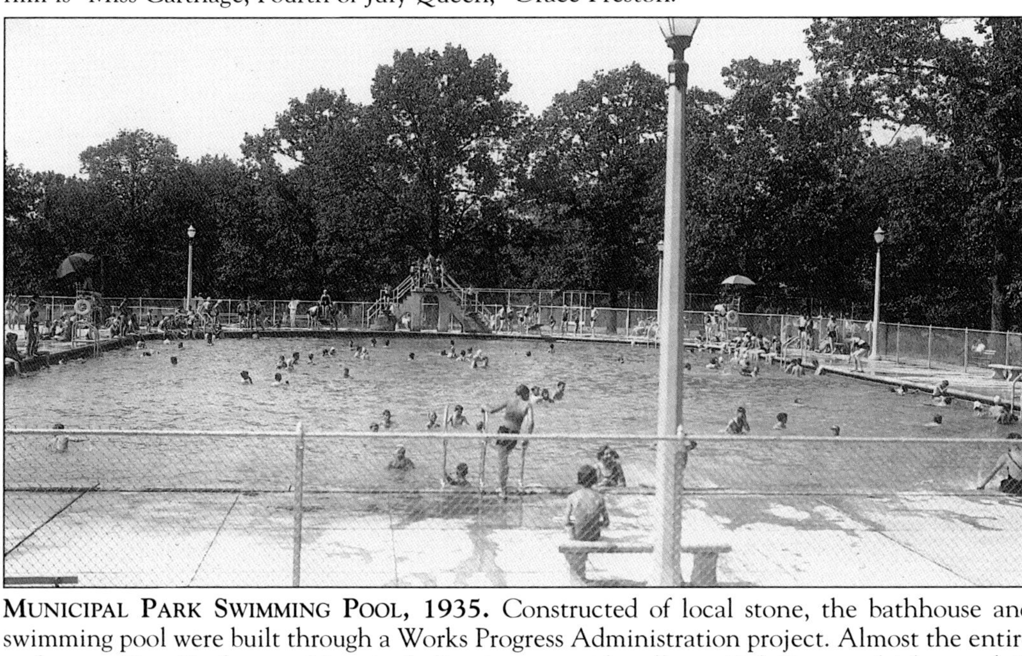

MUNICIPAL PARK SWIMMING POOL, 1935. Constructed of local stone, the bathhouse and swimming pool were built through a Works Progress Administration project. Almost the entire park was a New Deal proposition, including its stone sidewalks on Oak Street, which were laid by the National Youth Administration.

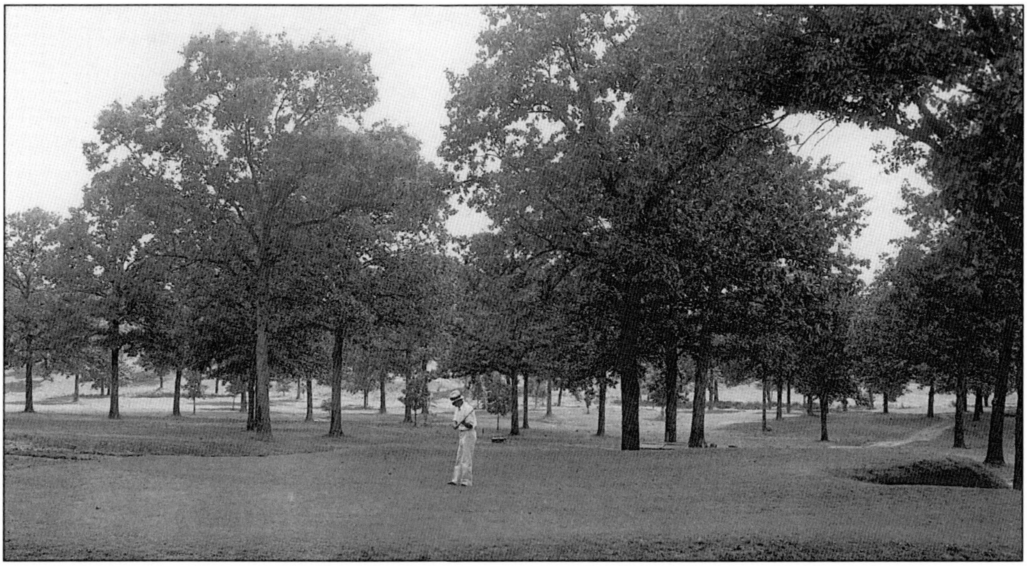

MUNICIPAL PARK GOLF COURSE, C. 1937. Beginning with nine holes, the golf course has since been expanded to eighteen holes as the park acquired additional land. When first proposed in 1934, the park's plan was developed by Hare and Hare, nationally-known landscape architects of Kansas City. Members of the Park Board when the park opened were Wilson Elrod, Willis Wallingford, George Stump, Dr. A.B Wheeler, Dr. LeMoine Cunningham, Dr. E.J. McIntire, Fred Nesbitt, Robert Redmond, and E.L. Dale.

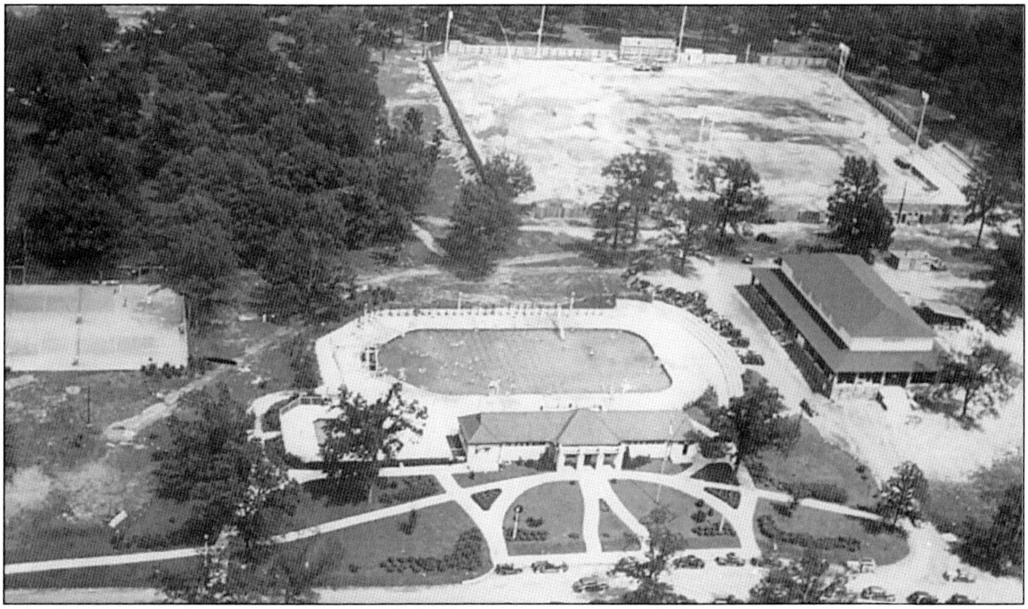

AERIAL VIEW OF MUNICIPAL PARK, C. 1938. The baseball stadium is under construction in this view showing the pool, bathhouse, dancing pavilion (now skating rink), and tennis courts. The stadium was used for Carthage's professional baseball teams including the Pirates, Browns, Cardinals, and finally the Cubs in 1950.

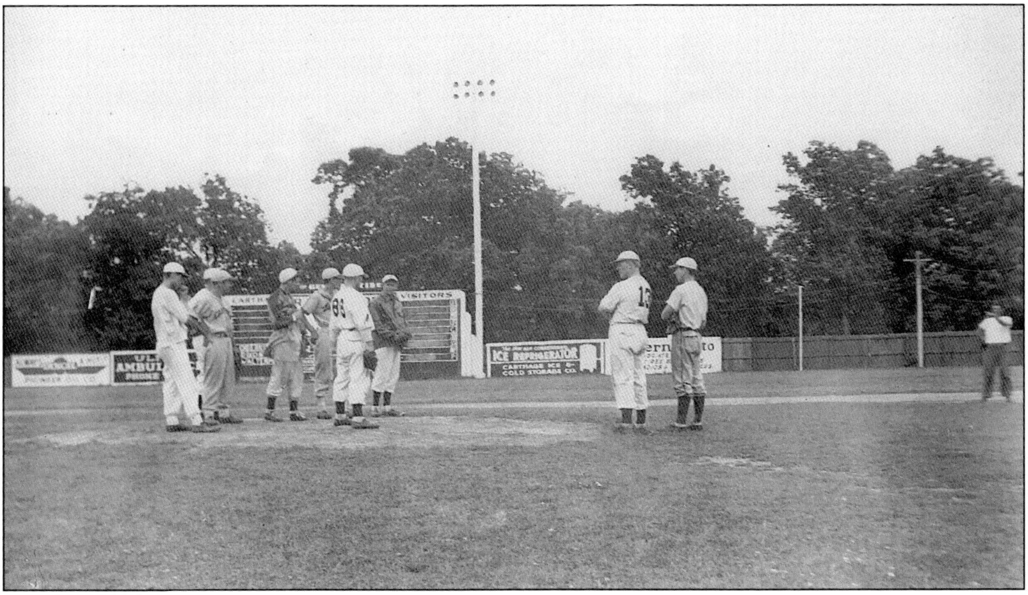

CARTHAGE CARDINALS, KANSAS-OKLAHOMA-MISSOURI LEAGUE BASEBALL TEAM, 1946. Coach Adolph "Buzz" Arlitt (off to right) is giving instructions to the following individuals, who are pictured from left to right: William Rogers, Oscar "Pappy" Walterman, Louis "Whitey" Ballou, Frank Borghi, Glen Koepke, Wilbert May, Laverne Etting, and Ray Coss. The scoreboard in the background features ads for Pioneer Oil, Ulmer Ambulance, Carthage Ice and Cold Storage, and Western Auto.

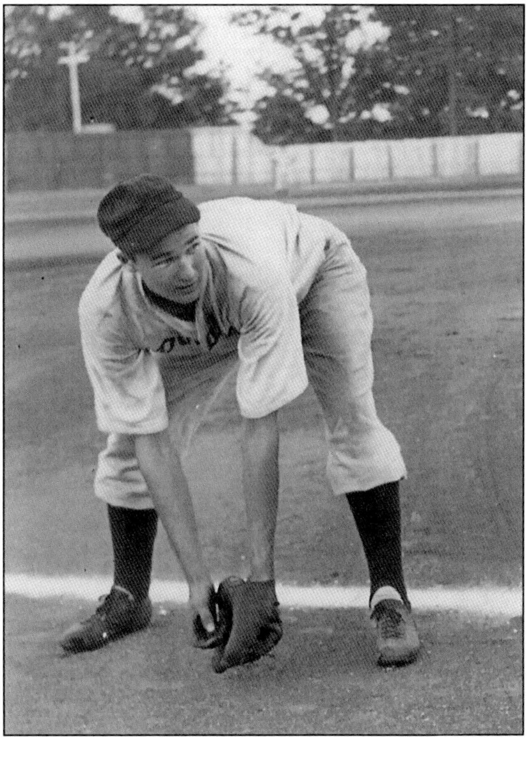

CARTHAGE PIRATE SECOND BASEMAN CHARLES KNOBLAUCH, 1938–39. Charles Knoblauch and his first cousin Irvin Knoblauch played for the Carthage Pirates of the Arkansas-Missouri League, which was a franchise of the Pittsburgh Pirates. The league disbanded in 1940 before finishing a full season. (The Knoblauchs are the uncles of New York Yankee Chuck Knoblauch.)

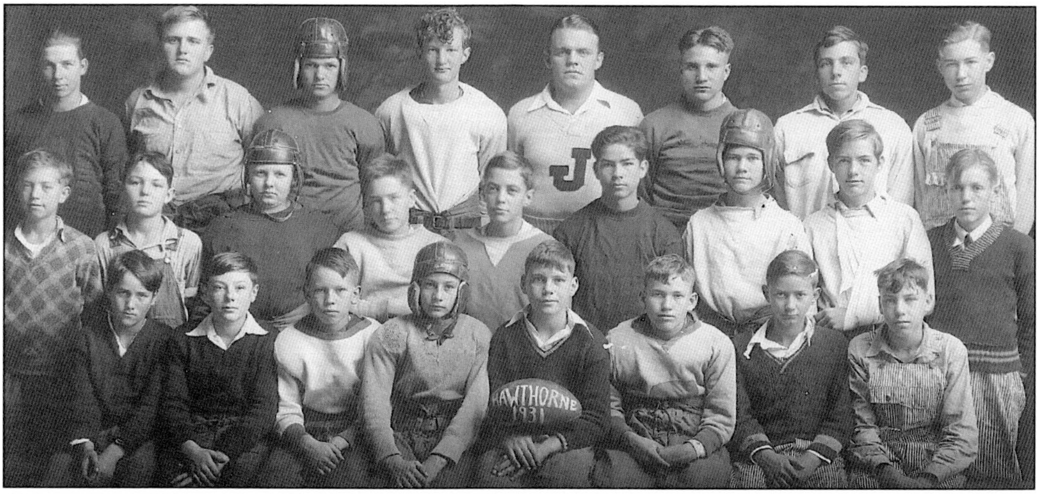

HAWTHORNE FOOTBALL TEAM, 1931. Grade school league champions that year are pictured from left to right: (front row) Elmer Ford, Jack Barton, Donald Williams, Kenneth Geisert, Max Croley, Virgil Hood, Roy Childers, Harry Sandidge; (middle row) Everett Martin, Floyd Dahlman, Elmer Allgeier, John Yancer, Bob Gadberry, Ray Ford, Rex Arnold, Harry Taylor, Johnny Taylor; (back row) Herbert Fasler, Denzil Coble, Edward Nash, Richard Murrell, Vernon Bridges (coach), Moochie "Little Rabbit" Baldridge, John Dennis, and Edgar Hurst.

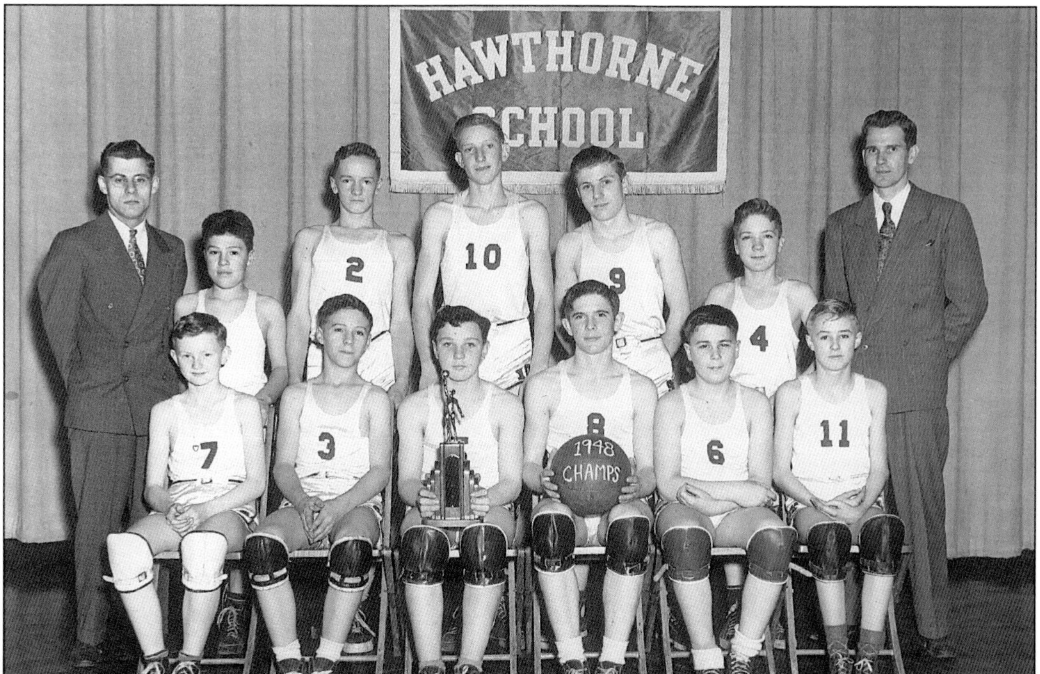

HAWTHORNE BASKETBALL TEAM, 1948. The Hawthorne Jayhawkers were junior high champs in 1948. Team members were, from left to right: (back row) Assistant Coach Bob Knell, Billy Southern, Harry Stout, Glen Moore, Bob Wilson, Leland Glaze, Coach Perl Dunn; (front row) Herbert Jennison, Terry Vogt, Max Dunn, Wayne Allison, Larry Dunphy, and Lloyd Coiner.

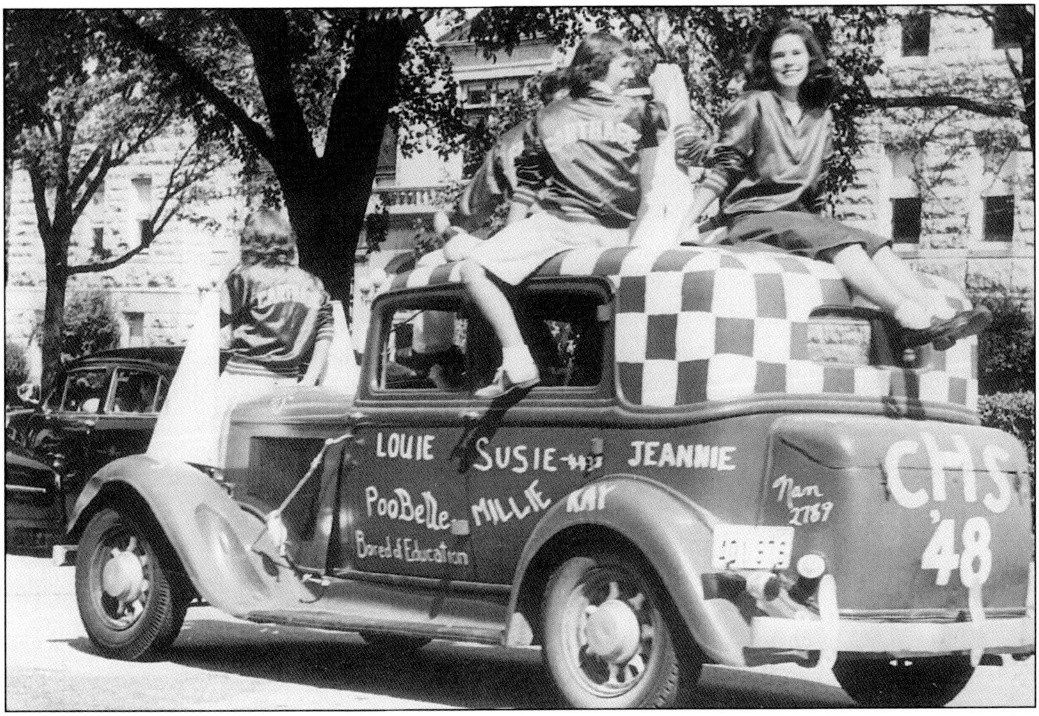

CARTHAGE HIGH SCHOOL HOMECOMING PARADE, 1947. These two views feature the Harrington girls and friends in their 1933 Dodge in front of the high school (top view) and in the 400 block of South Main Street (bottom view), with the facades of the YMCA and the Del Monte Apartments in the background. The spirited students are pictured from left to right: Pat Ennis Hays, Bill Moody, Janett Hurst Hodo, Nan Harrington Sprague, and Doris Swarens Gray on the front of the car. Mary Louesa Harrington Estes is driving.

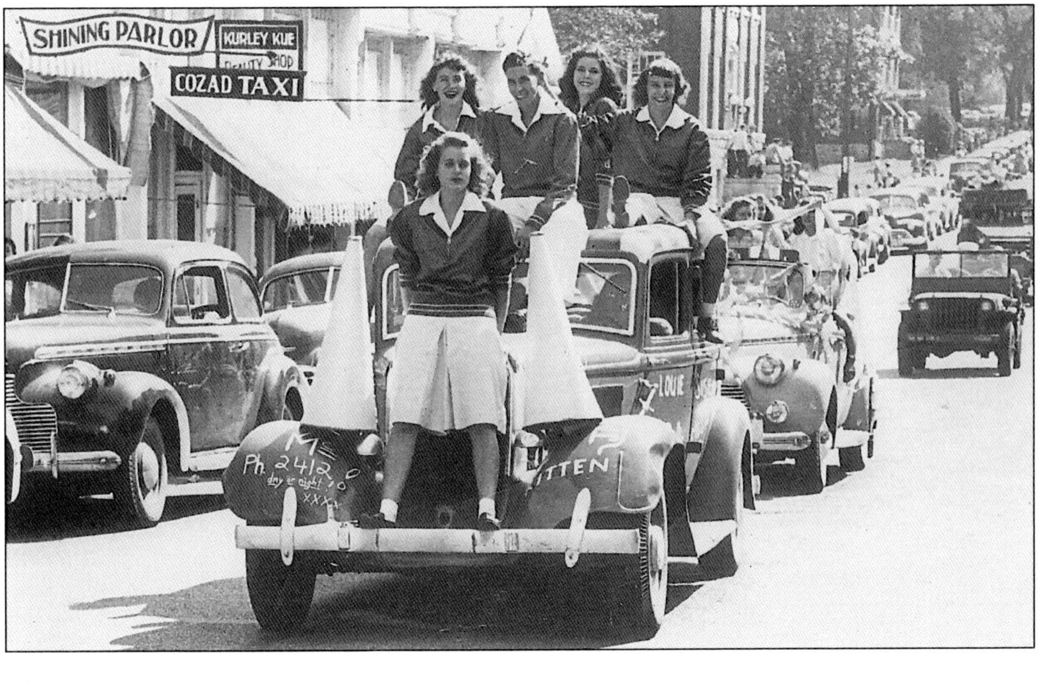

Six

Around Carthage

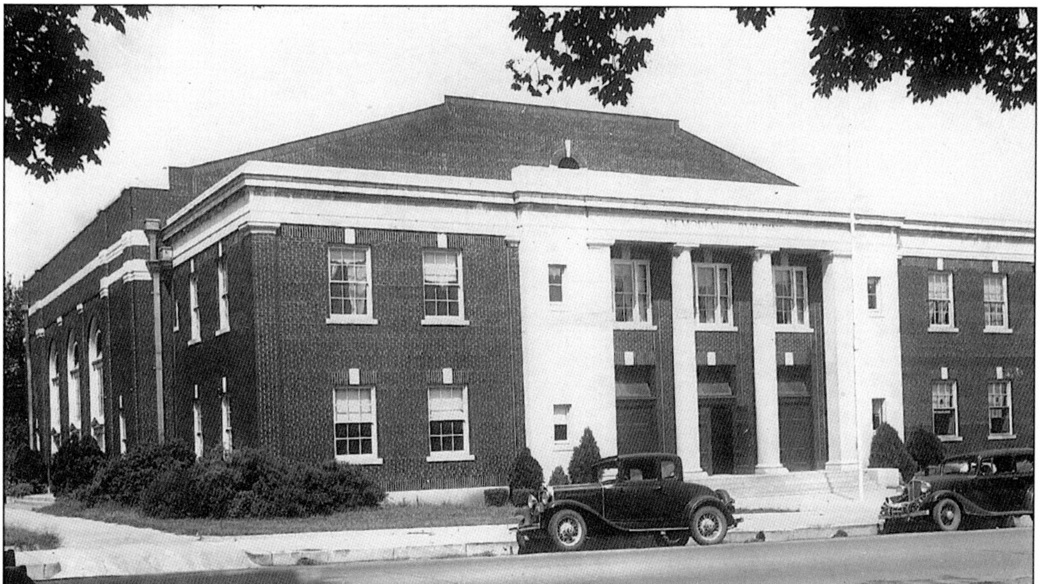

Memorial Hall, Oak and Garrison Streets, 1924. The idea for a soldier's memorial surfaced immediately after World War I and fundraising began in 1919, spearheaded by Rev. W.G. Clinton, who envisioned a building that would serve as a community hall and convention center. Together with a second fund-raising campaign under Rev. L.J. Marshall, funds collected from 2,400 supporters provided two-thirds of the money needed, and the other third came from a bond issue.

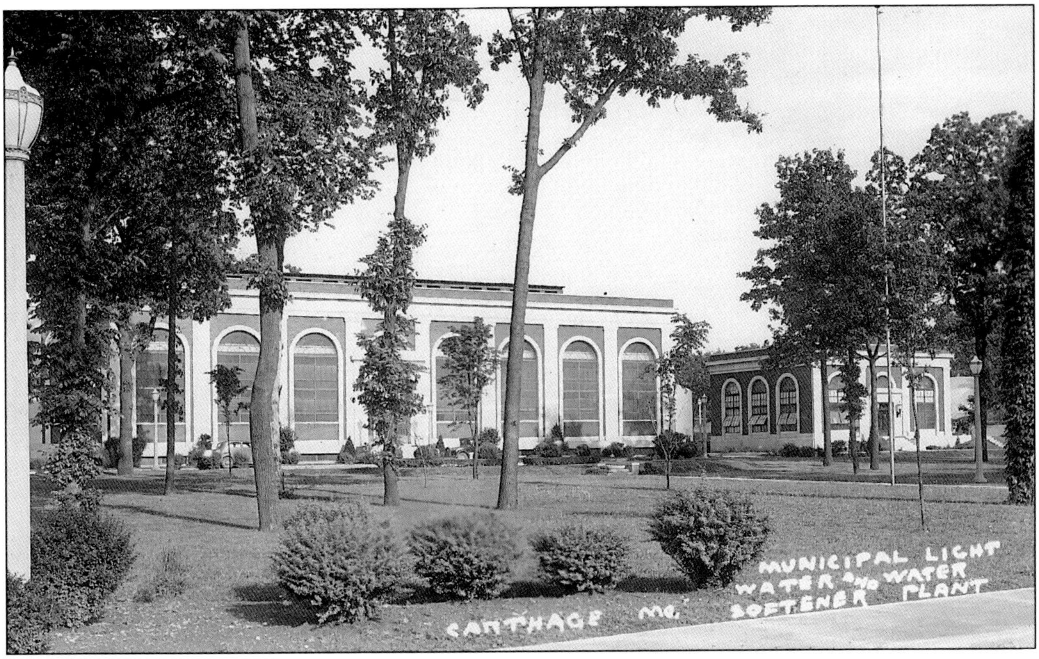

CARTHAGE WATER AND ELECTRIC PLANT, 3RD AND RIVER STREETS, 1927–31. One of Missouri's oldest municipally-owned power plants, this generating station was started in 1927 to house the Nordberg 750 and 1250-hp diesel generators (below) from the former plant across the street, plus one additional 1250-hp engine purchased during the building project. At the time of completion in 1931, Clarence Hoen was CW&EP general superintendent, while the Board of Public Works was comprised of D.G. Wells, E.L. Smith, F.C. Hodson, and H.E. Williams.

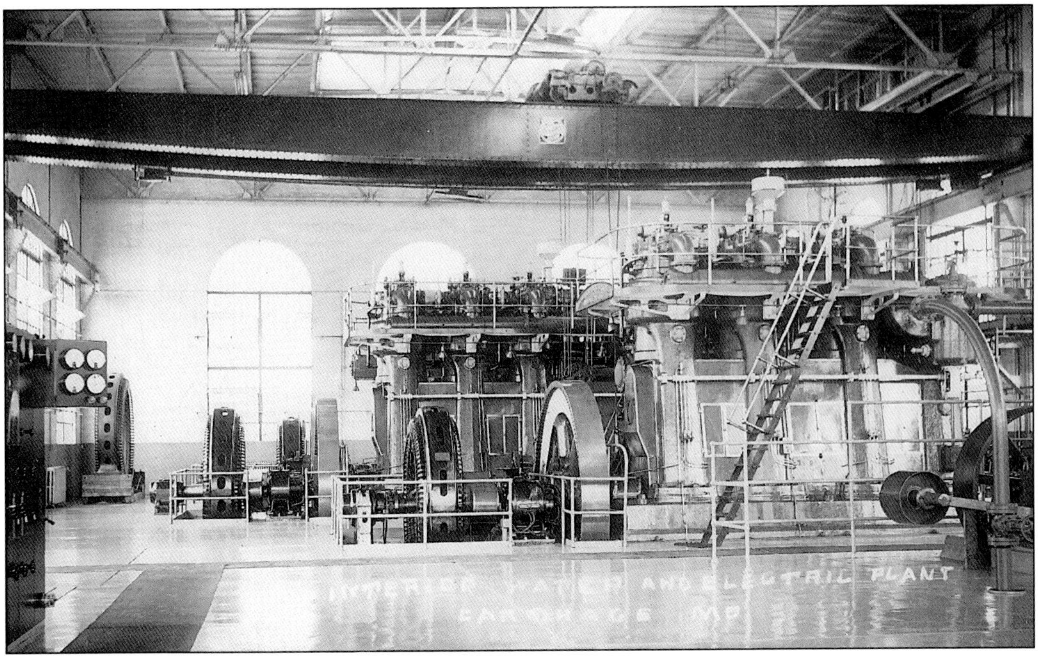

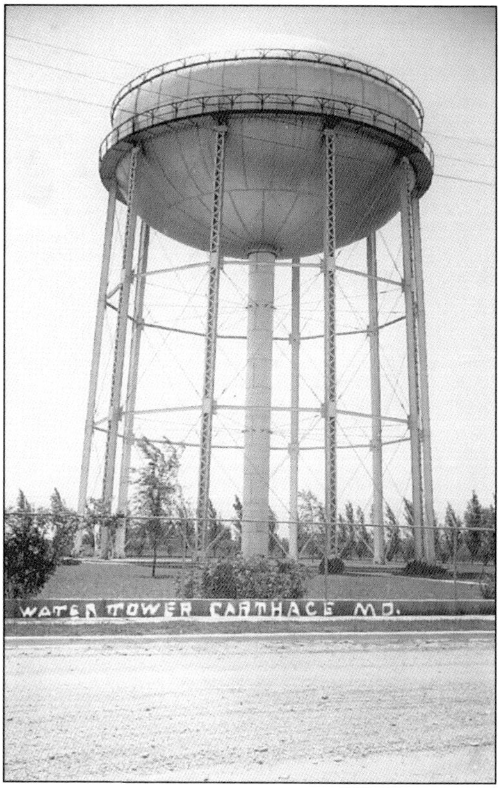

CW&EP WATER TOWER, MAIN AND FAIRVIEW STREETS, 1934. A 500,000-gallon elevated water tower was constructed, which served the city until 1955 when an additional 1 million-gallon elevated water tower was added on West Macon.

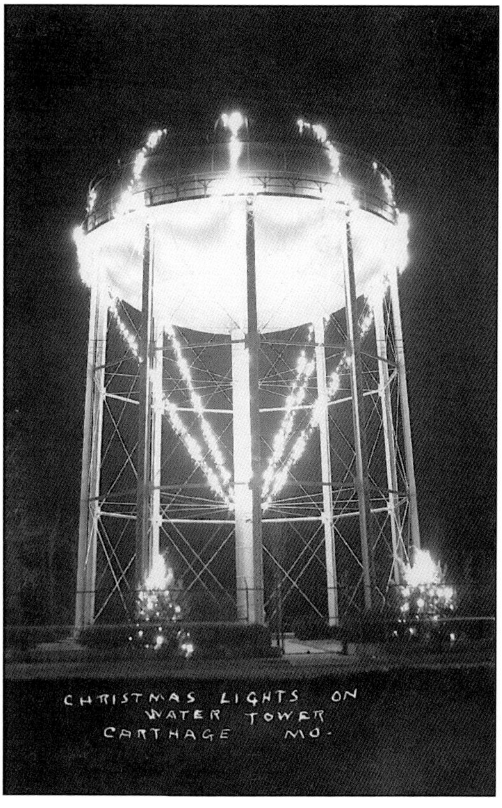

CW&EP WATER TOWER, CHRISTMAS, 1938. As reported in the *Carthage Press* that season, the one thousand lights used on the tower were "sensational in [their] attractiveness." Continued for many years, the custom ceased eventually, but was revived in 1996 as tribute to longtime CW&EP worker Robert "Buster" Lown through a gift from the Martin Lown family.

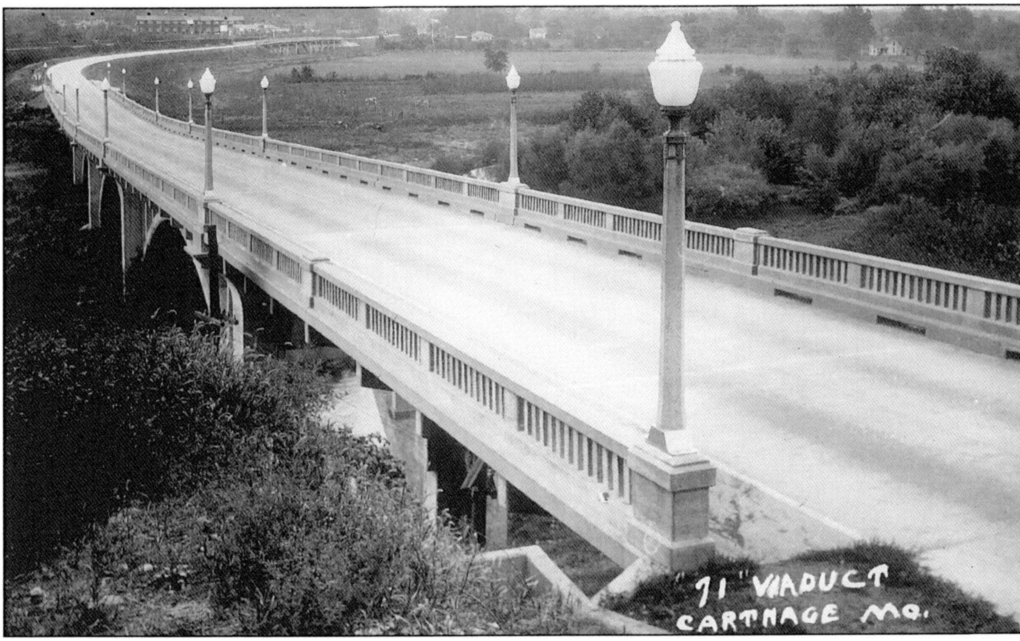

NATIONAL HIGHWAY 71 VIADUCT, NORTH OF CARTHAGE, C. 1935. Dedicated in 1930, a series of three bridges was built by the Missouri Highway Department for $205,000. They spanned Tiger Hill across the Spring River bottoms and over the river to the edge of Kendricktown north of Carthage. A two-day celebration at the bridges and in Central Park was held to mark their opening almost a year after their construction in 1929.

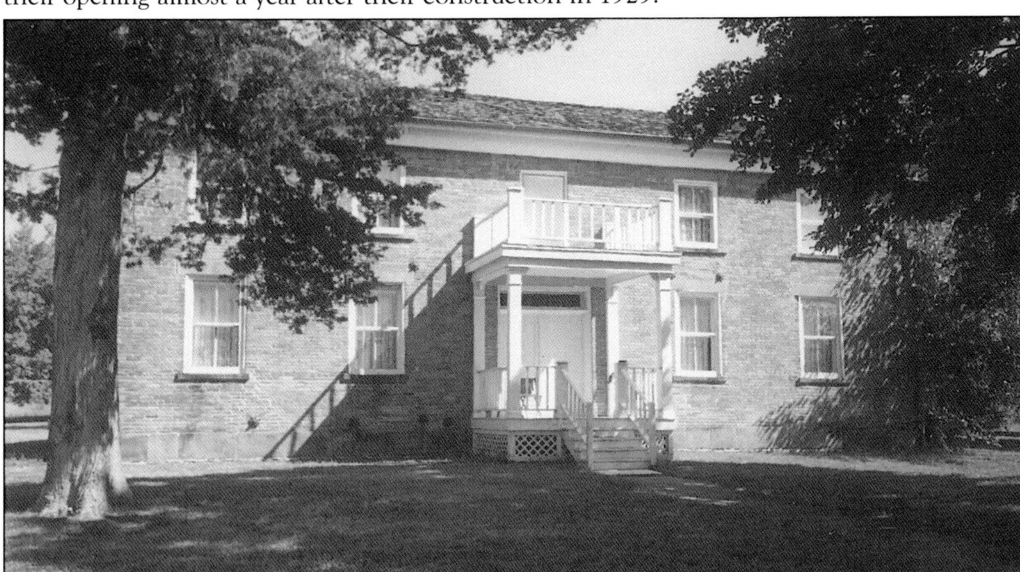

KENDRICK HOUSE, KENDRICKTOWN. Just beyond the viaducts sits one of the oldest structures in the Carthage area. Begun in 1849 and constructed by slaves who fashioned the brick from an on-site kiln, the house was acquired by the William Kendrick family before the Civil War. From their porch, the family stood and watched Carthage burn in 1863. Remaining in the Kendrick-Janney families until purchased by Victorian Carthage, Inc., the home is open today for living history tours.

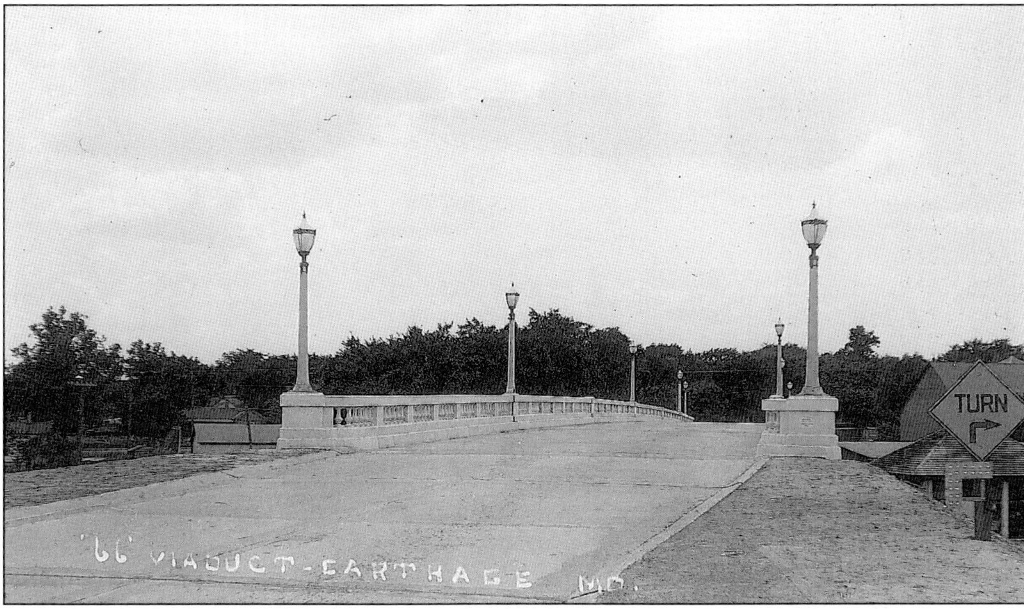

HIGHWAY 66 VIADUCT, APPROACHING EAST CENTRAL STREET, 1936. The opening of this bridge was celebrated at the same time as the opening of Municipal Park and a sister bridge west of the park on Highway 16 (now Oak Street Road).

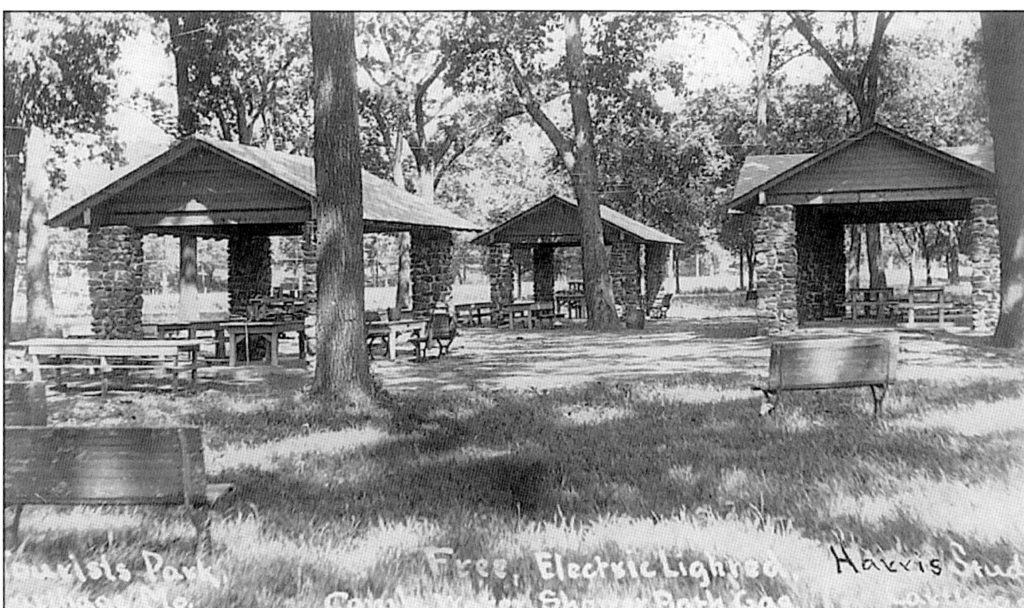

CARTER PARK (ALSO KNOWN AS CARTHAGE TOURIST PARK), RIVER AND CHESTNUT STREETS, C. 1930. In 1926, reporter Richard Martinsen wrote that "the two best municipal camps along the routes we've traveled recently are at Quincy, California, and Carthage in the Missouri Ozarks. Carthage's Carter Park offers a cook-house, two eating pavilions, running hot water, lights, and commodious shower rooms." The main gates are a memorial to the Battle of Carthage, and the park and area to the east were the location of the final round of action in 1861.

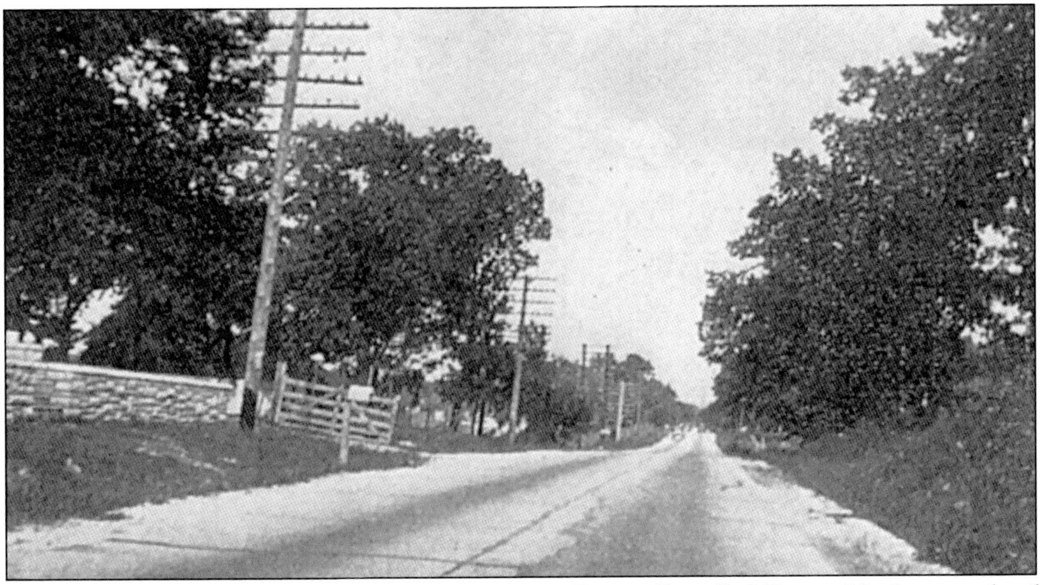

HIGHWAY 66 WEST OF CARTHAGE, C. 1926–27. Originally called Route 14, the stretch of road west from Carthage was the first concrete portion of Missouri's highway system. In 1926, the designation was changed to Highway 66, and this image, taken from an early Carthage tourist guide, describes the drive as "a seemingly endless aisle of oaks [as] Highway 66 winds its way westward."

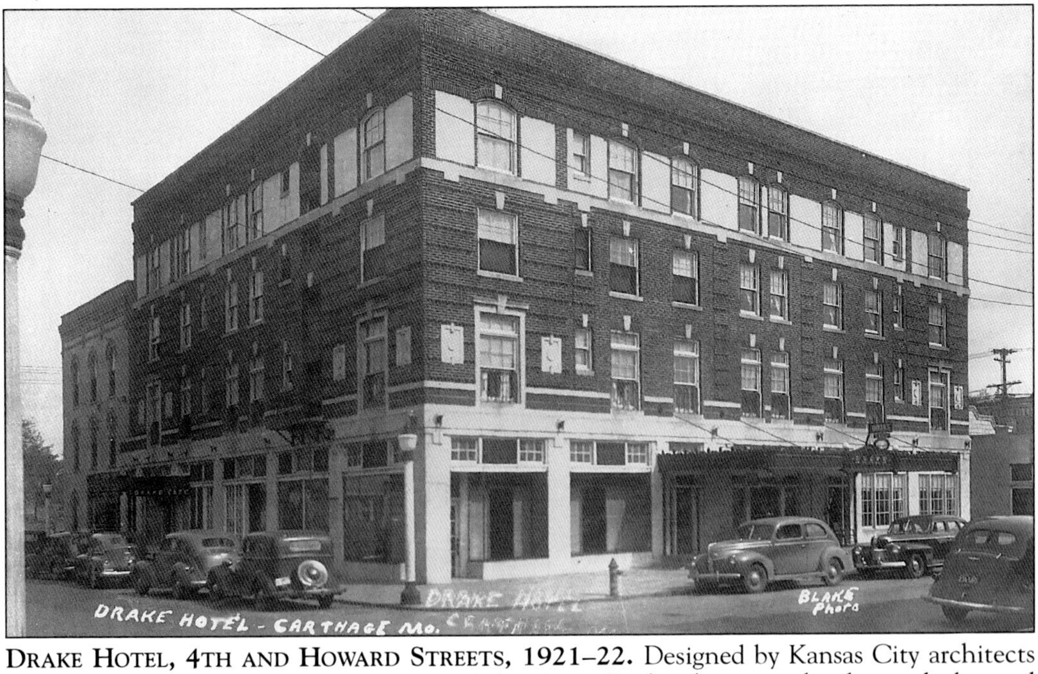

DRAKE HOTEL, 4TH AND HOWARD STREETS, 1921–22. Designed by Kansas City architects Shepard and Wiser, the hotel was named for A.M. Drake, longtime hardware dealer and stockholder in the new hotel. The building cost $200,000 to construct and joined the Arlington at Central and Main Streets, the Elk's Hotel (immediately next door to the Drake), and the Crane (popularly called the Harrington) in offering rooms to the traveling public. Rates at the Drake in the 1920s ranged from $1.50 to $2.50 per night.

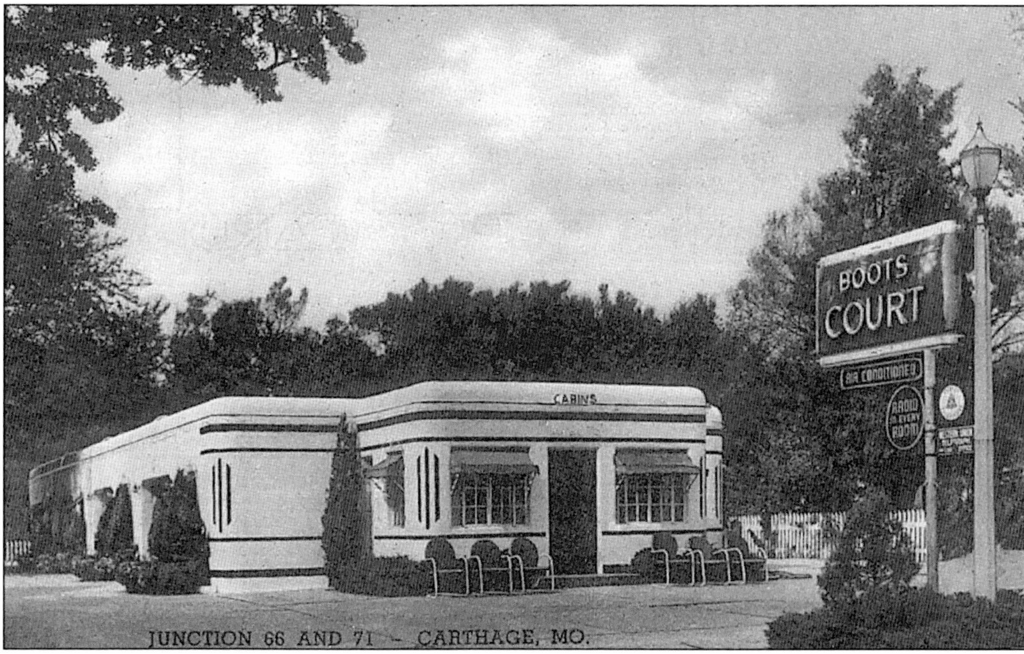

Boots Motor Court, 107 South Garrison Street, 1939. Many guests including Clark Gable, who stayed in room #6, have visited here. Built by Arthur Boots, the motel was sold in 1942 to Mr. and Mrs. Ples Neely who added the back units. Boots Drive-In across the street at 120 South Garrison Street, was home to the radio show "Breakfast at the Cross Roads of America," which featured many of the famous and not so famous traveling Routes 66 and 71.

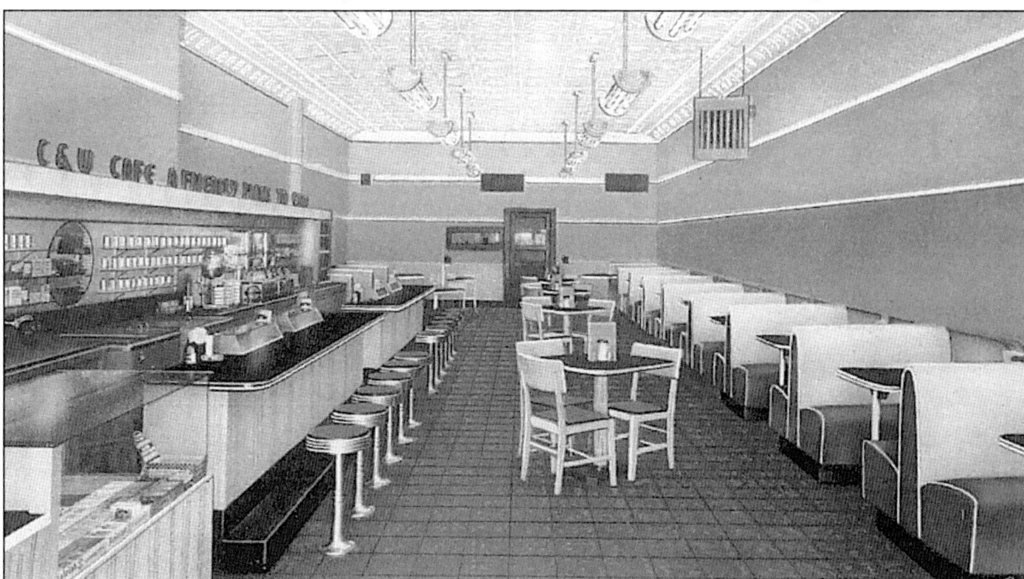

C&W Cafe, 111 East 3rd Street, c. 1936. A popular eatery for town folk and travelers alike, the C&W Cafe later moved to the east side of the square. Thanksgiving dinner in 1936 cost 25¢, and consisted of turkey and duck with all the trimmings. The cafe was operated by Mr. and Mrs. Bus White and Mr. & Mrs. Ray Carter. (Permission to publish this card courtesy of Lake County (IL) Museum, Curt Teich Postcard Archives.)

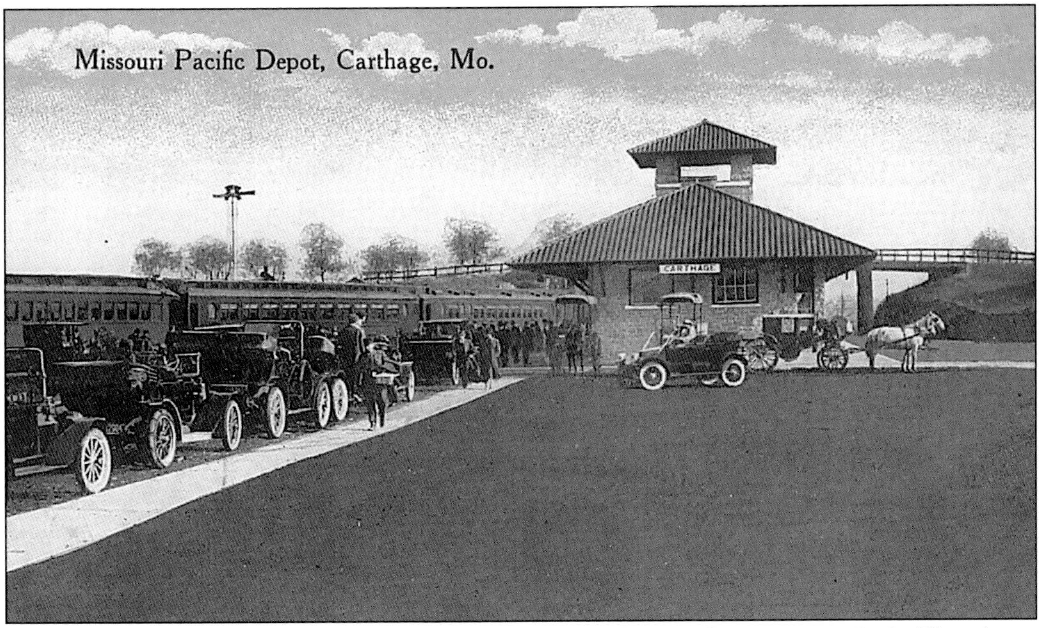

MISSOURI PACIFIC RAILROAD STATION, 517 NORTH ORNER STREET, C. 1915. This depot functions as the office for the Missouri and Northern Arkansas Railroad today, but was built in c. 1905–10 as the Missouri Pacific passenger station. The Missouri Pacific Railroad came to this area in 1881–2.

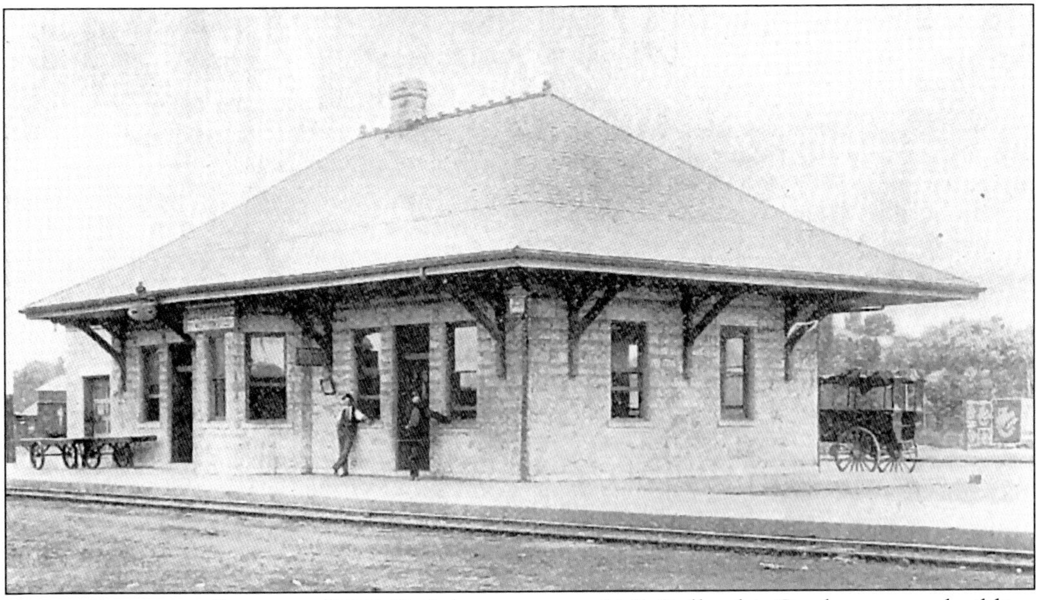

FRISCO RAILROAD STATION, 1895. Built by contractor N.E. Bolle, this Carthage stone building was located at Limestone and Main Streets, but was dismantled and moved to the former Dr. Carter estate off East Chestnut Road almost one hundred years later. The Saint Louis & San Francisco Railroad, or "Frisco," came to this area in 1879.

U S POST OFFICE, 200 SOUTH GRANT STREET, 1895. Built in the bustling year that witnessed the opening of the courthouse and electric railway, C.O. Harrington constructed this modest post office behind his massive hotel when the U.S. Post Office agreed to stay in that location for at least five years. In 1899, he built another stone-faced building to the south that still stands today along with the post office building.

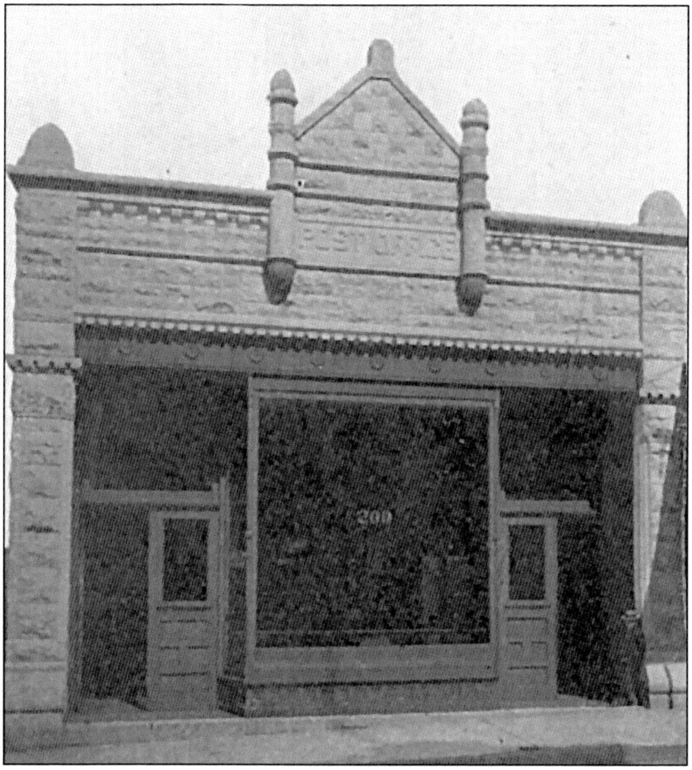

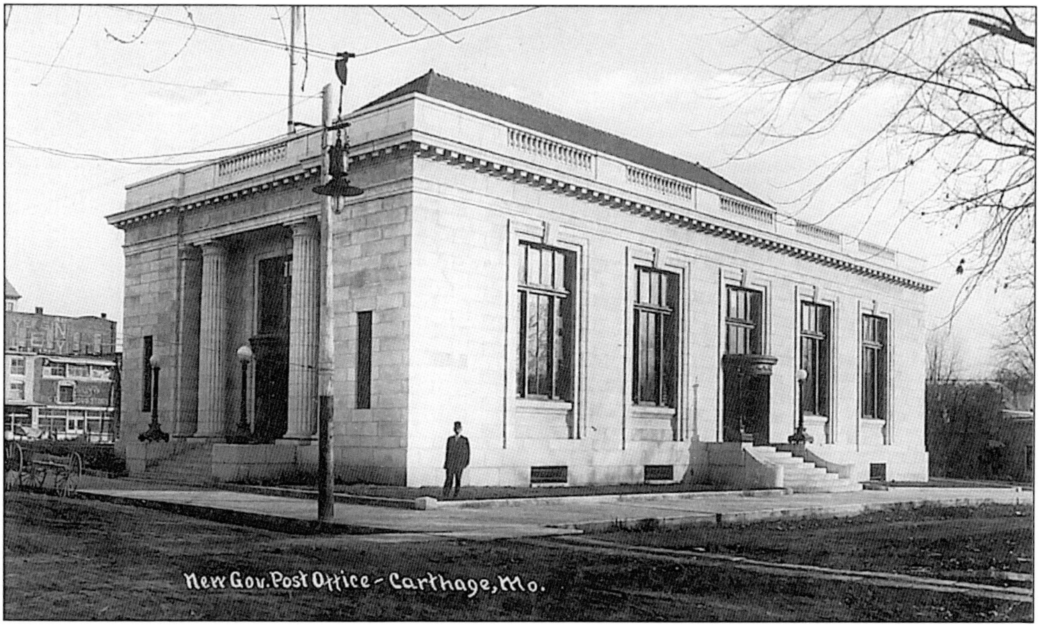

U S POST OFFICE, 3RD AND MAPLE STREETS, 1909–10. Within a short time, a larger facility was needed, and another post office was started on property donated by L.P. Cunningham of Joplin. When constructed, it was the only building in Carthage that had a fluted finish to the stonework, which was said to give the building facade a "soft" look.

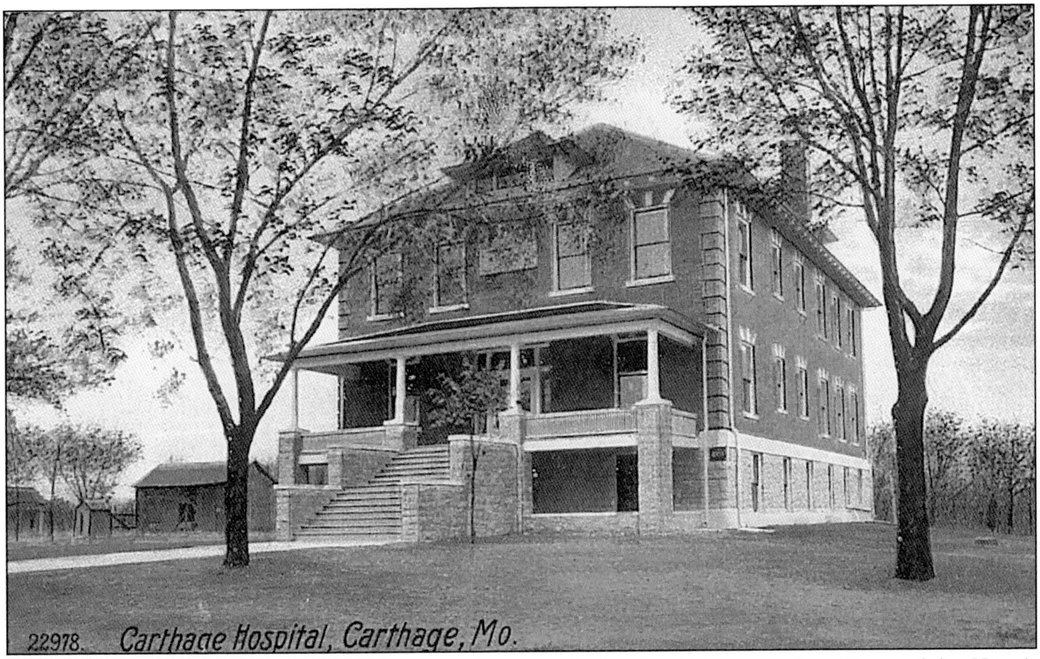

CITY HOSPITAL, 615 WEST CENTENNIAL STREET, 1906–07. Through the efforts of the King's Daughters of Carthage, ground was purchased for a hospital and construction began. Clubs and individuals alike, including W.H. Phelps, A.M. Drake, the Masons, Eastern Star, the Ladies Hebrew Benevolent Society, and others, furnished the rooms. Ninety patients entered the hospital the first year, and the cost for a single room per week ranged from $12 to $25.

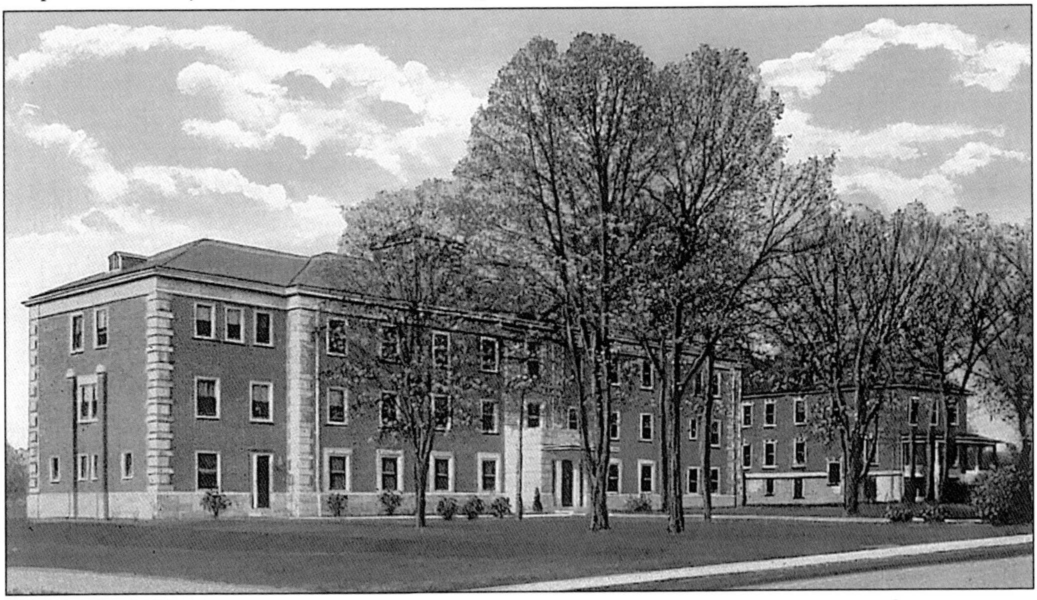

MCCUNE BROOKS HOSPITAL, 627 WEST CENTENNIAL STREET, 1929. Soon it was acknowledged that City Hospital was too small, and with a $75,000 gift from J.C. Guinn and matching funds, a new facility designed by Kansas City architects Hoener, Baun, and Frosse was opened in the fall of 1929 while Dr. Everett Powers was chief of staff. The 50 bed hospital was named for Dr. J.F. Brooks and Mrs. Lizzie A. McCune.

DOCTORS & NURSES AT CITY HOSPITAL, C. 1920. Standing on the steps of City Hospital are, from left to right: Dr. Everett Powers, two unidentified nurses, and Dr. David Wise. When McCune-Brooks opened, this hospital building became the nurse's home and was used for supply storage, until it was destroyed in 1973 to provide additional parking facilities for the ever-growing main structure to the west.

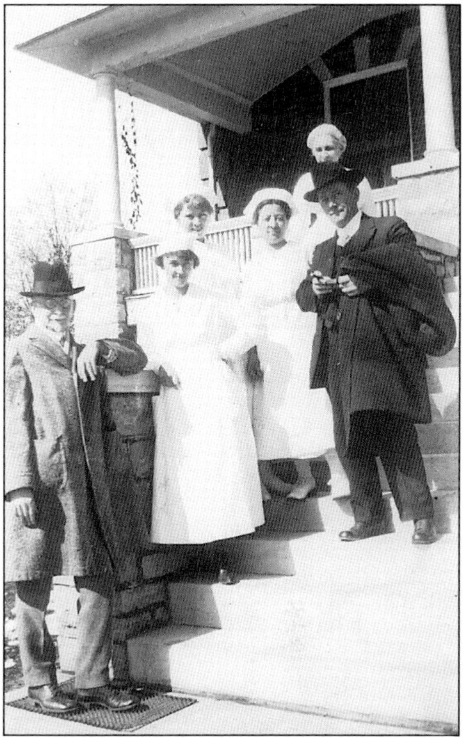

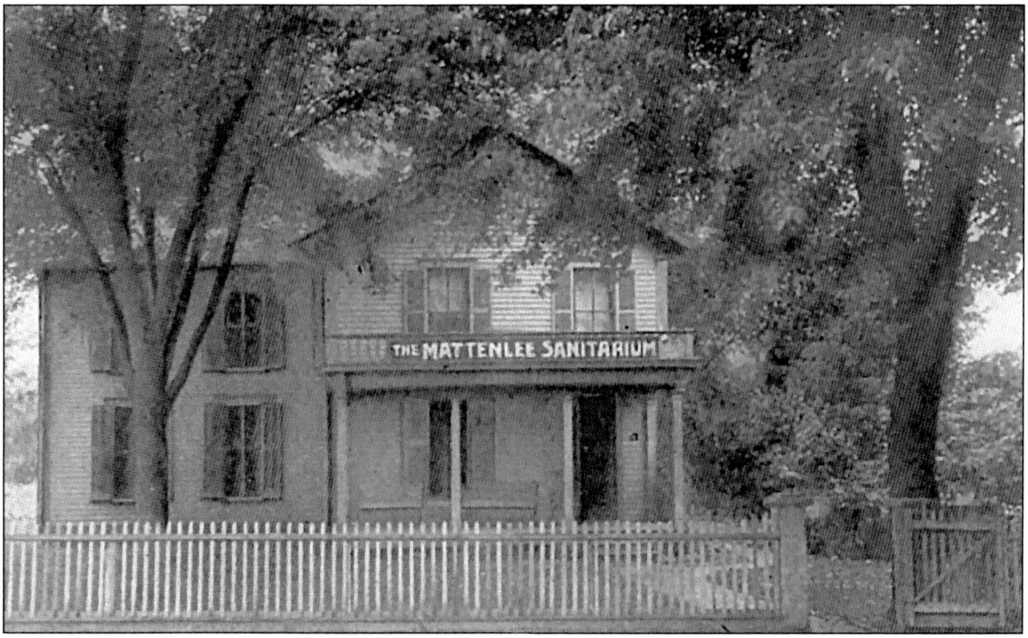

MATTENLEE SANITARIUM, AT 120 WEST 4TH STREET, C. 1900. Originally located on the upper floor of the Cassaday Building, Dr. J.M. Mattenlee operated a sanitarium for the treatment of alcohol, opium, morphine, and tobacco addictions. Alcohol patients took a three-week cure, while others took a four to six-week cure costing $17 a week. Patients boarded at 1133 South Main Street in this residence.

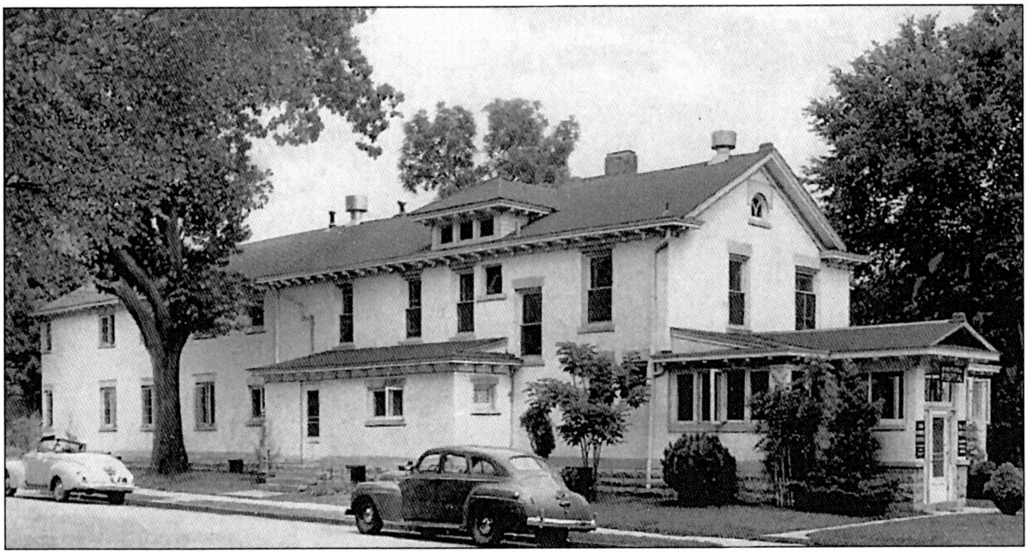

STONE MEMORIAL HOSPITAL, 1069 SOUTH GARRISON STREET. The osteopathic hospital moved from its first location at 1128 South Garrison Street to this residence that was remodeled for use as a hospital in 1939. Osteopaths were not permitted to use McCune-Brooks, therefore establishing the need for a separate hospital. (Permission to publish this card courtesy of the Lake County (IL) Museum, Curt Teich Postcard Archives.)

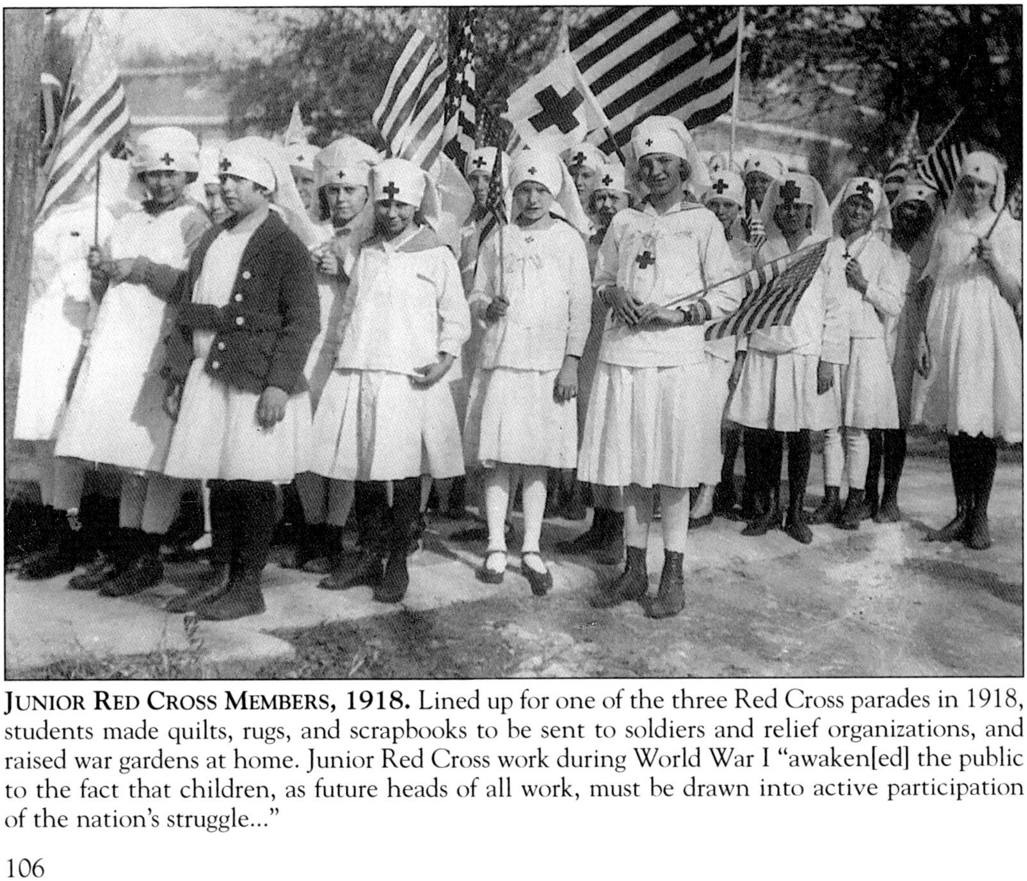

JUNIOR RED CROSS MEMBERS, 1918. Lined up for one of the three Red Cross parades in 1918, students made quilts, rugs, and scrapbooks to be sent to soldiers and relief organizations, and raised war gardens at home. Junior Red Cross work during World War I "awaken[ed] the public to the fact that children, as future heads of all work, must be drawn into active participation of the nation's struggle..."

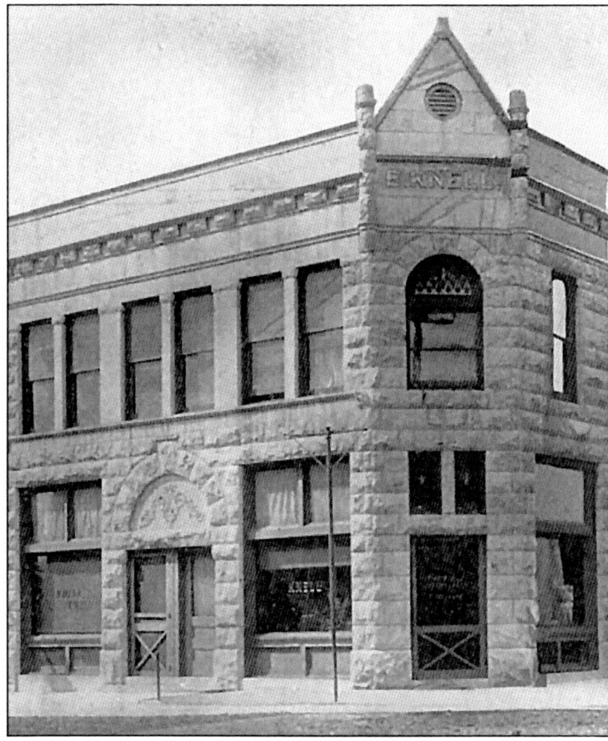

KNELL MORTUARY, 201 WEST 3RD STREET, C. 1897. Edward Knell arrived in Carthage in 1882 to pursue the undertaking and furniture business. Initially located on the upper floors of the building at 111 East 3rd Street, the firm conducted its business from this address until the late 1930s.

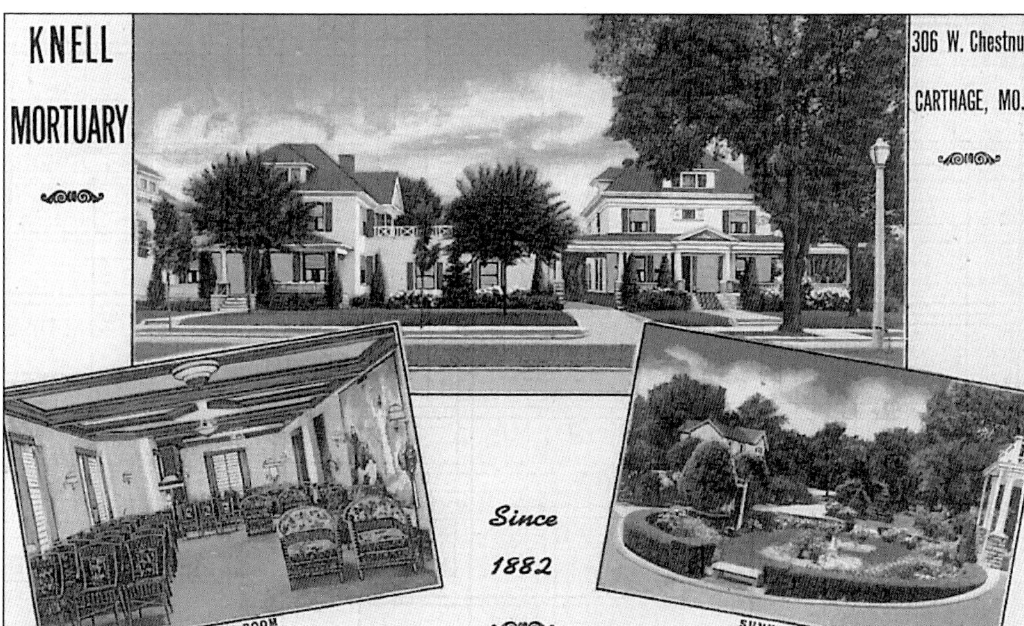

KNELL MORTUARY, 306 WEST CHESTNUT STREET, 1940. Seeking new quarters, the Knell firm purchased homes in the 300 block of West Chestnut Street. Among the directors at the time was Emma Knell, who was the third female mortician in Missouri when she got her license in 1898. (Permission to publish this card courtesy of the Lake County (IL) Museum, Curt Teich Postcard Archives.)

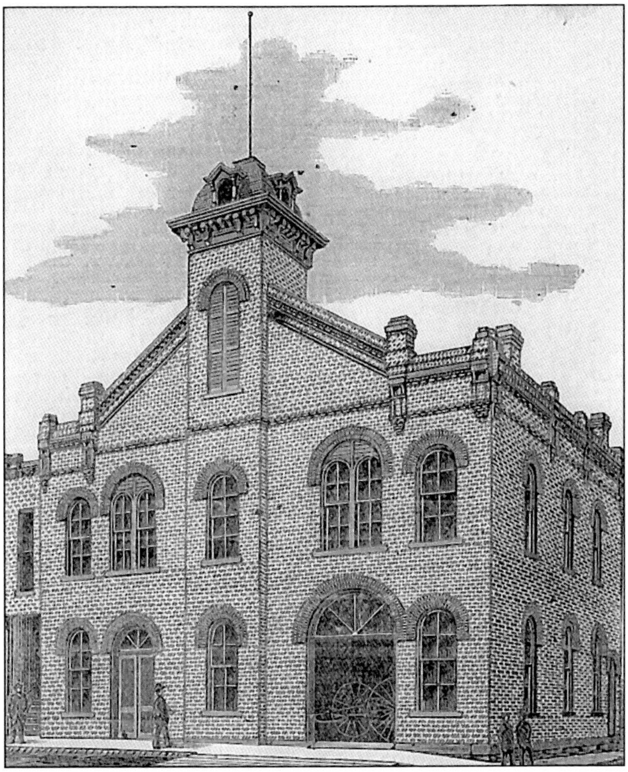

CITY HALL, 205 SOUTH GRANT STREET, 1883–84. Built to house city offices, the volunteer fire department, and the city marshall, this structure served Carthage until 1895 when City Hall was moved to rooms in the Jasper County Courthouse that were given in exchange for Carthage's $50,000 contribution to its construction. Fire and police functions contiuned in this structure.

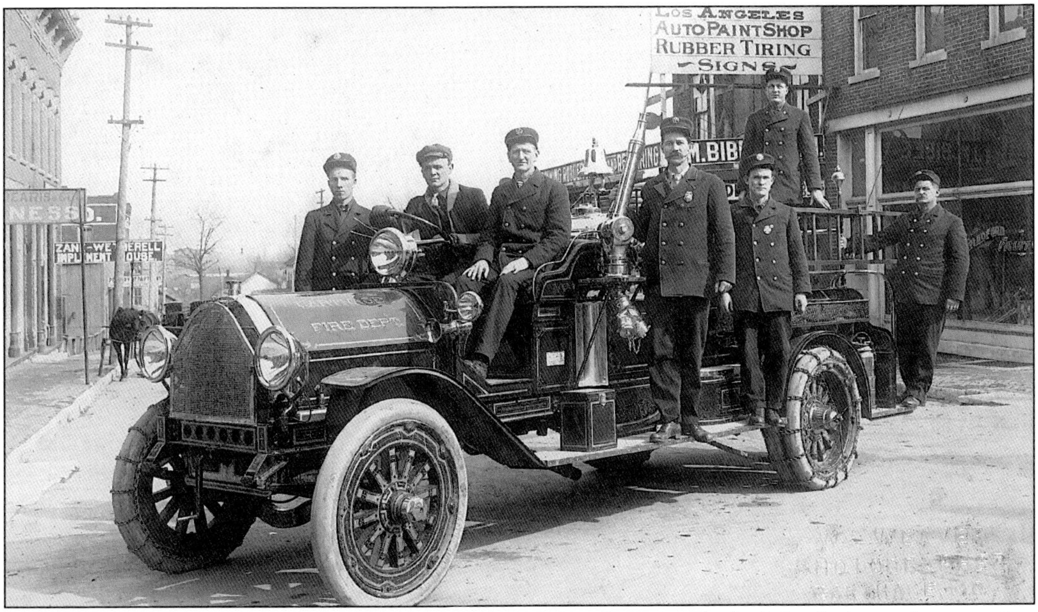

CARTHAGE FIRE DEPARTMENT, C. 1914–15. In 1895, council abolished the volunteer fire department and established a paid department. C.M. Shipps was the first chief, and part of his duties also included the sprinkling of the streets. The crew pictured in this photograph includes the second fire chief S.S. Mathews (third from left) along with firemen (left to right) Neely, Whiteman, Wheeler, Huffer, Ayler, and Woods.

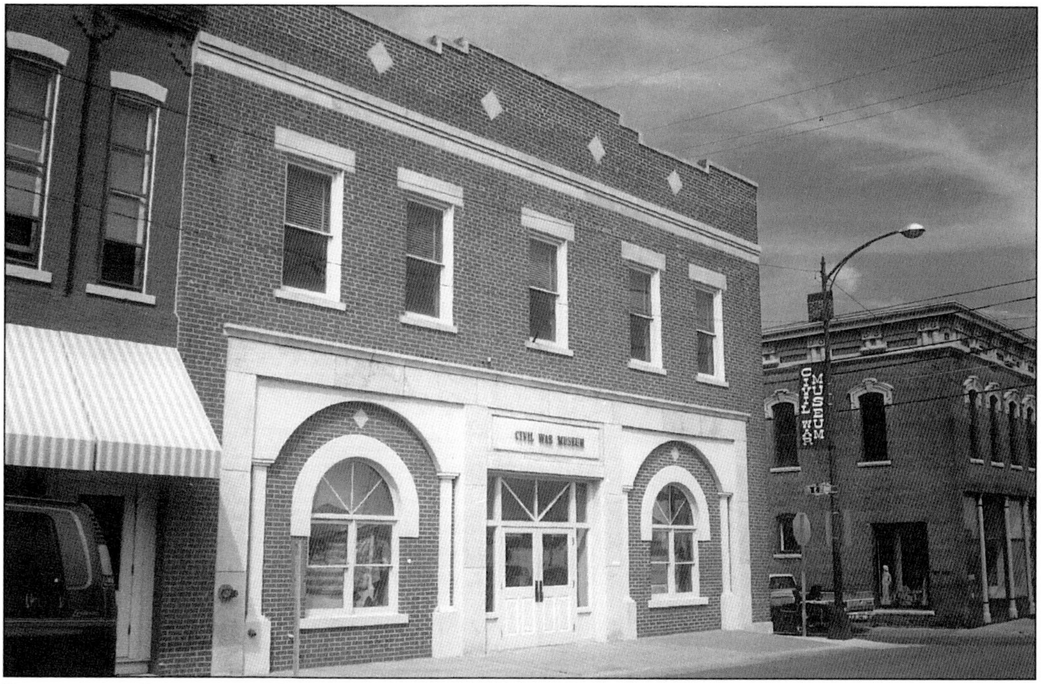

BATTLE OF CARTHAGE CIVIL WAR MUSEUM, 205 SOUTH GRANT STREET. The fire station was remodeled in the 1920s, removing the tower and providing garage doors on the first floor for the trucks, and continued to serve until 1980. In 1992, the City of Carthage recycled the building, establishing a museum dedicated to the Battle of Carthage.

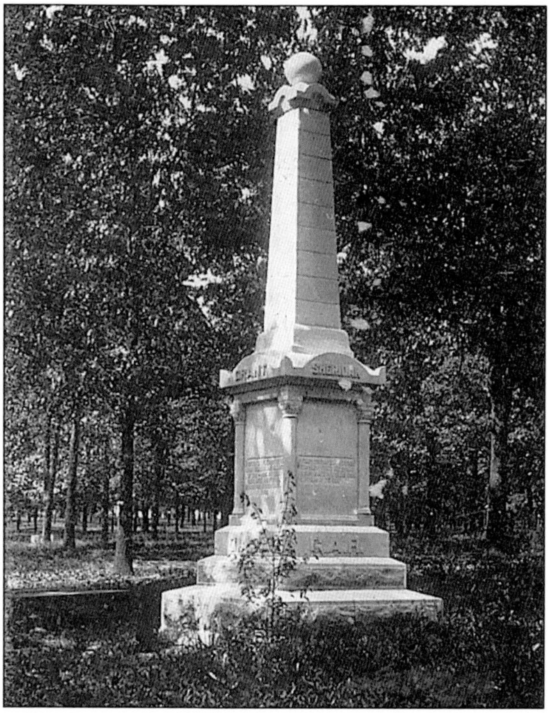

GAR MONUMENT, PARK CEMETERY, C. 1906. The Grand Army of the Republic monument honored federal soldiers of the Civil War, while in nearby Oak Hill Cemetery, an earlier monument had been placed in 1905 to honor the fallen of both sides of the Battle of Carthage by the Carthage Soldiers' Memorial Association.

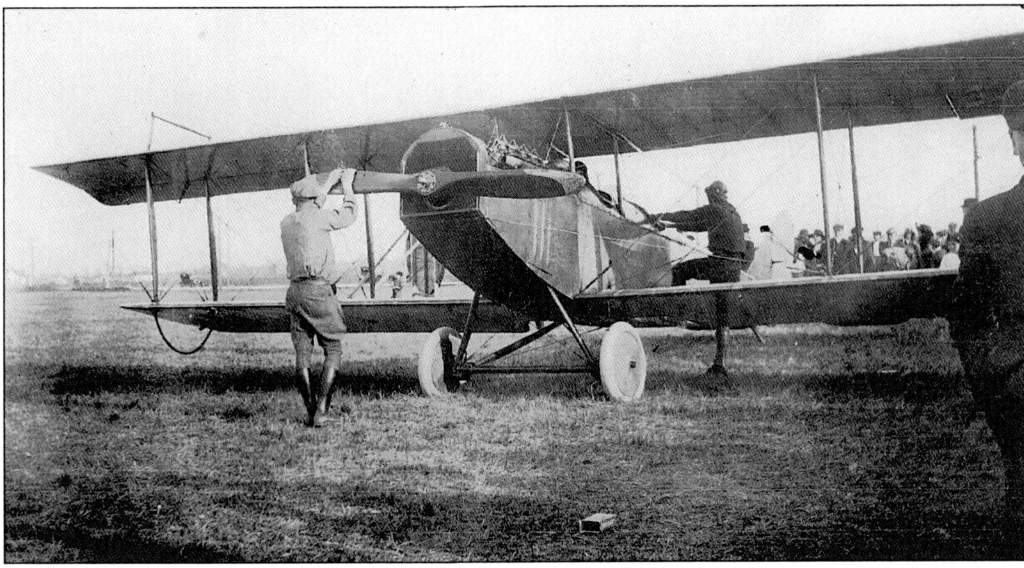

CENTRAL AVIATION COMPANY FLY-IN, 1919. On March 31, this Pittsburgh, Kansas, firm gave demonstration airplane rides in Carthage in an effort to promote their aviation school. Marian Wright Powers took one and remarked of the experience, "There is no disagreeable sensation about it.... I liked it and want to go again, but I will like it better when they put street car rates into effect for airplane passengers." She paid $10.00 for her test flight.

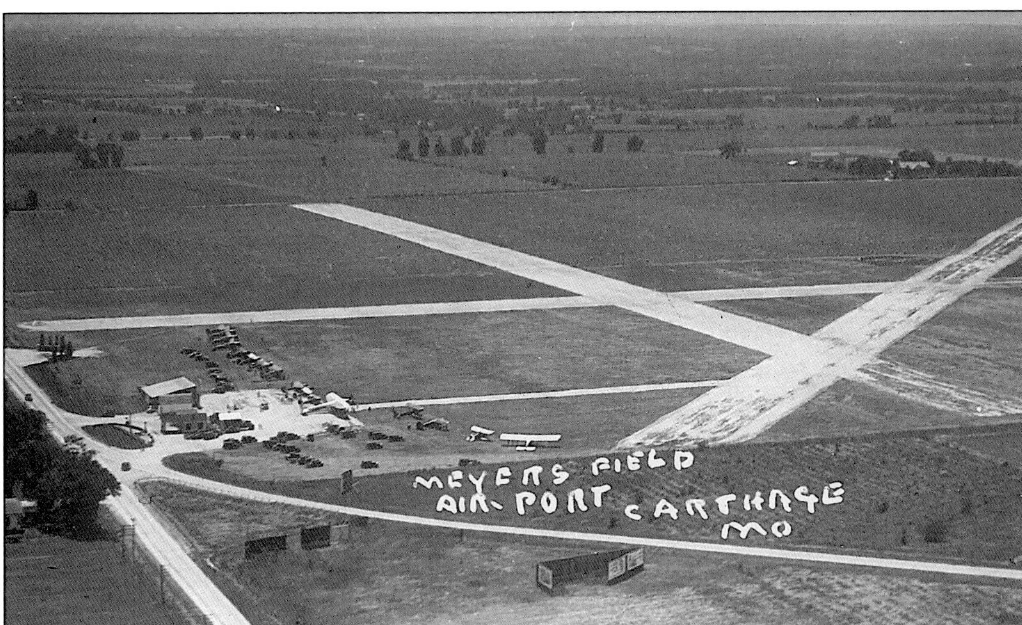

MYERS FIELD AIRPORT, HIGHWAY 71, SOUTH OF CARTHAGE, C. 1935. Myers Field represented 159 acres of land that had been in the Myers family since Enos Myers' arrival in 1868. Edna Myers and her husband Allen had been interested in aviation since leasing the land to O.L. Carrothers for a flying field. Although she died before the land was dedicated as a municipal air field on May 30, 1933, her property represented the largest gift to the city to that date. The airport was closed in 1997.

Seven

HOME

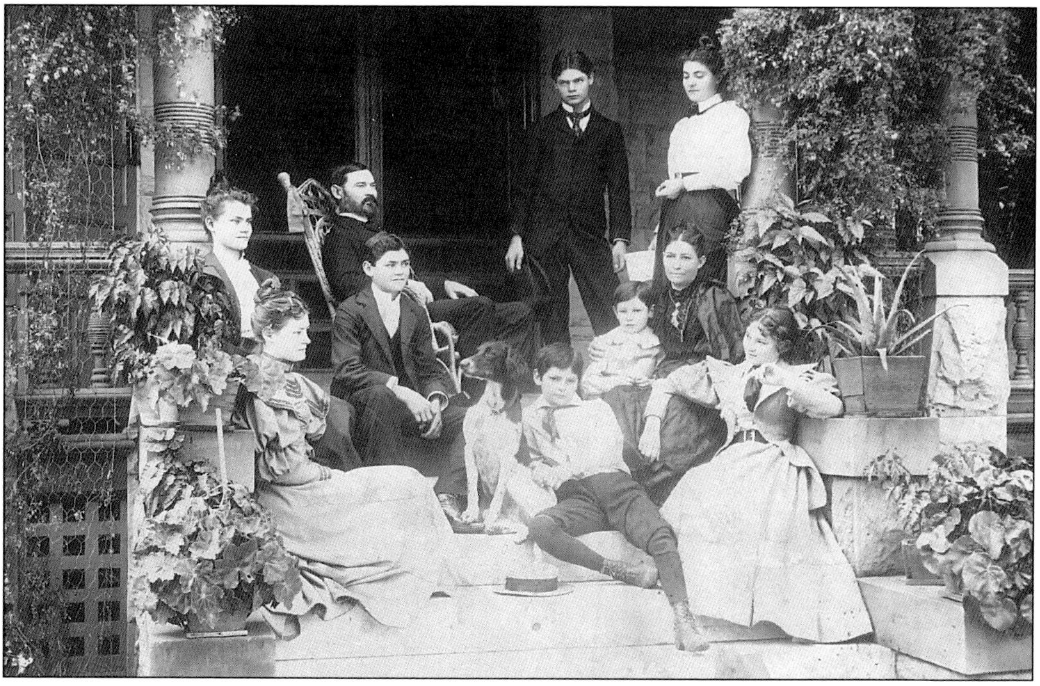

WRIGHT FAMILY, C. 1894. Posed on one of the porches of their home at 304 West Macon street, the members of the Wright family are pictured from left to right: Nira, Bess, Curtis Jr., father Curtis (in chair), Lark, William (next to dog Lark), Nathaniel (standing), Robert in lap of mother Nira, Marian (seated next to her mother), and standing above, Matilda (Tyd).

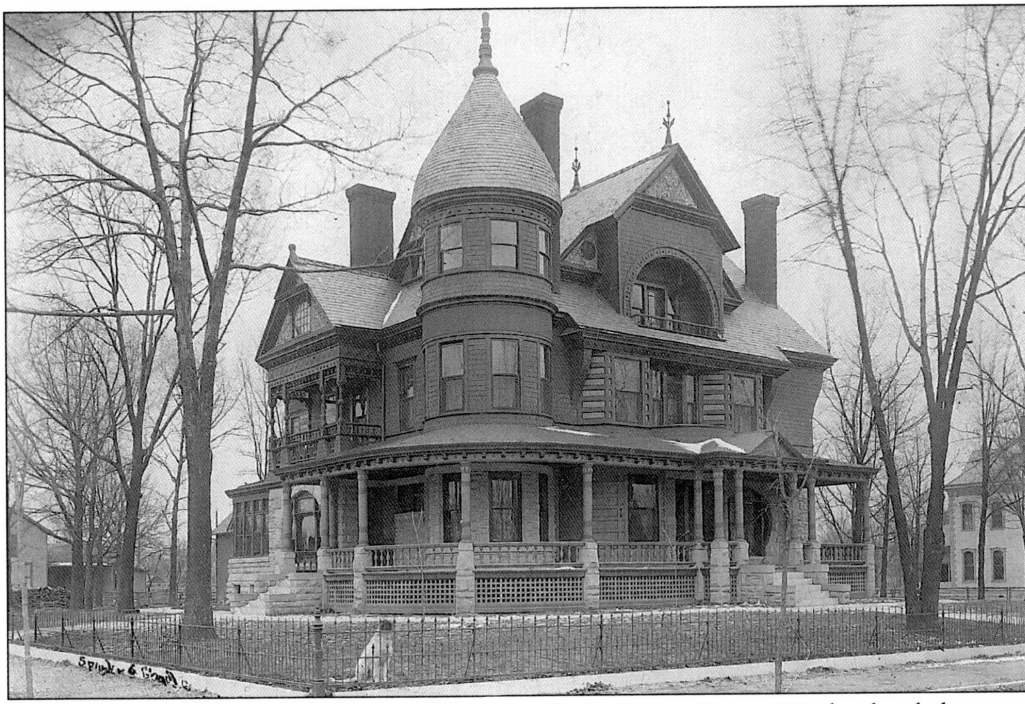

WRIGHT HOME, 304 WEST MACON STREET, 1891. When Curtis Wright decided to turn down a $20,000 bonus to start a furniture factory in Sedalia, Missouri, and invest instead in the mineral opportunities of this region, he promised his wife to build her the the finest house in town. This Queen Anne-style home is the result of that promise, and was designed by C.W. Terry and built at a cost of $15,000 according to the *Carthage Press*. In 1984, it was dismantled and moved to Eureka Springs, Arkansas.

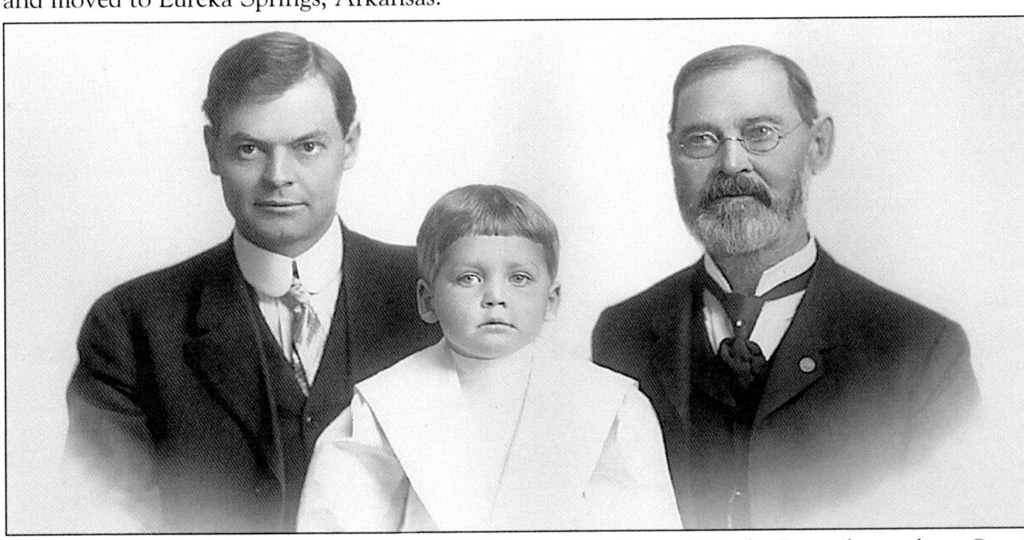

CURTIS WRIGHT (1844–1918), 1908. Pictured is son Curtis Wright Jr. and grandson Curtis Wright III, along with the elder Wright who was 64. Wright Jr. was a representative of Leggett and Platt in Oakland, California, operating the Pacific Spring Bed Company. Through his many letters, he had kept his family and the *Carthage Press* informed of the San Francisco earthquake and its aftermath just two years before.

NIRA KOOGLER WRIGHT (1845–1910). An active church and club woman, as well as an ardent W.C.T.U. worker, Mrs. Curtis Wright had overseen the running of the Wright home and the raising of her family many times without her husband, who traveled for the Carthage Stone Company and his Southwestern Slate & Manufacturing Company of Mena, Arkansas.

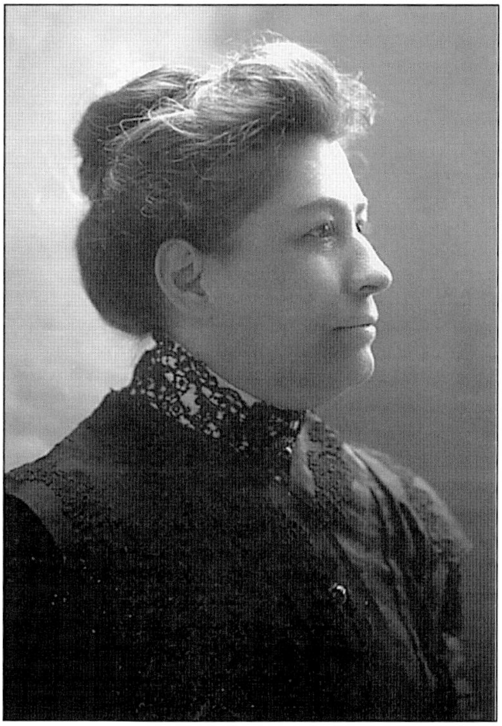

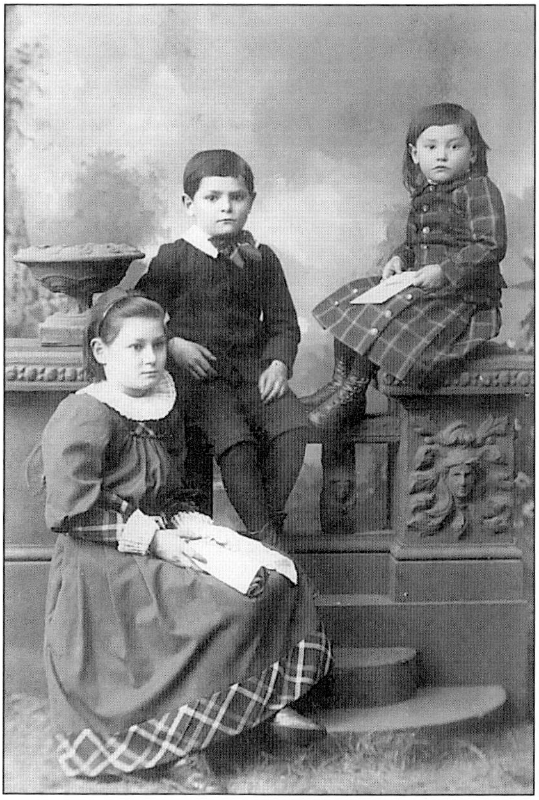

YOUNGEST WRIGHT CHILDREN, 1890. Taken shortly after their arrival in Carthage, this cabinet card photograph by the Roessler Studio on the east side of the square featured the three youngest Wright children, who spent their childhoods in Carthage. Marian is seated on the left, then William, and finally four-year-old Robert not yet in pants.

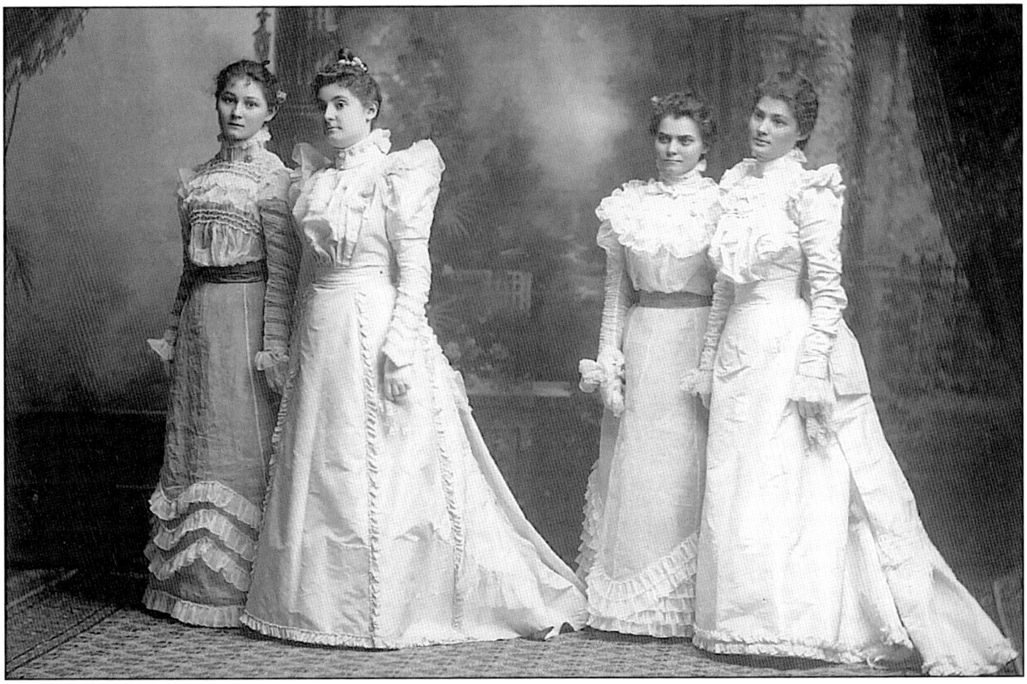

MARIAN, TYD, NIRA AND BESS WRIGHT, 1898. On the occasion of the double wedding of Bess (to Robert C. Briggs) and Tyd (to George C. Hench), the girls are pictured in their fine dresses as bridesmaids and brides. The First Presbyterian newsletter for May 6, 1898, remarked that the wedding "was a very pretty and most delightful social event. We are sorry to lose two of our best girls but glad to give them into such good hands."

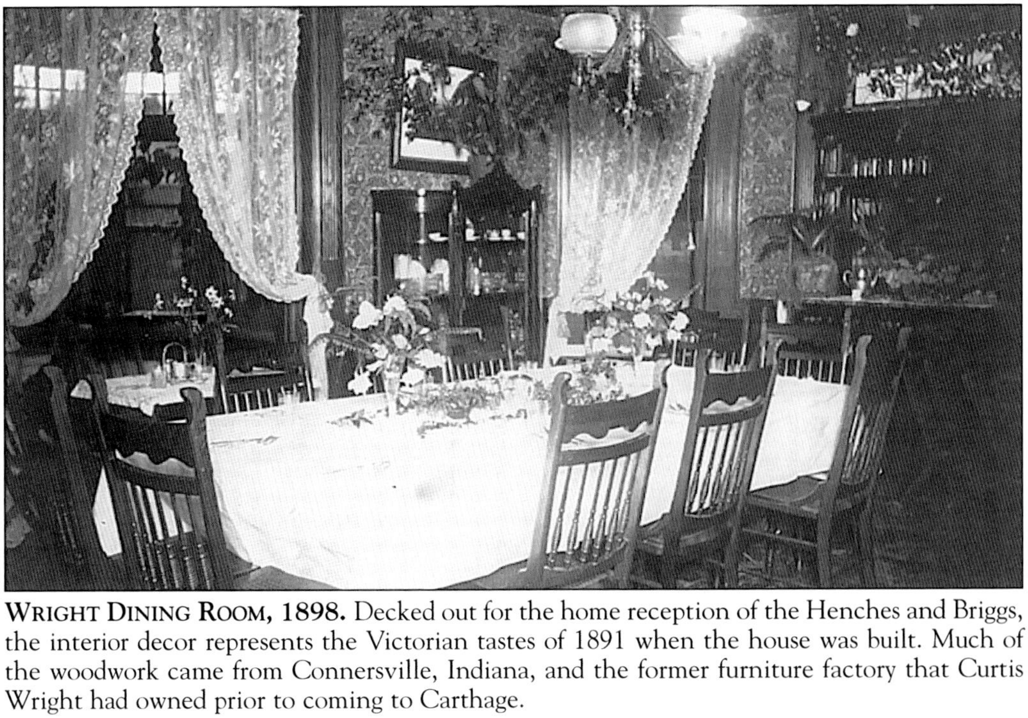

WRIGHT DINING ROOM, 1898. Decked out for the home reception of the Henches and Briggs, the interior decor represents the Victorian tastes of 1891 when the house was built. Much of the woodwork came from Connersville, Indiana, and the former furniture factory that Curtis Wright had owned prior to coming to Carthage.

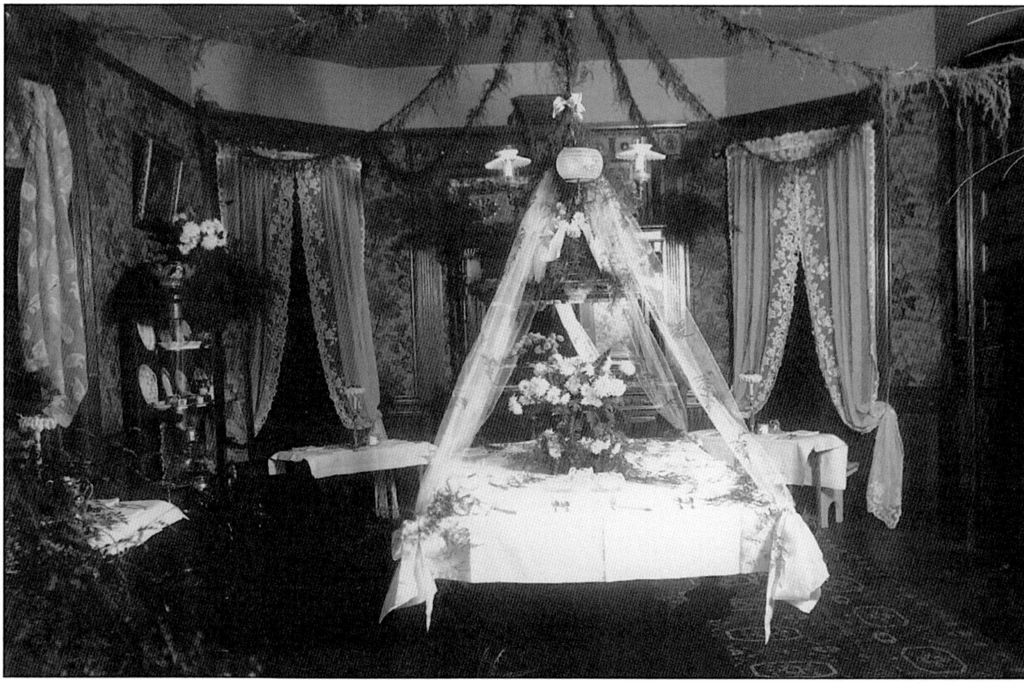

WRIGHT LIBRARY, 1903. Another wedding reception was held in the Wright home in October of 1903 when youngest daughter Marian married Dr. Everett Powers. Their gifts were displayed for several days so callers and family could inspect the bounty of cut glass, sterling silver, china, and other decorative items bestowed on the couple.

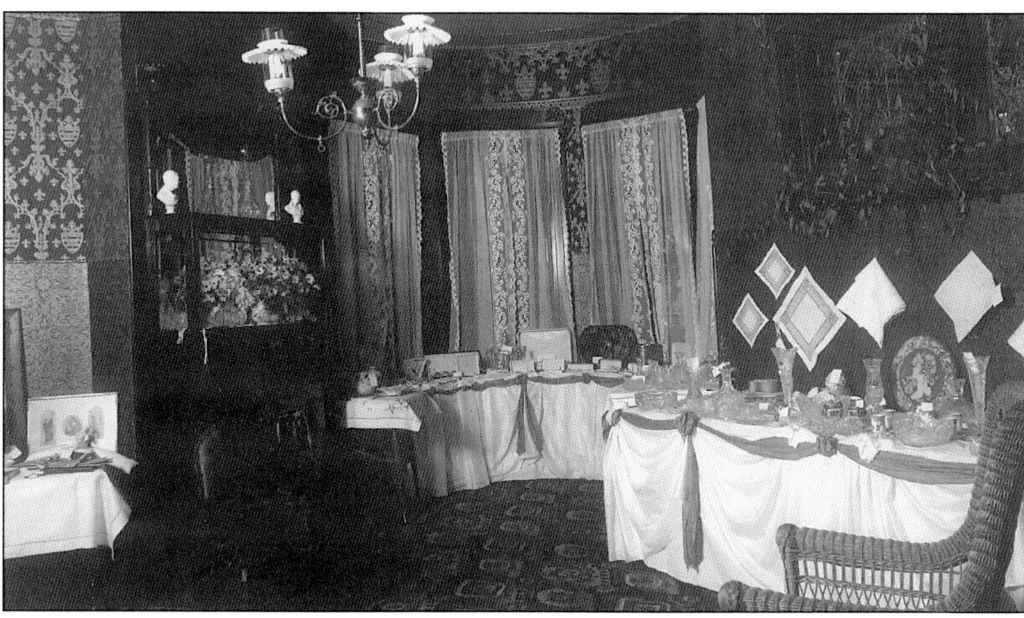

WRIGHT DINING ROOM, 1903. Compared with the view to the left, differences in decor can be noted. Just one year earlier, in preparing for retirement, Curtis Wright had told his wife and two daughters to fix the house one more time. The china cupboard seen in both views was an anniversary gift to Mr. and Mrs. Wright from his former furniture factory employees.

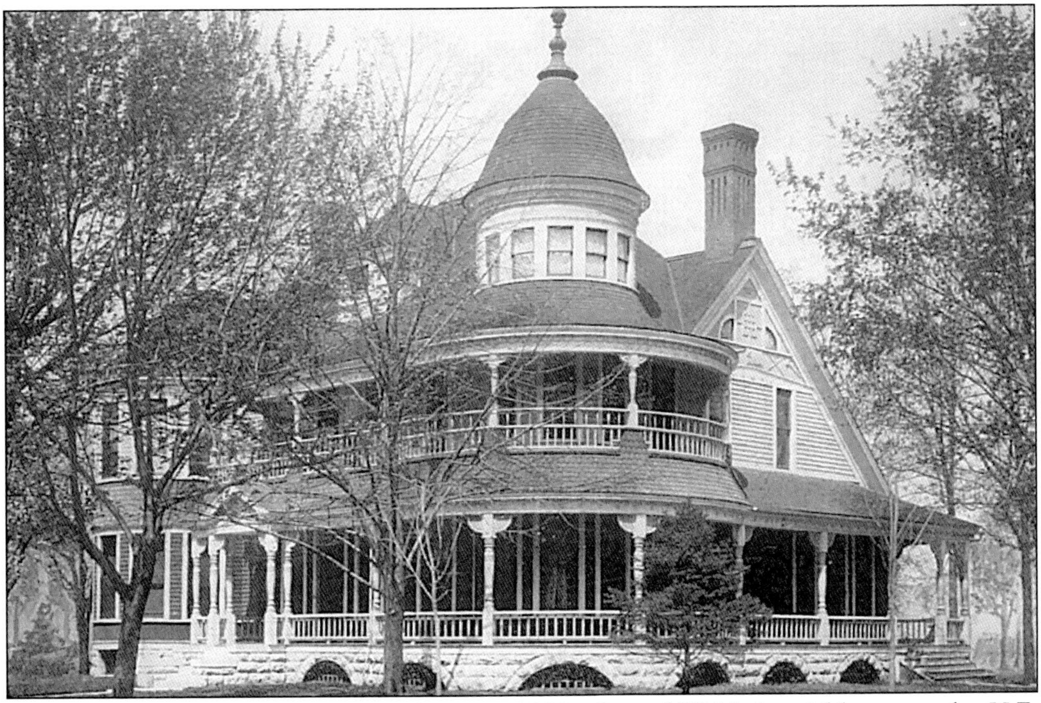

Baker House, 205 West Macon Street, 1893. One of Wright's neighbors was the H.E. Baker family, who built this Queen Anne-style home in 1893 at a reported cost of between $8,000 to $10,000. Designed by C.W. Terry, it is the house that "jack" built—jack being the by-product of lead and zinc that Baker mined on property located near Oronogo to the west of Carthage. A pick, shovel, and ore samples can be found in the gable on the east side of the house.

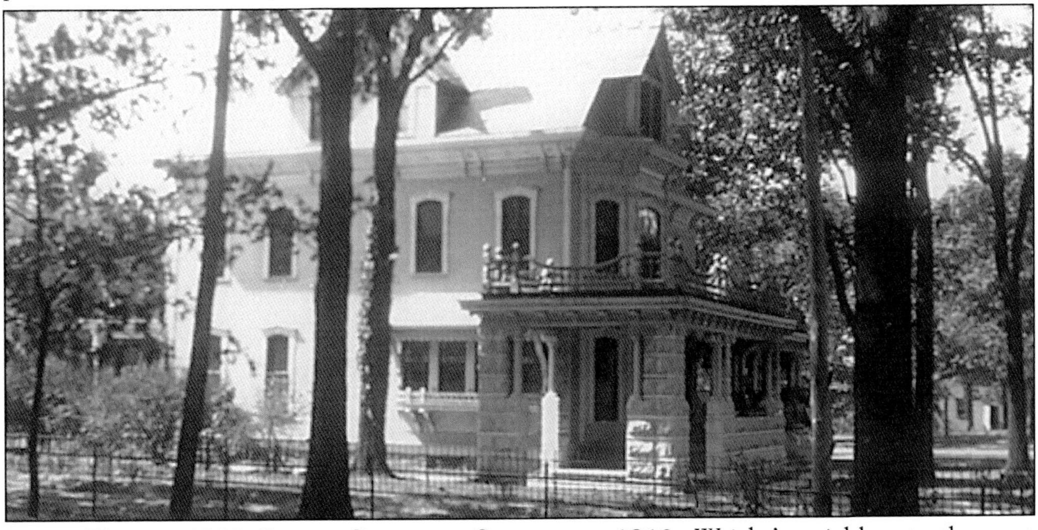

Johns House, 1208 South Garrison Street, c. 1910. Wright's neighbor to the west was E.W. Johns, another mine owner, whose daughter Emma was a concert pianist and contemporary of the Wright daughters. The house became the Cooperative Kitchen in 1909, and families pooled their resources to have meals cooked and served to them in this home. National attention was focused on the operation when local writer Emily Newell Blair's feature was published in *Woman's Home Companion*, October 1910.

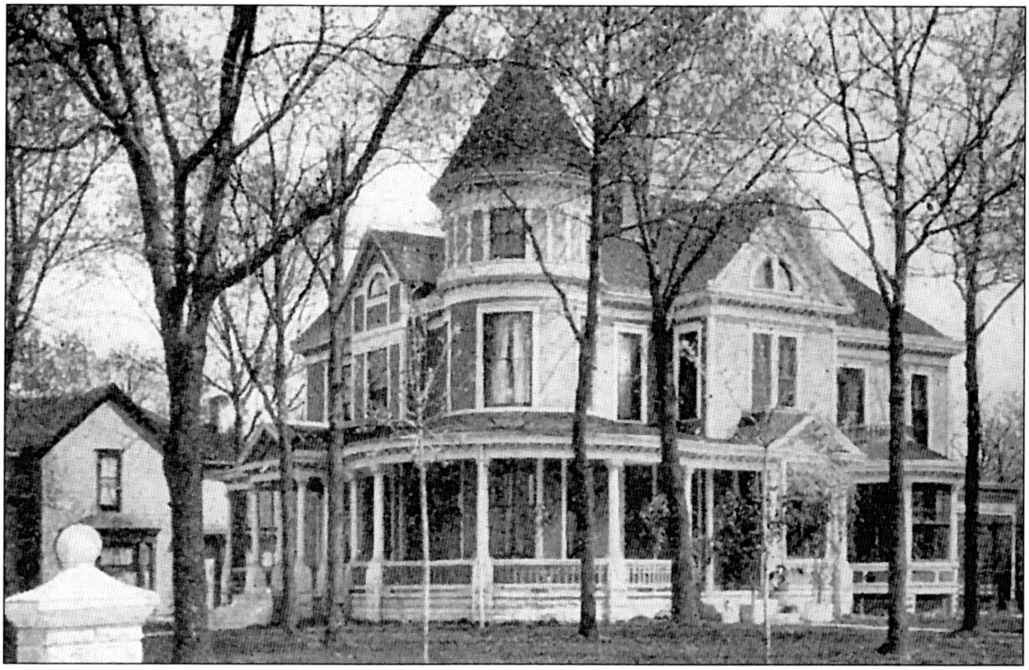

GROUND HOUSE, 1128 SOUTH GARRISON STREET, 1897. Another mining neighbor of the Wright family was J.W. Ground. His Queen Anne-style home had a cyclone shelter in the basement, along with a winter conservatory for the family's plants. It was said that this home cost $7,500, which probably did not include the cost of the formal gardens planted behind the house.

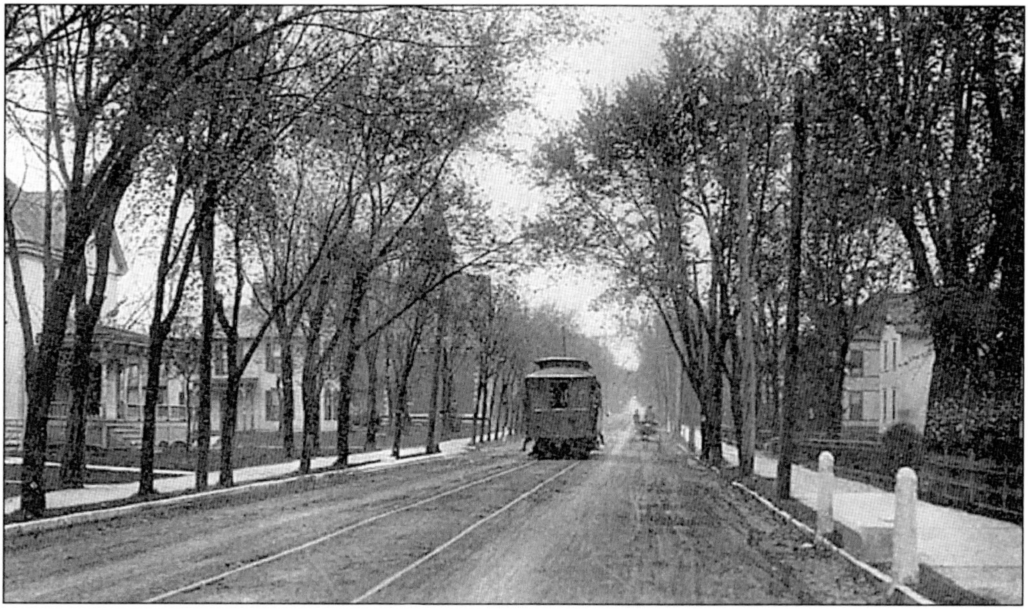

SOUTHWEST MISSOURI ELECTRIC RAILWAY, ON 900 BLOCK SOUTH MAIN STREET, C. 1904. Interurbans or trolleys kept cities of the tri-state mining district connected. With its central location, Carthage was home to mine owners and "mine employees as well, [who] took advantage of the opportunity to reside in a city free from the turbulent environments incident to those cities actively in the midst of mining operations" as a 1900 booklet proclaimed.

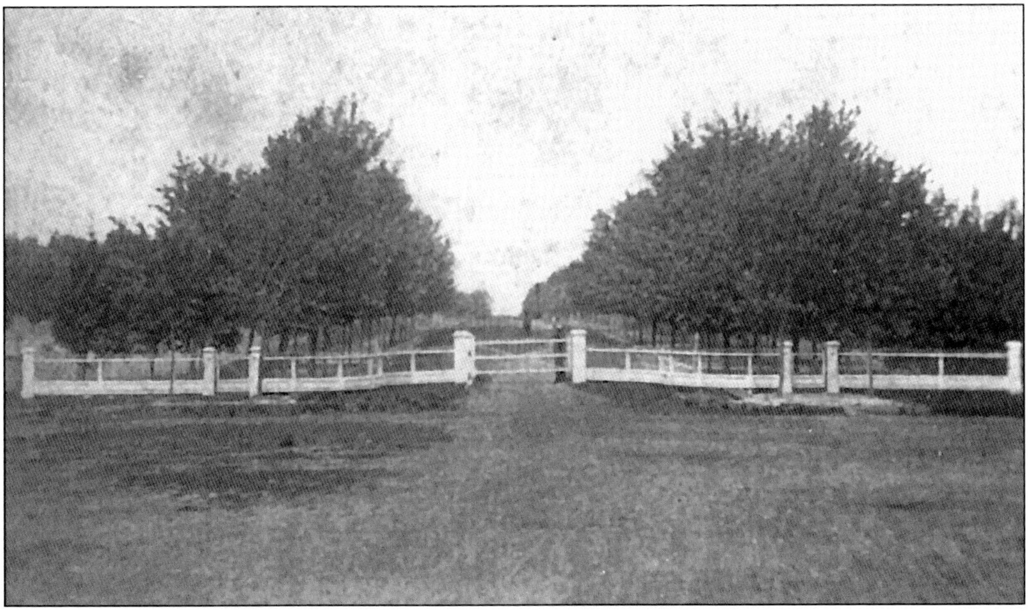

Gates to Cassil Place, c. 1875–80. One place the trolley did not go was the private and gated neighborhood of Cassil Place at 700–800 West Central Street. Platted by G.A. Cassil in the late 1870s, the stone entrance that graced the neighborhood was later moved to Carter Park and used for its northern entrance. Cassil made his money developing real estate, in banking (specifically the Bank of Carthage), and through other investments.

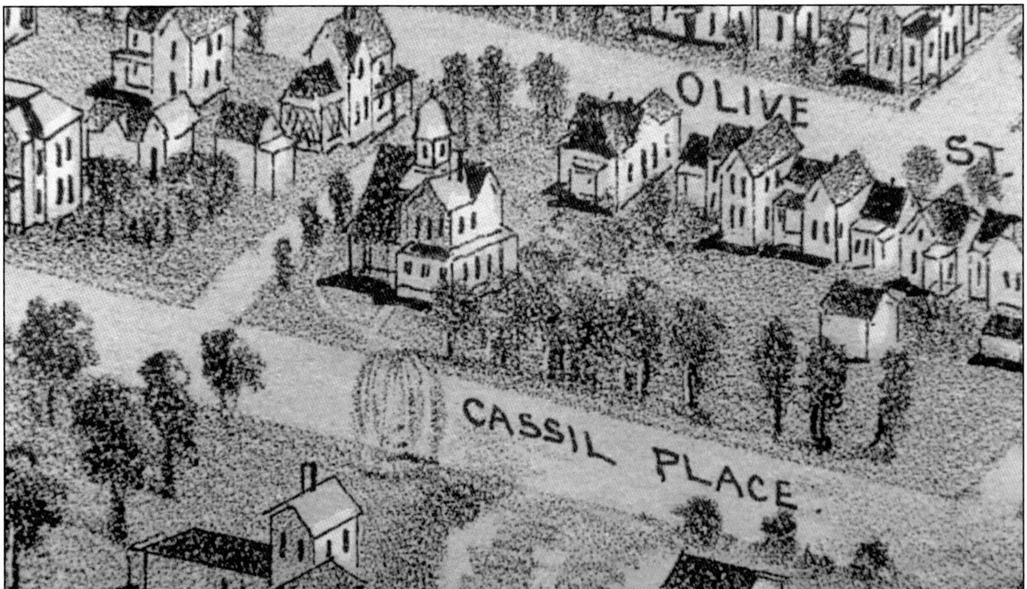

Cassil Place Detail From *Bird's-eye View of Carthage, 1891*. The estate-like layout of the area can be seen in this detail when compared with the closeness of the homes on Olive Street to the north. The house with the tower above the word Cassil is the R.A. Montgomery home built in 1885, which was said to have been designed by architect Stanford White. In the 1930s, this home was moved to 1500 Grand Avenue.

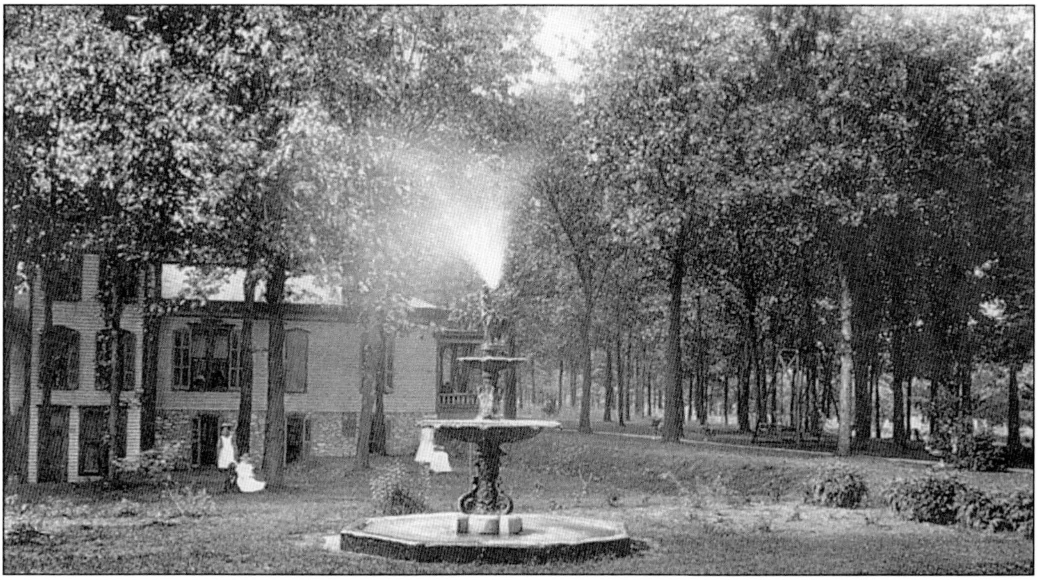

CASSIL HOUSE (#1) AND FOUNTAIN, 801 WEST CENTRAL STREET, 1878. The Cassil family's home was an Italianate-style house with several additions. To the west was a garden area that featured a fountain. This area, which was called Cassil Park on this c. 1910 postcard, was the location of the construction site of Hawthorne School in the 1920s.

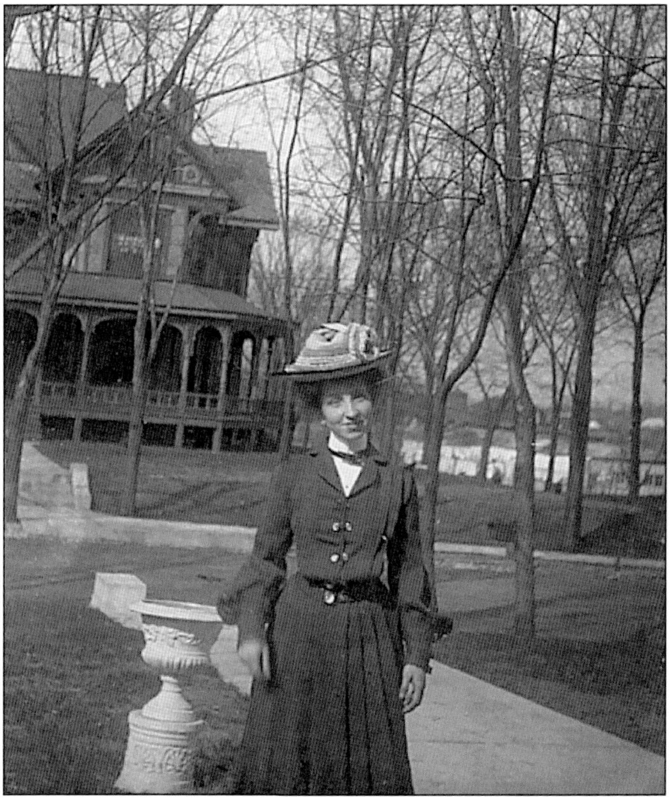

CASSIL HOUSE (#2), 729 WEST CENTRAL STREET, c. 1895–8. Behind Kitty Herrin, who is standing on the walk of her home at Cassil Place at 728 West Central Street, is the second home of G.A. Cassil, built in 1890 just a few houses away from his first home. The remaining two blocks of the original Cassil place were placed on the National Register of Historic Places in 1986 through the efforts of Carthage Historic Preservation, Inc.

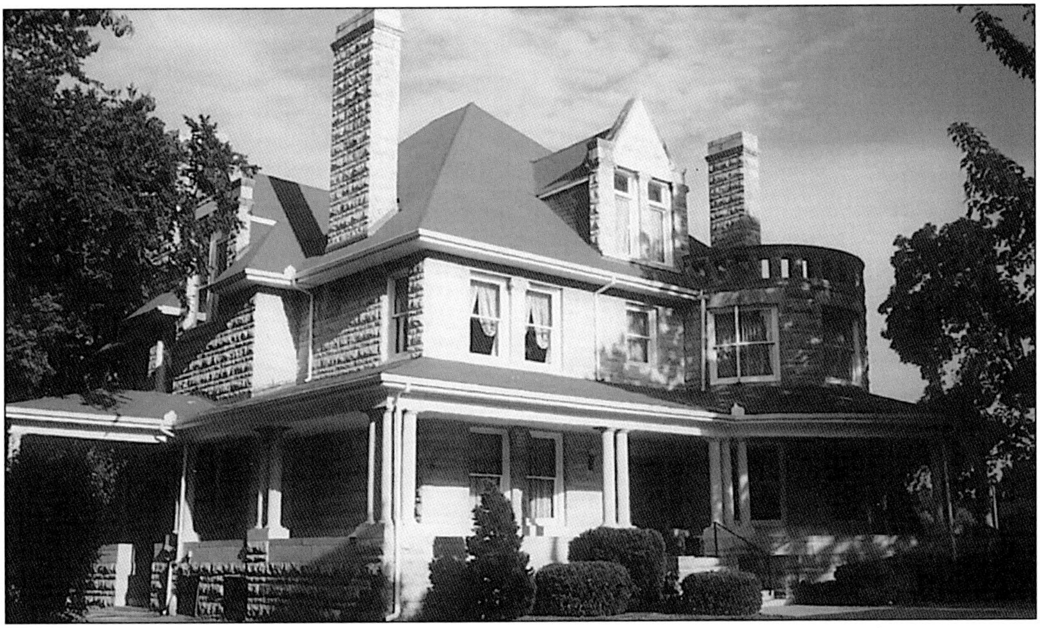

PHELPS HOUSE, 1146 GRAND AVENUE, 1897–9. William H. Phelps, state legislator, attorney, Democratic Party boss, and Missouri Pacific lobbyist, had come to Carthage in 1867 and witnessed the town's transformation from an ugly duckling to a beautiful showplace, much like his residence. Decorated with wooden paneling, stained glass, and hand-painted decorations, it was the scene of many social functions. Carthage Historic Preservation maintains it today for tours and rental engagements.

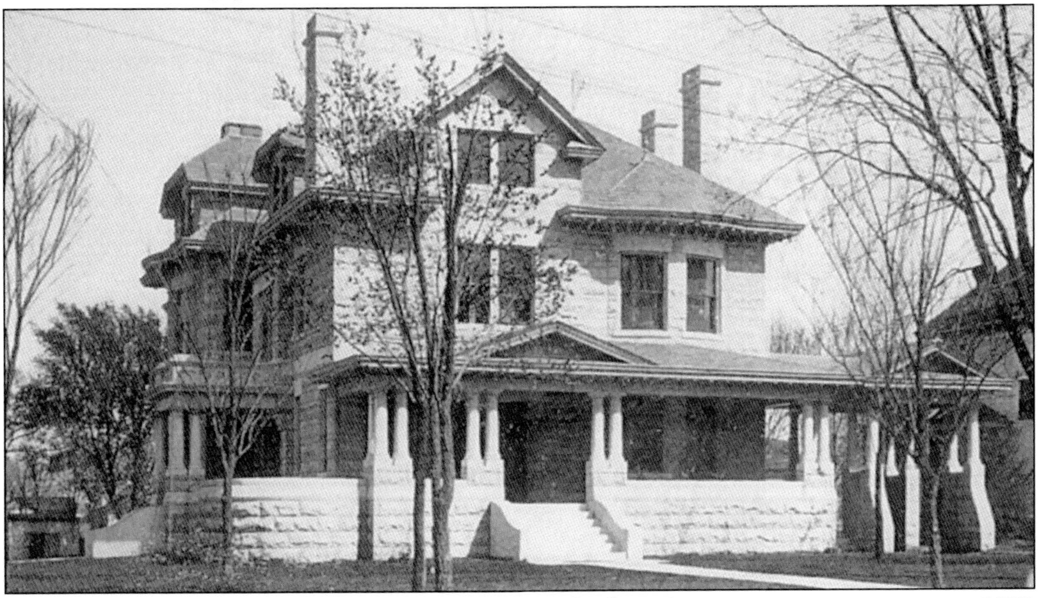

LEGGETT HOUSE, 1106 GRAND AVENUE, 1901. Built with a companion structure at 1131 Grand Avenue, this was the home of Joseph P. Leggett, while the twin across the street was the home of Cornelius B. Platt. Joseph Prather was the builder for both, and originally buff-colored brick was considered for use, but finally Carthage stone was selected for the exteriors. Today, The Leggett House is a bed and breakfast establishment.

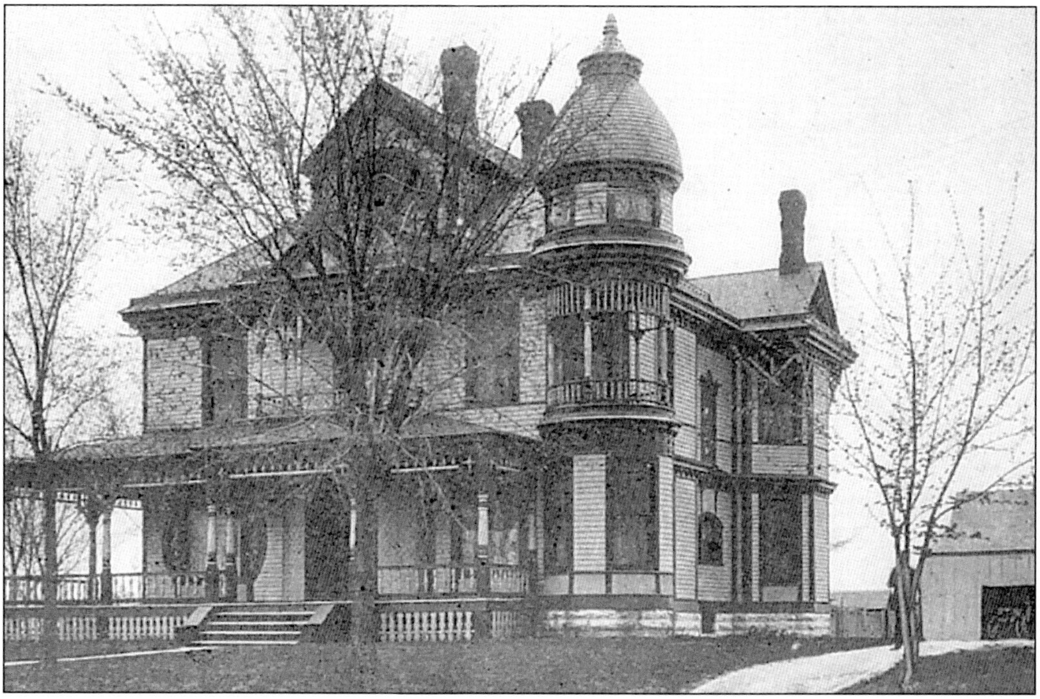

CARMEAN HOUSE, 1615 GRAND AVENUE, 1893. Known as the Carmean home for its third owner, who was a county official, mine owner, and hardware dealer, the structure was built by S.H. Houser for a reported cost of $6–8,000. Like the Leggett house, this Queen Anne-style home is operated today as a bed and breakfast named Grand Avenue.

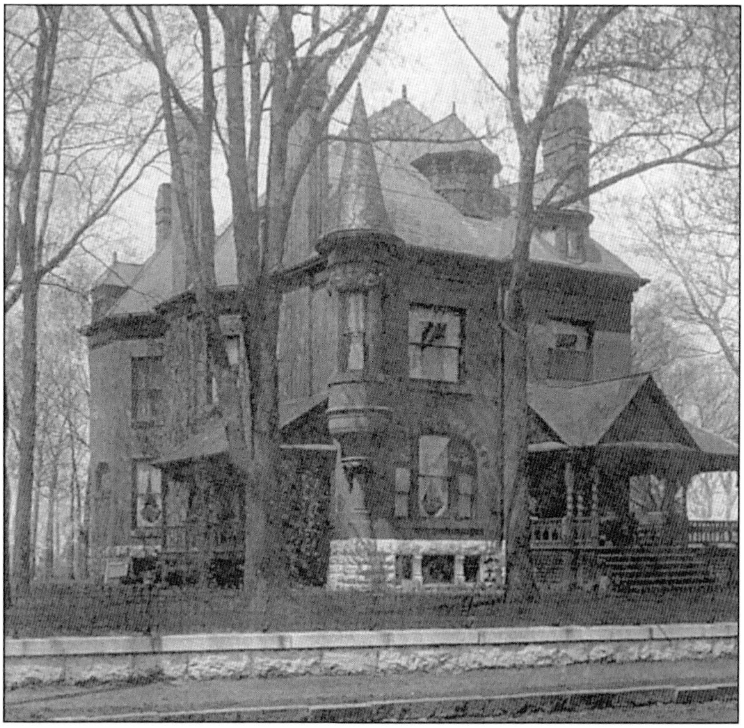

HILL HOUSE, 1157 SOUTH MAIN STREET, 1886. Designed by J.B. Legg along with the Carthage Collegiate Institute, this home belonged to Frank Hill, Carthage industrialist. Besides banking, Hill also was part owner in the Carthage Woolen Mills and the Cowgill and Hill [Flour] Mills. Opened for tours in the 1980s, this home has returned to serve as a private residence.

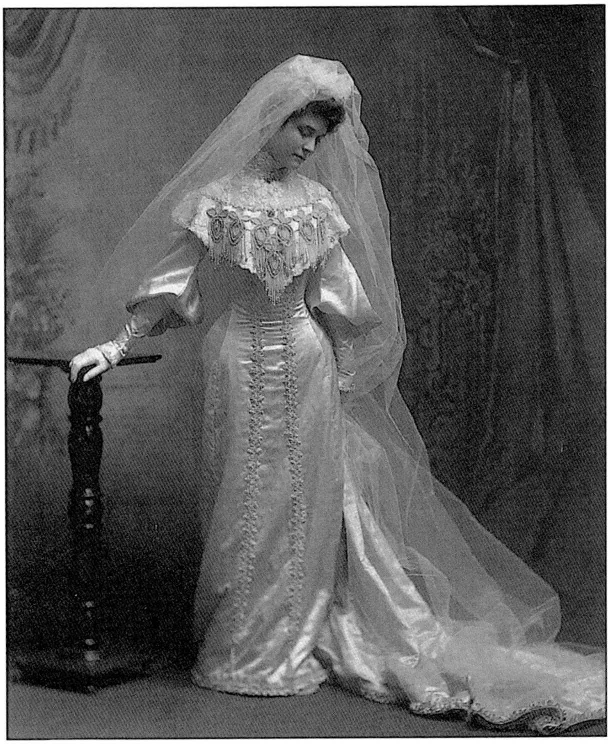

MARIAN WRIGHT POWERS IN WEDDING DRESS, 1903. The wedding of Marian Wright to Dr. Everett Powers on October 29, took place at the First Presbyterian Church. The bride wore a white satin, princess-style dress, with a train, and the bodice was trimmed in lace and pearls. The gown is now part of the collection of the Powers Museum.

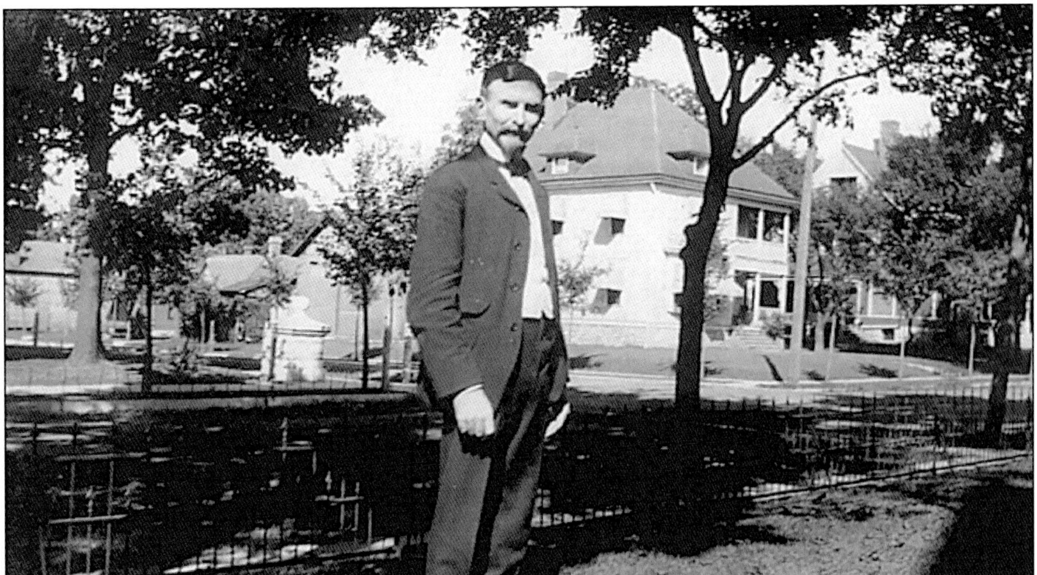

DR. EVERETT POWERS, C. 1910. Dr. Powers was raised in Labaddie, Missouri, and followed his father, John Alexander Powers, into the medical profession. He studied in Cincinnati, Philadelphia, New York, Austria, and Germany. Originally a general practitioner in Monett, Missouri, Powers opened an eye, ear, nose, and throat-specialty practice in Carthage in 1902. Standing on the lawn of the Curtis Wright house, the home visible in the background of this image is 213 West Macon Street.

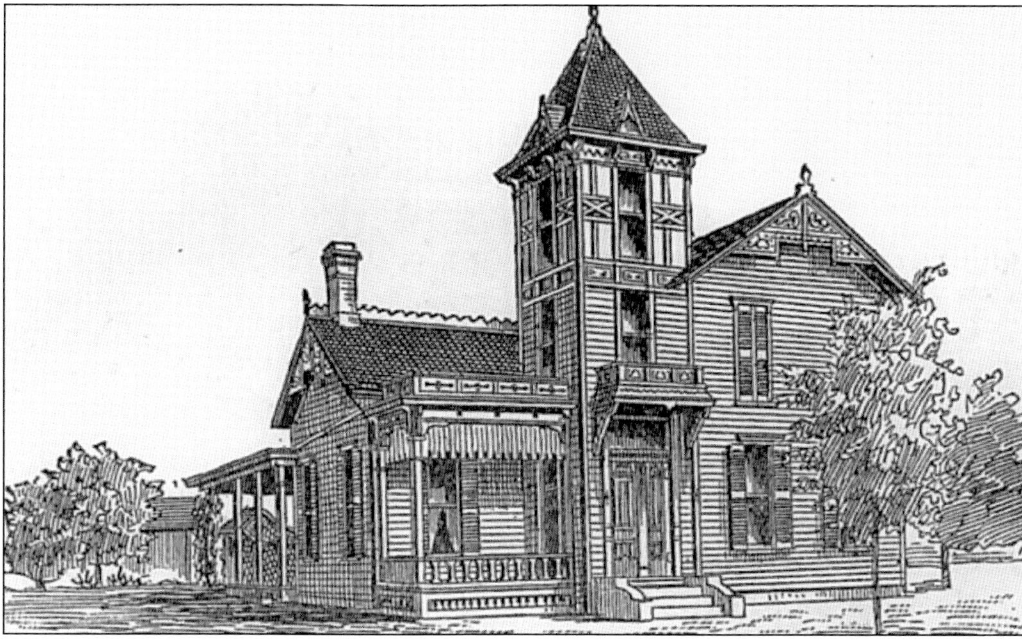

UPDEGRAFF-RITTENHOUSE-WRIGHT HOUSE, 208 WEST MACON STREET, C. 1882. This cottage was built by J.F. Updegraff and later owned by Curtis Wright's stone partner, T.J. Rittenhouse. The Wrights bought the house eventually, and most of the Wright children started out housekeeping in this home including the Powers family. Daughter Marian Louisa Powers was born in this house in 1905.

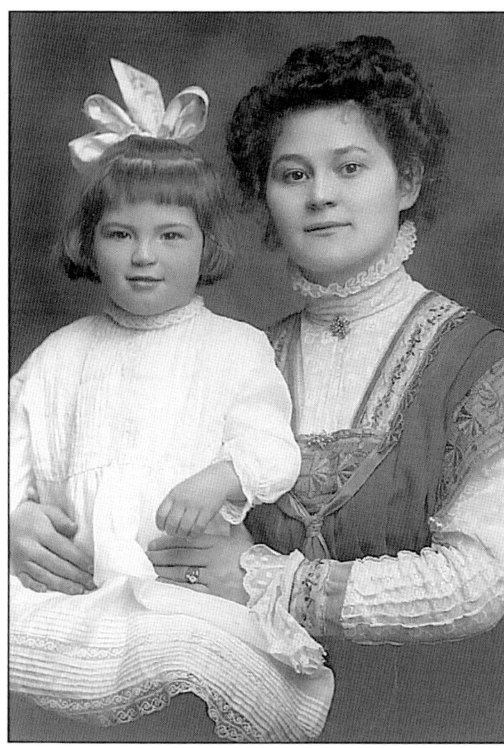

MARIAN WRIGHT POWERS AND DAUGHTER MARIAN LOUISA, 1908. All of the Wright daughters were musically gifted, but Marian Wright Powers aspired to a professional career as a coloratura soprano and studied prior to her marriage. After the birth of her daughter, Mrs. Powers began to think of a career again and returned to study in New York and Paris. Often daughter Marian accompanied her mother, and even attended school in Paris during one of her mother's educational sojourns.

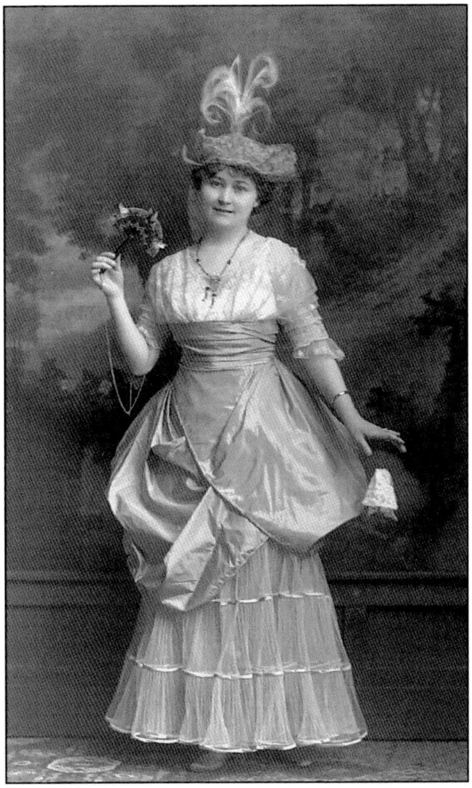

Marian Wright Powers in recital costume, c. 1910–14. Mrs. Powers sang a varied repertoire of opera, sacred, popular, and folk songs including an entire program of Civil War-era songs sung in period costume, but this recital gown is more contemporary. Mrs. Powers performed throughout the four-state region and used to remark that she had "married and buried half of Jasper County." Other musical engagements found her signing with the symphony orchestra of Kansas City, Saint Louis and Saint Paul, Minnesota.

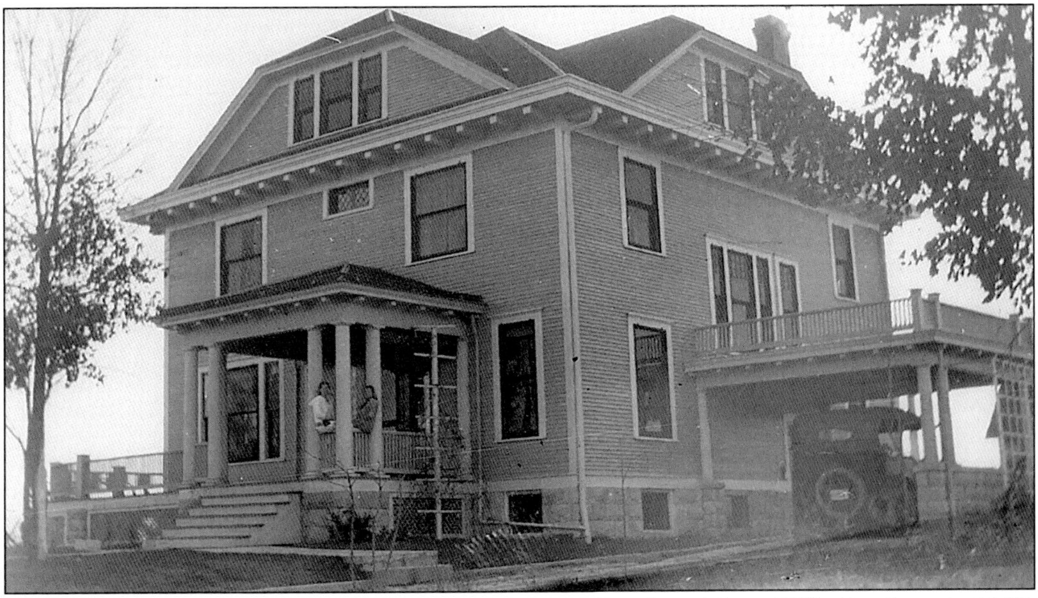

Powers House, 314 Euclid Boulevard, c. 1920. Purchased from W.R. Caulkins in 1917, Mrs. Powers was left to supervise the move and decoration of this house by herself, as Dr. Powers joined the U.S. Medical Corps and was sent to Camp Dodge, Iowa. The home was built in 1908 and included quarters in the basement for a chauffeur who had been employed by the home's former owner.

Euclid Boulevard, c. 1920. Located in an undeveloped area of town with just a few homes scattered about, the extra lots the Powers purchased with their home were developed into gardens. The street where the house sat was nicknamed "Lover's Lane," but it was eventually developed into a landscaped boulevard as the area was divided off and sold in the 1930s and 1940s.

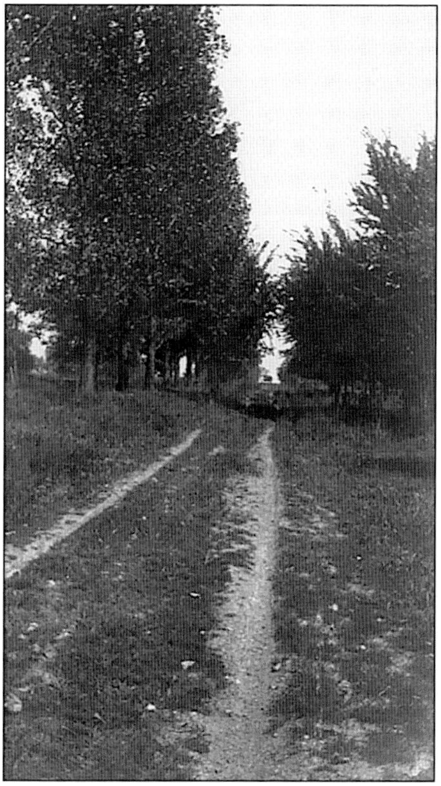

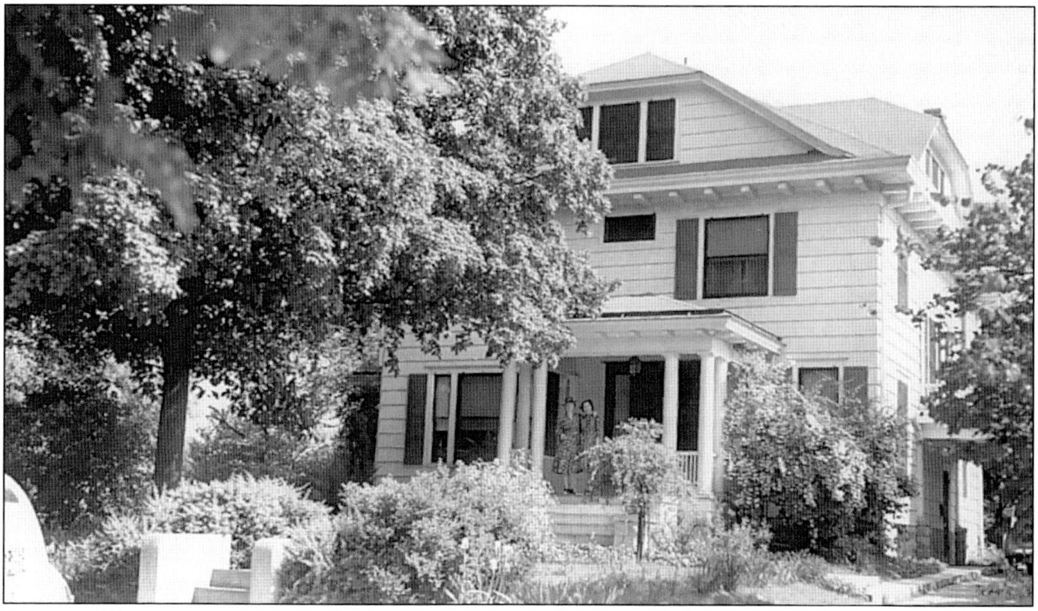

Powers House, 314 Euclid Boulevard. Remodeled in the late 1930s, the original veranda that wrapped around the house was removed and replaced with a small entrance porch that mother and daughter stand on this 1941 Easter morning. Daughter, Marian Louisa Powers Winchester continued to reside here until her death in 1981.

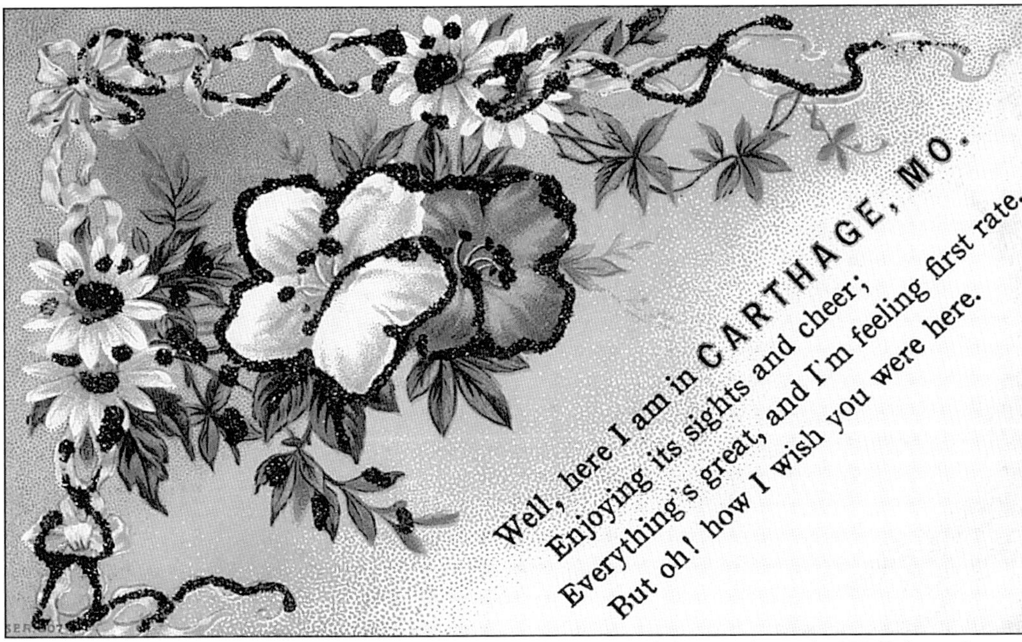

WELCOME TO CARTHAGE POSTCARD, C. 1910. The verse of this cards reads: Well, here I am in Carthage, Missouri. Enjoying the sites and cheer; Everything's great, and I'm feeling first rate, But Oh! how I wish you were here.

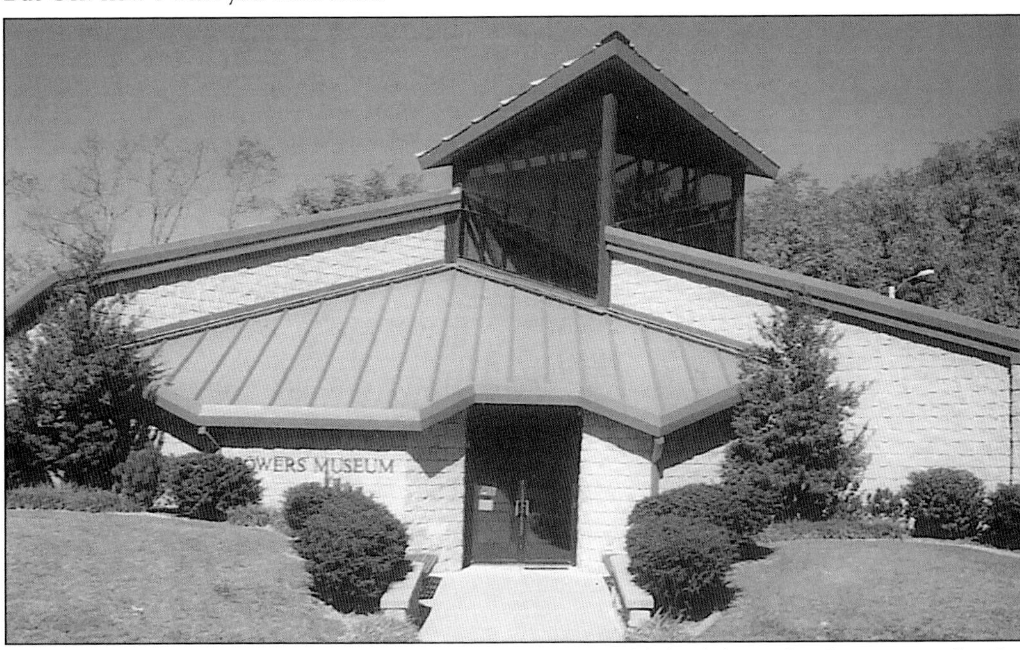

POWERS MUSEUM, 1617 WEST OAK STREET, 1988. Established through a bequest to the City of Carthage in 1981, Marian Powers Winchester requested that the museum be named for her parents, Dr. Everett and Mrs. Marian Wright Powers. The majority of photographs for this book have come from the founding collection left with this bequest. For more information on any of them, write to P.O. Box 593, Carthage, MO 64836, (417-358-2667), or consult ***www.powersmuseum.com***.

INDEX